THE MAN-MADE FUTURE

THE MAN-MADE FUTURE

C.H. WADDINGTON

ST. MARTIN'S PRESS   NEW YORK

St. Martin's Press Inc., 175 Fifth Avenue, New York, N.Y. 10010
Printed in Great Britain
Library of Congress Catalog Card Number 77-29043
ISBN 0-312-51045-4
First published in the United States of America in 1978

Library of Congress Cataloging in Publication Data

Waddingon, Conrad Hal, 1905—1975.
    The man-made future.

    Bibliography: p.
    Includes index.
    1. Human ecology.   2. Social problems.
3. Forecasting.   4. Systems theory.   I. Title.
GF41.W29 1978   301.31   77-29043
ISBN 0-312-51045-4

CONTENTS

FOREWORD

It gives me a very special pleasure to write this foreword, if only as a way of reliving the forty years during which I was privileged to know C.H. Waddington. Over four decades we discussed the series of problems which concerned him as he moved from the most exquisite experiments in embryology to larger and larger questions of evolution, of the relationships between science and ethics, science and art.

In this volume and its companion piece, *Tools for Thought* (Jonathan Cape/Basic Books, London and New York, 1977) he is concerned with the world problematique and the contributions which a biologist can make to the preservation of human civilisation and human life. As a young anthropologist who had grown up in a tradition of scientific inexplicitness, I first learned what scientific conceptualisations were about from conversations between Waddington and Gregory Bateson, as they leapt from one science to another in the gloriously permissive atmosphere of thinking which was given to young Cambridge biologists in the 1920s. *The Man-Made Future* contains materials to think with, carefully, imaginatively, meticulously assembled from all of Waddington's interests, years of laboratory experiments in embryology and evolution, active participation in the organisation of science, nationally and internationally, and in his final years, dedication to a long look at the present state of our society.

He was clear about what science could and could not do, which problems urgently needed more scientific work and which had to be left to other fields and aspects of the total culture. But he did believe firmly in the scientific method and the need to ask questions that would produce answers.

The Man-Made Future is essentially a work book for those students and their teachers who wish to give direction and meaning to the human condition in the current crucial state of an emerging global culture. Undogmatic, ruthlessly honest in his acceptance of the twists and turns of the new biology, always sensitive to the beauty and value of human life — he has produced a real curriculum for the development of the future.

The American Museum of   Margaret Mead
Natural History, New York, NY,
February, 1978

BETTER MIND Your P's and Q's

It appears probably impossible to prevent
the philoprogenitive propensities of persons
peopling the planet with two-times
its present population of two-timers

The pressure to provide provender
and prevent pestilence
will be portentous

People science-perceptive enough to empathise
　　the problems and proposals
Will profit from a propitious posture
to promote their personality potentials

The querulous who merely question the qualifications
of the scientific enquiry after quantity *and* quality
will find that their eternal quest is querying
whether their quasi-quietude qualifies them
for equality, quashiokor, quod or the quietus,
unless these quondam Quixotes
quite quit their queasy quibbling
and take as quarry their quota of quotidian quiddities

They will earn their quittance when they
can qualify as equating
ZPG with a quorum of the quick
rather than an unquiet queue of the untimely quenched

INTRODUCTION

Whatever the future will be, it will have been made by Man. The great
problem the world-wide species is facing is essentially and inescapably
complex. It is made up of a series of major world problems — of
population, food supplies, energy, natural resources, pollution, the
conditions of cities, and others — and they are inextricably inter-
connected, so that no one of them can be properly dealt with in
isolation. Taken together, they constitute not just a problem, but
what has been called a *Problematique* — a multi-problem. And even
if, as a first step, we try to come to grips with any particular one of
the topics, such as population, we find that it is itself internally complicated, in the sense that, for instance, the immediate effect of an
increase in population is not to produce a great number of useful
workers, but rather to lay a greater burden for some years on the
existing labour force to feed and look after the young children before
they grow up to be effective. Anyone who wishes to take a responsible
attitude to the affairs of mankind, or, on a more pragmatic level,
would like to feel some competence to deal with the problems that
are likely to come his way during his lifetime, will have to acquire at
least an inkling of understanding about all of the major problems and
about how they interact with one another to produce the *Problematique*.
Expertise in one or other field may be the way to earn a living; it will
not be enough by which to navigate over the rough seas ahead.

At present we cannot have more than a beginning of an understanding of each problem area, and of how it interacts with the others.
The theoretical schemes and practical knowledge for a satisfactory
grasp of the situation are simply not there at the present time. The
type of complexity with which we are confronted is one which mankind has not often encountered in the past. We have been used to
analysing phenomena and events into simple causal sequences, in
which it seemed meaningful to ask what is the cause of A, or to say
that P brings about Q and that in turn produces R. It is only recently
that people have realised how inadequate simple causal sequences are
to express the real nature of the problems of the world of today.
Nearly always we find we have to deal with a network of causes and
effects. For instance, A, B, C and D may all contribute to producing
'effects' P and Q; and those in turn, with contributions from X and Y,

produce K, L and M; and M perhaps has an effect, backwards as it were, on C or D, while A might have an effect forward, not through P and Q, but directly on to K. Complicated networks of interactions of that kind can behave in ways quite unlike those of simple causal sequences. A process controlled by some such network may show great resistance to the effects of outside influences which one might have expected to change it; or again it may show unexpected discontinuities in behaviour, remaining apparently unaffected by some outside influence until it suddenly switches over into another alternative type of activity. There may have been many recent developments of methods of understanding and dealing with systems which have various kinds of complex internal structure. I have attempted to give a sketch of many of these in a companion book to this, called *Tools of Thought about Complex Systems.* The ideas have often been first expounded in somewhat awe-inspiring jargon, but in general their basic notions are fairly simple, and can be expressed well enough in plain English; although, for anyone who thinks he already knows the general principles of the way things work in the real world, it may require a little imagination to grasp the nature of these systems which actually operate in more subtle ways than we have been used to.

It would be nice to be able to take each of the major topics in the world's problems, such as population, the food supply, the energy crisis and so on, and expound them clearly in terms, either of the conventional linear causal sequences, or of the more sophisticated recent types of thinking just mentioned. Unfortunately, that again is asking too much at the present time. Most of the newer methods of thought have only been developed in the last couple of decades; it is only in the last year or two that it has been realised that the major world problems require these newer types of theory for their understanding; and the application of these theories is only in its very beginning. What I have aimed to do in this book is only to open a gate, as it were, into a new area of countryside, to indicate the main obvious features, the hills, the streams, the woods, as an introduction to an area, the full exploration of which will take many years.

If a set of processes is controlled by a network of causes, and even more if one is really facing a network of networks, like the world *Problematique* today, one has to have some outline of the whole system before one can do anything with any particular part of it. This is the exact opposite of the way in which our understanding of the world has been pursued in the recent past. The universities, and other organisations of intellectual life, have been aiming for a greater and greater degree of specialisation. Very detailed knowledge of some particular topic is, of course, a necessary tool when it comes to carrying out the operations of a complicated society. However, it is only one tool, and to rely on specialisation alone is like having a very powerful drilling machine, but nothing to hold steady, and in the correct orientation, the piece of material to which the drill is to be applied. If the world's problems do actually have anything like the character which is described here, and I do not see how this can be easily denied (although, of course, many of the details are controversial), then the world does very definitely need people who can claim to be generalists with an over-all picture, as well as specialists with great detailed knowledge. I am a professional university teacher, and I believe it is now the responsibility of the universities to provide courses for generalists which will complement the many specialist courses they give at present. The contents of this book and *Tools of Thought about Complex Systems* were in fact originally meant to provide a basis for a possible university course of this type. The books have, however, not been written in the usual style of a university text book, since the type of understanding they are trying to provide is needed by every thoughtful citizen, a much wider group than those who are attending universities as students at present.

Anyone who tries to write about topics of this kind must face two circumstances which are rather daunting. In the first place, he must inevitably be to some extent out of date. The world's problems are moving so fast that in the interval between finishing a manuscript and finding the bound book on your desk, it is much more than likely that some major new event will have occurred such as the quadrupling within a period of a few months of the price of one of the most basic raw materials (oil), or that some new step of understanding will have been achieved, such as the quantitative estimation of the energy inputs into the production and distribution of foodstuffs in industrial nations, the knowledge of which was almost negligible as little as a year ago. The best one can hope to provide is an over-all picture the general outlines of which will not have to be altered very much in spite of new discoveries and events.

Secondly, the author is bound to be controversial. The problem areas in mankind's affairs have become the centres of vigorous and vociferous debate. Readers will be tempted to think that any new book must belong to one or other of the 'sides' which are beginning to be recognised. Roughly speaking, one can discern about three schools of thought. There are 'the doomsters' who see almost inevitable calamity – not always the same calamity; nuclear war for some, pollution for Rachel Carson and Barry Commoner, population for Ehrlich, multiple causes for Heilbrunner and the Blueprint for Survival group – but calamity nevertheless. Then there are their opposite numbers, 'the cheerleaders' for growth and more growth – Buckminster Fuller, John Maddox, Beckerman and others. Finally – because there are very few, if any, authors who think there is nothing very special about the present and that things can go on quite quietly, although Zuckerman did at one time take this line – there are 'the reformists', who argue that we shall have to make some kind of discontinuous change in the way society works, but that it is quite possible for us to do so. They include a spectrum of opinion. Some expect fairly mild but quite definite alterations, such as the development of alternative technology for the developing world, and advocate left-of-centre policies in the industrialised nations. There are others who expect considerably more drastic changes, which, however, will still be focused on values which are recognisable components of western civilisation as it has developed since the Renaissance. Lastly, there are those who argue that salvation is possible, but will demand really revolutionary changes, probably back to pre-Renaissance value systems such as those advocated by D.H. Lawrence, or to the ideas of hippie culture, flower people, drug culture, or other counter-culture groups. However, the purpose of this book is not to advocate any programme. It is intended to provide an outline of the situation, a sketch map if you like, without describing a definite path to follow through it. Of course, the mere description given in a map is bound to imply that, in the map-maker's mind, certain lines will be easier and more profitable to follow than others. Probably I have done this to some extent, but my intention was to describe, without prescribing.

The general point of view places me somewhere among the reformists. I accept that an ever-accelerating (i.e. exponential) rate of growth cannot continue indefinitely, but must eventually slow down; and I agree that we are reaching, and probably have already reached, the time when this slowing becomes appreciable. A great deal will have to be done to accommodate societies to this situation; different changes will be called for in different parts of the world, at different stages of 'development' or industrialisation, but there is no society which is likely to be able to go straight ahead along the paths it has been following in the last few decades.

Now of course all these changes will have to be brought about by political actions. Some readers may feel that it is politics to which everything in this book has been leading, and to a large extent I should agree with them. But I am not going to try to provide here either guidelines about how to be politically effective, or a discussion of political philosophies. This is partly because these are both enormous subjects in themselves, and one must stop somewhere; partly because I have no particular competence in either field. So this must remain (merely, if you like) the basis for politics, rather than the full-blooded article; but it is as well to get the basis right if any blood that gets spilt is not to be wasted.

A word about the structure of this book. It is organised into twelve chapters but, as pointed out above, all the topics in fact interact with one another, and the dividing lines between them are to a large extent a matter of convenience. Where appropriate a good deal of the factual material has been presented in visual form. It must be emphasised that most of these so-called 'facts' are actually estimates; many are not very reliable, and they will be changing as time passes, but they are at least attempts at quantitative statements. The diagrams are therefore not of the same character as those of *Tools of Thought*, which dealt only with qualitative concepts and relations. These diagrams have mostly been made by Mr E.D. Roberts, the draughtsman at the Institute of Genetics Laboratory in Edinburgh and, in order to emphasise the approximate nature of the estimates involved, they are in a style appropriate to a blackboard illustration to a lecture, rather than with the precise finish of a scientific publication.

1 POPULATION

At the very centre of the difficulties which the human species faces is the problem of people; their sheer numbers and the rate at which they are increasing. The more population, the more food has to be produced; the more houses, schools, hospitals, factories have to be built; the more resources used and pollution produced; the more difficult it becomes to find satisfaction in periods of leisure; and one runs up against the paradox that the healthier the population, the faster its numbers grow, bringing these other problems with them.

Population increase is an example of 'exponential growth'. The number added to a population in a given time depends on the number who are already present, who may act as parents. The precise form of the dependence will vary from one population to another; in some populations people will marry young and have many children, in others the marriage-rates, or birth-rates, or death-rates, may be different; but there will always be some connection between present numbers and new additions, so we will always be dealing with exponential growth of some kind. Actually it has been an 'accelerated exponential growth', since the fraction of itself which a population has added on in a given time has been increasing throughout history, as people have lived longer and more of the babies have survived.

So 'the population problem' deserves first place in this discussion. The two main points to be emphasised are, firstly, that in most parts of the world it is at present the rate of population increase which is the cause of difficulty, rather than the absolute numbers of people, and, secondly, that the rate of population growth is enormously influenced by the desires and wishes of people, as well as by the external factors (food, health, care etc.) which condition the human ecology.

There is considerable uncertainty in all figures relating to the human population. Even the numbers of the existing populations are in most cases only estimates. Counting people is a laborious and time-consuming procedure. In the richer countries censuses take place at intervals of about ten years, and there are intermediate summaries of births and deaths compiled from local records. In such cases the figures are reasonably accurate. In many of the more populous and poorer countries, such as most of Africa, South America, India,

Figure 1.1: Population through History

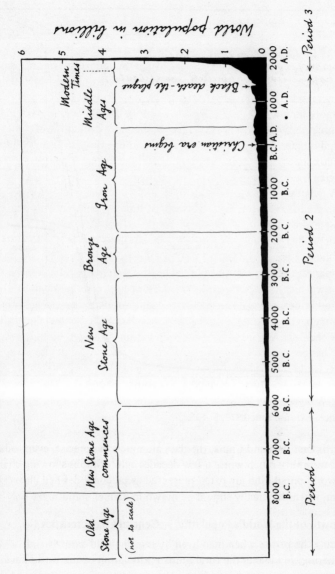

Source: *Population Bulletin*, April 1971, p. 4.

Figure 1.2: Six Projections of World Population

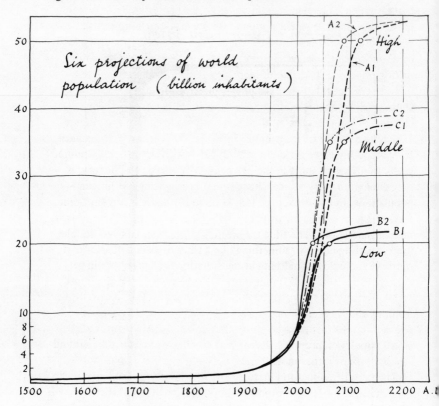

Source: *Ekistics*, June 1972, p. 435.

South East Asia and China, the data are much less precise, even today, and were very much worse a few decades ago.[1] Graphs showing changes in world population are often presented as precisely defined clear lines, when they really should be drawn in a much more fuzzy way.

Growth of the World's Population – General Characteristics

During the period when man lived by hunting wild animals and gathering wild plants the total human population of the world never reached more than a few million. The invention of agriculture and the formation of the first permanent settlements made possible a considerable increase in numbers. The figure of around 10,000,000 probably rose fairly rapidly, over a period of 1,000 years, to perhaps one or two hundred million.* However, even about three centuries ago, when there is much more evidence on which to base an estimate, it seems most likely that the world's population was not much more than 500 million. In the last three centuries the number has been increased by about seven times, to approximately three and a half thousand million. Moreover, the rate of increase has been accelerating.

It is very hazardous to extrapolate such figures into the future. Quite small differences in the figures assumed make very large differences in the results reached in a hundred or more years. Figure 1.2 shows a family of projections, made by the Athens Technological Institute, using three different sets of assumptions. Further, a hundred years, though very short in the perspective of man's total history, is long enough for very radical changes in breeding habits of human populations. But whatever the long-term uncertainties there are some facts which look to be unescapable within the time span of one or two human generations. The time the world's population takes to double itself is getting down to something like a third or even a quarter of a century, and unless something in the situation is changed it will get even shorter. People who are just entering their adult life are almost certain to find, by the time they are in late middle age, that the world contains about twice as many people as it now does. The general opinion of most people who study the subject seems to be that the world population around the year 2000 is almost certain to be around 7 billion, if not rather more.

The rates of population increase are, of course, not the same in all countries. Figure 1.3 gives the annual rate of growth, and the population doubling-time, which is simply another way of expressing the same facts, for a few countries chosen to show the range of variation. Figure 1.4 expresses the same 'facts' — which are really only estimates, of various grades of reliability — in terms of the contributions which various regions seem likely to make to the total world population in the near future.

We need to ask: is this population increase a good thing; and if not, what, if anything, can be done about it?

If, as I think one should, one starts from the point of view that on the whole people are likeable and to be desired, a first answer to the question would be to say the more the merrier. However, if one tries

---

*Since so many of the writings about world population are American it is as well to remember that in American usage 1,000 million is called a billion, whereas in orthodox English usage the word billion should mean a million million. Since the American usage is so widespread in this subject it will be used in this book.

Figure 1.3: Annual Rate of Growth and Population Doubling-time

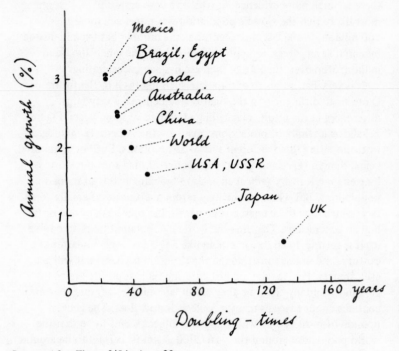

Source: After Figure 3/5 in A, p. 32.

to go more deeply into the matter, it becomes difficult to reach a clear-cut evaluation. Two points of view are very often expressed;[2] one is that the numbers of people in the world already pose problems of providing food, natural resources, housing, and so on, which are extremely difficult to resolve, and can in fact only be resolved by procedures which will rapidly deplete the available natural resources, will produce waste products which pollute the whole planet, and involve living conditions of such crowding and stress that the amenities of life will be destroyed and civilisation impoverished. This point of view tends to be held in two sorts of countries. Firstly, those which are already rich, and in which the rate of population increase is relatively small; many of them (e.g. Western Europe) have already high densities of people to the square mile, though others (particularly in the United States) do not. Secondly, this view is becoming accepted in some countries such as India, which have a very high density of people to the square mile and only a small supply

Figure 1.4: Contributions of Various Regions to Total World Population in the Near Future

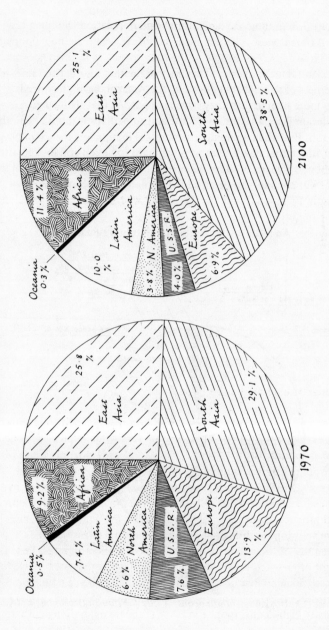

Source: *Population Bulletin*, September 1974, p. 25.

of their own natural and agricultural resources.

A different view is held in many countries which are now poor and have a low density of people to the square mile, as for instance much of Africa and South America. They may argue that in order to tame the wilderness of sub-Saharan Africa or the Amazon basin they need many more people than they have now got. At first sight, then, population increase seems welcome and so perhaps it should be in the long run. But when a population increases in numbers the extra people are at first either new babies who will have to be fed and looked after for about 15 years, or older members of the community, who will live longer but are likely to be an added burden rather than a source of strength, Figures 1.5 and 1.6. Thus even when an increased population

Figure 1.5: Analysis of the World Population by Phases

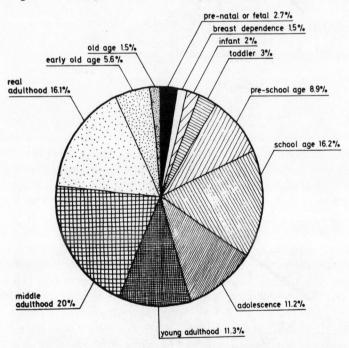

Source: C.A. Doxiadis, *Anthropopolis: A City for Human Development*, (Athens Technological Institute, 1974.

would be desirable the rate of increase should, ideally, be adjusted to the rate at which the new people can be properly looked after and usefully employed.[3]

Considerations like these show that it is not sensible to try to define a population policy for the world as a whole. What is required is that each state (or region in which there is free movement of population) should determine its own population policy to suit its own circumstances. It is urgent that such regional policies should be worked out, and implemented as soon as possible. There is probably no part of the world today in which sheer population pressure is resulting in a decrease in the average expectation of life of the new-born baby, although it is possible that this is already beginning to happen in the most densely populated poor regions. But conscious attempts to regulate rates of population increase are bound to be slow acting, requiring several decades before their effects are felt, and there is good reason to be apprehensive whether production of food and resources can keep ahead of the naturally growing population for that length of time in many parts of the poor world.

Factors Affecting the Rate of Population Increase

Broadly speaking, the main factors which control the rate of population increase are the number of babies born, and the length of time they live.

Expectation of Life

The average length of time a new-born baby can expect to live ('the mean expectation of life at birth') is one of the best over-all indicators of the state of health in a society. Although people may die at any age, they are most likely to do so in early childhood or in later life. The maximum age to which people live has probably not changed much during human history. Even today, and even in the richest countries, anyone reaching the biblical three score years and ten is getting quite close to the end of his lifespan. However, advances in public medicine and general health care in the richer nations in the last century or two have very considerably increased the proportion of the population which actually does approach old age. The most recent changes in mortality have been in childhood. In unimproved situations there is normally a very great loss of children in the first two years of life, from malnutrition or from a large number of children's diseases. If these children are preserved, as they have been with great success in any countries in which modern medicine has been made available, they will not only go on forming part of the population for the next fifty or sixty years or more, but will probably add to it by having children of

Figure 1.6: Infant Death-Rates, Selected Countries

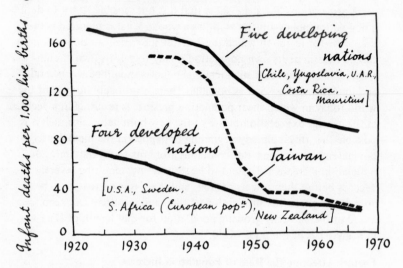

Source: *Population Bulletin*, April 1971, p. 16.

their own. This reduction of childhood mortality therefore adds greatly to the rate of population increase.

Number of Babies Born

The number of babies born depends basically on the number of women of child-bearing age. Populations may differ in this respect to a surprisingly large extent. These differences depend on the pattern of mortality to which the population has been subjected in its recent past history. To simplify the argument to its bare bones, suppose we had a population of 10 million people, in which every baby born lived to the age of 50 and then died. Clearly any 10-year age-group — say those between the ages of 20 and 30 — would have to amount to one-fifth of the total, that is to say 2 million; and there would also be 2 million between the ages of 0 and 10, and so on. If on the other hand you had a population in which a certain number of babies had died by the age of one, some more by the age of two, and more still by the age of three, and so on, each age group would be getting smaller as you went to more advanced years. If one made a diagram of the population as a stack of bars, each bar representing the size of a particular age group, the former population would make a parallel-sided stack, while in the latter population the sides of the stack would

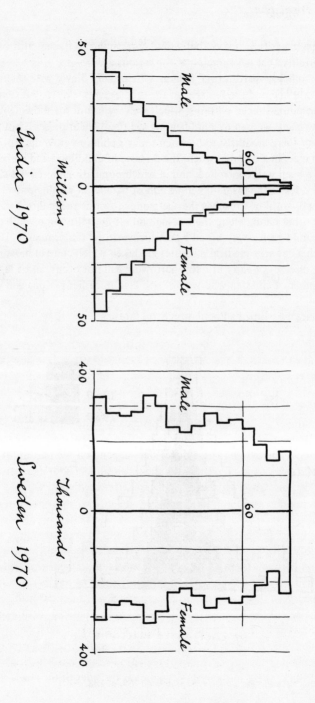

Figure 1.7: Age Distribution Diagram

Source: *Population Bulletin*, November 1970, p. 3.

slope inwards, in a way that would correspond to the amount of mortality that had gone on at the various ages.

Such 'age distribution' diagrams are usually drawn with the males on one side and the females on the other, giving a variety of domed or even onion-shaped patterns, which are very useful for showing not only how many women of child-bearing age there are at present, but how many there are likely to be when today's children grow up. For instance, in a country where the diseases of childhood and early life have been well controlled, and in which population increase is slow, the sides of the diagram will be almost parallel or sloping only slowly, until one reaches the age-groups towards the end of life. On the other hand, where there is high infant mortality, one will have a pyramid with a very broad base which narrows fairly quickly. If in such a country medical measures are taken which control most of the diseases of early life, this narrowing will not occur, and a large number of children who would have died in earlier periods will now

Figure 1.8: Brazil's Population Structure

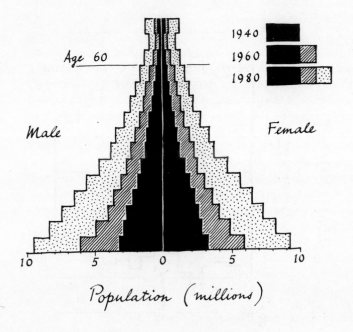

Source: *Population Bulletin*, September 1969, p. 108.

reach the reproductive stage of life. If we optimistically suppose that by contraceptive or other means the number of children that each woman bears is considerably reduced, the initial effect of this will only be to produce an onion-shaped diagram, since for a decade or two there will still be a lot of already-born children coming up to the child-bearing age.

The 'Demographic Transition'

In most of the richer countries the decline in the mortality-rate, which tends to bring about an increase in population, has been followed by a fall in the fertility-rate which has more or less brought the two rates into balance again, so that the over-all rate of population increase is fairly slow. This sequence of changes is known as 'demographic transition'. In the richer countries it was brought about by the personal preference of the individuals concerned, for having a smaller number of children with better opportunities for education and advancement. There was no official compulsion, and indeed very little persuasion other than that arising from the unconscious forces of a high standard of living.

One would like to think that similar changes would take place in the countries that are at present poor, but there are two major difficulties. In the first place, it is very difficult to raise the standard of living of these countries fast enough for it to have much effect in tempting people to limit the size of their families in order that their children may secure its benefits. Secondly, such a transition, even if it did occur, could be effective only rather slowly, in periods to be measured in decades. This is because of the great momentum of the population process, which follows from the age distribution pyramids described above. Where there has been a recent reduction in infant mortality not accompanied by any reduction in fertility, as in India, the pyramid has a very broad base indicating that there are a great many young children already born who will soon be entering their child-bearing phase. Thus, even if Indian families decided now to bring their family sizes down to the replacement level of about two children, the population would continue to grow quite fast for several decades because, while the existing children are growing up, in each year there would be more mothers to begin on their new families.

Methods for Controlling Population Growth

The factor which in the main controlled the rate of growth of

Figure 1.9a: Explosive Growth-Rate: Sri Lanka, 20th Century

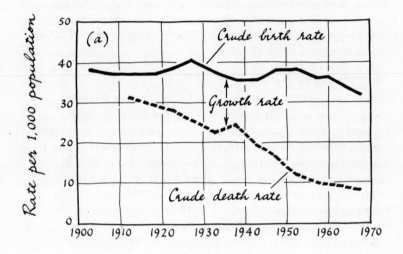

Figure 1.9b: A Demographic Transition: Sweden 1750–1968

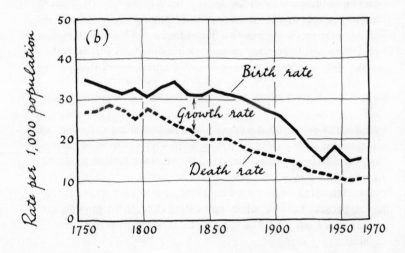

Source: *Population Bulletin*, April 1971, p. 18.

population before the advent of the industrial society was mortality. Usually this was the natural mortality from diseases consequent on life in an unimproved natural environment. Occasionally, in some places and times this has been supplemented by additional mortality consciously contrived by man, particularly by the practice of infanticide, in which certain babies considered to be surplus to requirements were allowed to perish, either by being abandoned or by being given inadequate care. It is difficult to believe that the world as a whole will ever be willing to go back to such unsympathetic measures, though one does occasionally hear the argument advanced that we should go slow in improving health provisions for young children and thus reducing infant mortality as we have been doing in the past. In general most people would hope to see effective population control exerted by the voluntary action of the reproducing couples concerned. This involves both the availability of effective contraceptive methods and a will to use them.

Societies differ considerably in the number of children which most people desire. In general, the surveys and questionnaires show that in countries in which women actually bear rather few children, they express a wish to have families of fairly restricted size; most of these countries are rather rich by world standards. By contrast, in many of the (mainly poor) countries which have high fertility-rates, the family size the women say that they desire tends to be larger. There are several factors here which seem to be of general importance. In rich countries there are educational, recreational and other facilities, which are within reach of a large proportion of the population, provided their families are not too numerous. Particularly important perhaps are schemes for old age or retirement pensions, which ensure that an elderly couple can live in decent circumstances even if they have not got a battery of young and active children to support them. In most poor countries, on the other hand, children in small families do not have much more opportunity for education or other advancement than do members of large families; and it is an age-old tradition in cultures living near the subsistence level, that the existence of an ageing couple will be miserable indeed unless they have active sons who can provide for them. Moreover, in very many religions it is imperative for a man to produce sons to perform important ceremonies at the tombs of his ancestors. Even in the rich urbanised western world many families feel that they need to produce at least one boy 'to carry on the name'. Of course, when there is high infant mortality and not more than half the children born are likely to

Figure 1.10: Desired Number of Children in Some Countries

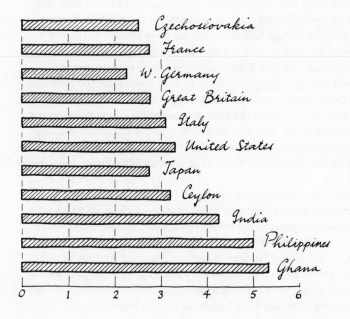

Source: *Population Bulletin*, April 1971, p. 20.

become adult, let alone survive their parents, it is necessary to have several sons born before one can be sure that one of them will still be there to worship at one's tomb.

While the sex of a person's next offspring remains the chancy thing it is — just about 50:50 boy or girl — even if parents set out with the laudable aim to have only two children, but insist that one must be a boy, quite a lot of families would have to go on well beyond two children to achieve the essential male child. If you want to be sure of getting at least two boys, you would on the average have to set your sights at something like four or five children, as so many families in the developing countries seem to do. It seems very doubtful, therefore, whether one could really hope to persuade parents in general to accept a family of two as about the normal to be desired, unless one could also provide them, not only with efficient contraception, but with some way of making sure that at least their second child was a boy, even if the first one was a girl. The ability to choose the sex of off-spring may be one of the most essential requirements for an effective policy of regulating the rate of population increase. We shall see later (Chapter 9) that it is not at all impossible that acceptable means of doing this might be developed, if sufficient research effort were put into the subject.

A change in religious values might be another very important factor in persuading people to wish for small families; or rather, a change in the events in the life history to which religious significance is attached. In the past nearly all organised religious bodies have asserted, and society as a whole has accepted, their right to interfere with private freedom of choice in sexual activity. They argued that this was such an important element in a person's life that it had religious significance, and that it should not be engaged in without the sanction of a sacramental ceremony approved by society at large. In general, the part of human sexual behaviour singled out to require the endorsement of a sacramental approval has been copulation. The sacramental ceremonies have been marriage ceremonies. In past societies in which effective contraception was not available the licence to marry and copulate has in practice also been a licence to produce offspring. By placing their emphasis where they did, the churches have acquired the great power which comes to any institution to which society concedes the authority to regulate the powerful drives of individuals to engage in sexual activities.

In societies in which contraception is widely practised and accepted the situation is very different. The force of religious prohibition of premarital sex is rapidly whittled away when there is little likelihood that such behaviour will lead to the production of children. This has already occurred in most western or westernised populations, and in them we are perhaps already beginning to see what one might expect to be a new stage in the historical development of religious thought, namely a realisation that it is the actual reproduction — the adding of a new member of society — which is the undeniably important thing. In so far as people have the sentiment that certain actions demand the sanction of a sacramental ceremony, it would seem natural to select for such treatment not copulation, but the conception and bearing of offspring. If the decision to have a child were taken with as much conscious thought, and as much dependence on social approval, as was devoted to marriage, this might have a very large influence in restraining the rate of population growth.

Another suggestion is on a less high moral plane, and may even be considered frivolous by some. One of the most powerful arguments to persuade people to use a contraceptive method would be the assurance that it would increase the pleasure they would derive from the sex act. A really effective aphrodisiac contraceptive would have a great appeal. There would seem to be several possibilities; it might act mechanically to prolong the male erection,or postpone ejaculation, or to provide additional stimulation to the female genitalia. In certain African tribes, men are said to have tied small bands of feathers or bristly fur around the penis, just below the glans, which produce sensations much appreciated by their partners and postpone or even prevent ejaculation. Again the steroid hormones have such a varied battery of effects on sexual desires and performances, as well as on the many stages of the maturation, fertilisation and implantation of eggs, that it seems by no means impossible that a suitable formula could be worked out that had both aphrodisiac as well as con-traceptive effect. I am not aware that at present any research is going on in either of these directions.

It is, of course, not at all certain that attempts to control rate of population increase, depending only on the voluntary activities of individuals, will be successful fast enough to avert the natural but un-pleasant controls that would be exerted by starvation or pestilence. In countries in which population pressures are greatest, such as India, suggestions have been made for mass temporary and reversible sterilisation of the population as a whole. The idea would be to develop a chemical contraceptive which would, as a matter of official governmental policy, be added to some staple foodstuff — salt has been suggested as one of the most appropriate. So long as people ate this they would not conceive. If they wanted to have a baby, they would have to get an official permit, either to be given a supply of an antidote which would restore their fertility, or access to untreated food to which the sterilising compound had not been added. There are very obvious dangers for the development of a black market, and for bribery, corruption and nepotism of various kinds in the adminis-tration of any such scheme, but in spite of these difficulties it has already been very seriously discussed.

However, at the present time no suitable chemical for producing reversible sterilisation of this kind is available. The research necessary to produce one, and to test it adequately so that it could be used on a population-wide scale, over a period of years, would be a very formidable task requiring quite a number of years.

Some Case Histories

1. *India*[4]

India is an example of a nation which officially and publicly acknowledges that it is faced with very serious problems of population pressure. It covers about 2.4 per cent of the world's total land area, but has to support 14 per cent of the world's total population, i.e. around 550 million people. This population produces about 21 million births a year. That is a crude birth-rate of around 39 per thousand per year. This is high by the standards of the rich western countries, but not particularly high in comparison with other Asian countries. However, the health services initiated in the days of the British Empire in the middle of the last century have been so successful that the death-rate is only about 14 per thousand per year, that is to say 8 million persons per annum. Thus the Indian population is growing at the rate of about

Figure 1.11: Forecasts of Indian Population

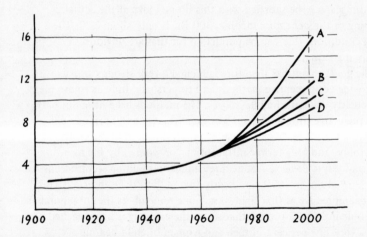

(A)	Fertility in 1965
(B)	Replacement fertility reached in 2025
(C)	,, ,, ,, ,, 1995
(D)	,, ,, ,, ,, 1985

Source: *Population Bulletin*, November 1970, p. 4.

13 million people every year, which is about the same as the total population of Australia or Holland. At this rate, the population would double itself in about 28 years and would reach a billion by the end of this century. However, health conditions are still improving and the death-rate coming down still further. The life expectancy has risen from the low figure of 32 years in 1950 to about 52 years in 1970. While it is difficult to deny that it is a 'good thing' for people to live longer lives, this will still further increase the rate of growth in population numbers.

When India became independent in 1948, its total national income was estimated at 86 billion rupees, and by 1966 this had increased to almost 150 billion, an increase of nearly 75 per cent. However, owing to the increase in population by almost 200 million during this period the income per head had risen by only about 20 per cent from approximately 250 Rs. to nearly 300 Rs.

One could conclude from these figures that the rate of population increase is at any rate not so enormous that the situation is actually getting worse; it is getting better, even though very slowly. However, one can scarcely be satisfied with this if one looks at the actual meaning of the *per capita* income. 300 Rs. is only about £20. The living conditions that can be purchased for that are obviously grossly inadequate.

The government has therefore launched a very strong campaign to provide contraceptive methods and to persuade Indians to use them, particularly since the middle 'sixties. The methods used have not only been the conventional ones such as sheaths, caps and hormone pills, but India has made extensive use of the sterilisation of males by vasectomy, and long-term contraception for women by the insertion of intra-uterine devices. About three and a half million sterilisations were carried out in 1970, and nearly two million IUDs inserted. This sounds impressive at first sight, but if one remembers the total number of people in India it is clear that so far the campaigns have reached only a very few per cent of men and women of child-bearing age. Moreover, investigation by the Indian family planning programme shows that the great majority of people seeking contraception do not do so until they have already had more children than would be needed to meet India's target birth-rate. Apparently nearly one-third of all sterilised Indian parents already have six living children.

The situation is in fact still profoundly influenced by four age-old traditional beliefs: that children are required to provide security for their parents' old age; that children can earn their keep as they are growing up and are an economic advantage, particularly in the country; that the Hindu religion requires a man to have sons to perform religious duties; and finally, the belief dies hard that even with modern methods one must expect that at least half the children born into the family will die before they become adult. And in many parts of India there is another factor: the fear of one linguistic or religious group being swamped by another. For instance, in India's neighbour Sri Lanka, the dominant Buddhist Sinhalese group is so afraid of finding itself outnumbered by the Hindu Tamils that they still refuse to acknowledge publicly that a population problem exists, although it is at least as bad as in India.

In a recent talk Professor Chandrasekhar,[5] former Minister for Health and Family Planning in India, concluded that the three major problems are: firstly, motivation — how to persuade people to wish to limit their families; secondly, communication — how to bring a knowledge of contraceptive techniques to the largely illiterate masses; and thirdly, development of contraceptive methods better suited to actual conditions in the poorer parts of India, where things such as bathrooms with running hot and cold water, privacy, electricity, chemists' shops, and so on are not available.

2. The United Kingdom

The population problems of the United Kingdom, and particularly of England, give an opportunity to emphasise several points of general importance. In the first place, England has been a fairly well-recorded country from Domesday Book onwards, so that one can obtain estimates of the population during the last 1,000 years which are probably as reliable as any available in the world. These reveal amongst other things that real crashes of population have occurred in the past, and might presumably do so again. The major one in English history was caused by bubonic plague (the Black Death) in the middle of the fourteenth century. The population, which had been just over 1 million at the time of Domesday had by that time climbed to nearly 4 million. Within a few years it was approximately halved. It soon started climbing again, but it took almost three centuries to get back to where it had been when the Black Death struck. Of course, it continued beyond this point and soon exhibited the 'explosive' rise which is characteristic of a continuing exponential increase. However, during the latter half of the nineteenth century, with the improvement of medical care, particularly the reduction in infant mortality, and a rise in the standard of living of larger and

Figure 1.12a: Population of England and Scotland, Domesday to Present

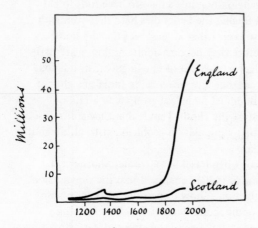

Figure 1.12b: Effect of Black Death in England

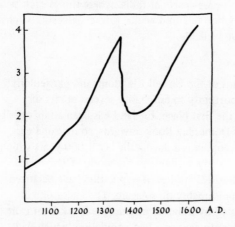

Source: After Figures 4/1 and 4/3 of A.

larger sections of the community, the population underwent the demographic transition. The shape of the age pyramid gradually changed from a pyramid to something more like a cupola, with sides which were almost vertical up to the age of about 50. It was, however, only in this century that this change became very marked, and the size of families was reduced from the large numbers characteristic of the Victorian era.

Figure 1.13: Changing Age-Structure of British Population

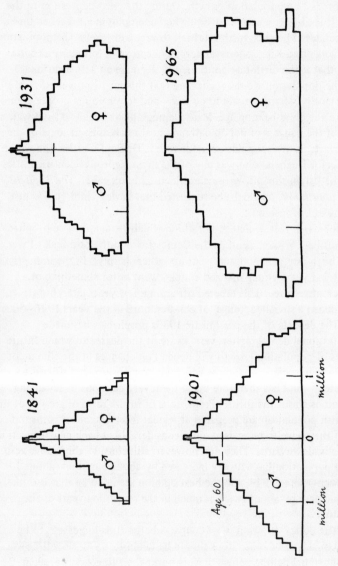

Source: After Figure 4/5 of A.

Another interesting point about the English population is that it has provided the classical example of the difficulties and dangers involved in forecasting population growth. During the great depression of the late 'twenties and early 'thirties, when unemployment reached unprecedented heights, birth-rates fell to very low levels. The population of the United Kingdom never actually decreased, but many experts saw that if the birth-rate continued to decrease an actual shrinkage of the population would occur, and that this might prove self-reinforcing, since every year there would be fewer and fewer young people coming up to the child-bearing age. Many demographers began to issue warnings about the dangers of depopulation almost as alarmist as some of the forecasts of over-population made today. Dr Enid Charles, the wife of Lancelot Hogben, who was one of the most vigorous scientific critics of the Establishment, wrote an influential book called *The Twilight of Parenthood*, in which she suggested that having children was just going out of fashion.

It was, in fact, a change in fashion which rendered these prophecies unfulfilled. With the end of the Depression and the outbreak of war, the birth-rate per thousand went up rather sharply. In the immediate post-war years young married couples went in for something of a procreative spree. This tapered off again a few years later, but it produced a so-called 'bulge' of children born in the years 1946–50.

The debacle of the pessimistic 1930s prophecies has made professional demographers very aware of the degree to which future rates of population growth will depend on changes in the climate of opinion in society – changes which are obviously very difficult to foretell – and has therefore made them very cautious in advancing opinions about the future. Projections of future rates of growth of the British population are prepared at regular intervals, but it turns out that they have to be revised quite considerably at each new inspection, usually downwards. They are, however, still considerably above zero. The population has actually increased by about 6 million (about 12 per cent) since 1949, and the best opinion seems to be that it is likely to increase by about twice as much in the remaining years of the century.

The policy question is, of course, whether this increase is to be welcomed, or whether steps should be taken to try to slow it down. Professional demographers, having burnt their fingers once, seem now very reluctant to get mixed up in the question. For instance, in May 1970 the major journal devoted to demography in Britain (*Population Studies*) produced a special supplement entitled 'Towards a Population Policy for the United Kingdom'. In spite of its title and its distinguished contributors, this supplement is entirely devoted to describing the demographic facts, the situation of the family planning movement, the bases of contraception, and similar subjects, and no mention is made of the question of whether the population is too big, too small, or growing too fast or too slowly.

Such interesting if awkward questions have, however, been raised outside the Establishment. In general most people who raise them seem to consider that the population of Britain is already perhaps too large. They put forward two main grounds. The first is the pressure of population on available land area.

At the time of Domesday there were nearly 29 acres per head; by the middle of the nineteenth century this had come down to something under 2 acres, which is still quite a lot of space; by 1950 it was only about three-quarters of an acre, and if the population goes on increasing at the relatively moderate rates forecast, by 2050 it will be less than a third of an acre.[6] This, of course, is rather an artificial figure, since people do not live evenly scattered over the moors and hills and woodlands. It is, however, of some interest if one sees these figures in connection with the fact that the use of land for leisure activities is very rapidly increasing, as is its use for motorways, airports and so on. Perhaps a less quantitative, but ultimately more useful, indication of the kind of changes that are occurring may be seen by comparing some accounts of what the countryside of Britain was like in the recent past with what it is like today.

Here is an extract from a story, of a period around 1840, set in the south of England.[7]

It was two or three hours past noon when I took my departure from the place of the last adventure, walking by the side of my little cart; the pony, invigorated by the corn, to which he was probably not much accustomed, proceeded right gallantly . . . I went on for a considerable time, in expectation of coming to some rustic hostelry, but nothing of the kind presented itself to my eyes; the country in which I now was seemed almost uninhabited, not a house of any kind was to be seen — at least I saw none — though it is true houses might be near without my seeing them, owing to the darkness of the night, for neither moon nor star was abroad. I heard, occasionally the bark of dogs; but the sound appeared to come from an immense distance.

And here again another more recent piece:[8]

In June 1957 I bought a small derelict cottage in mid-Wales. It had at one time been the home of a railwayman working on the line whose nearest station was about a mile away. I was attracted to this area by the quiet beauty of the rolling hills, whose sides were aflame with broom and gorse and whose crests were heather moors, and the nesting grounds for wheatears and whin-chats and the home of grouse, fox moths and oak-eggars. Marshland filled the hollows and, in consequence, the summer air was liquid with the calls of peewits, curlews and snipe. Redstarts flitted along the hedges beside the country lanes and insect life seemed plentiful.

In 1972 I spent Whitsuntide in this same cottage and saw no redstarts along the tarmac roads. The nearest railway is now 20 miles away and many of the neighbouring cottages are either empty or used only as holiday homes for visitors. All the heather and gorse have disappeared from the hilltops. Instead there is a dreary expanse of grass, barbed wire fences, sheep and thistles. The marsh-lands too have nearly all been drained and in their place rising conifers now cast their gloomy shade. Dawn breaks almost silently, for the curlews and plovers have gone. A few small-whites, tortoiseshells and an orange-tip or two are all that seem to be left of the previous abundance.

There has been no cataclysm of Nature to account for these changes, only the influence of 'Mankind bumbling along in much the same way as he has done for centuries', if I may quote from Professor Beckerman's myopic and insensitive lecture, as quoted in *The Times* (31 May 1972).

It is, of course, a matter for discussion whether one considers that this impoverishment of the natural environment, together with the increased stresses arising from the necessity to live in larger or more crowded cities, is sufficient evidence that the population of England has already got too large for comfort. Probably the most thorough examination of this issue published so far is that by Jack Parsons in his book *Population Versus Liberty*, in which he maintains that the limitations to our freedom, which we have to accept to accommodate ourselves to other people in a population of the present size, already surpass any gains in opportunities for individual development which may be offered by a larger and more flourishing population.

Another argument arises from Britain's dependence on imported foodstuffs. The country produces not much more than half the food consumed by its population and, even of that amount, a large part is dependent on imports of foodstuffs for cattle and other domestic animals (see Chapter 3). This situation could not be very greatly changed without extremely radical technological advances. The materials at present imported to feed our domestic livestock in this country are quite largely bought from developing countries, which really need the protein themselves for their own populations, and we cannot expect to carry on this economic system indefinitely into the future.

It certainly would seem sensible to devote a massive research effort to finding ways to produce protein-containing animal foodstuffs within this country, for instance by the cultivation of algae, or other methods, which we will discuss in Chapter 3. Even so, it is by no means certain that in the long run we shall have a strong enough base of industrial exports to sustain a population of our present size at a standard of living high up in the world league-table of the future. The pamphlet *Blueprint for Survival*[9] argues that we are not likely to be able to do so and that we should plan for a reduction in population. It is suggested that we ought to go down to about 30 million which is approximately what we could support from our own soil with present agricultural technology. It puts this target well into the future — about 200 years hence. This is so far ahead that we probably should not take this suggested figure of 30 million at all seriously. However, the argument does suggest that it would be wise and circumspect to try to restrain the growth of the British population, even if not actually reduce it, at least until we have much more confidence in our ability to extract from the rest of the world the wherewithal to feed it the kind of diet it would wish to have.

3. *Ireland*[10]

Probably the most dramatic example of the influence of social attitudes on the size of family is that of Ireland in the last century and a half. Up to the beginning of the nineteenth century, the growth of population in Ireland was much like that of any other Western European country rather poorly endowed with first quality agricultural land. However, the Irish economy gradually got hooked on the 'green revolution' of that time, and came to rely more and more on a single crop — the potato. At the beginning of this process Ireland's population increased rather rapidly, and by 1840 had reached about 8 million (6.5 million in what is now Eire, and 1.5 in Ulster). In the 1840s a new strain of the Blight fungus devastated the Irish potato fields. Probably more than a million Irish died as a direct or indirect effect of starvation, and another 2 million emigrated, mostly to the United States.

Then, on the evidence of what actually happened, rather than what anybody in particular stated, the Irish changed their whole idea, not only of how to produce their food — they went in extensively for breeding dairy and beef cattle, partly to provide for their own needs and partly for export — but also in connection with family structure and numbers. They shifted into a pattern of life in which people marry very late (or even do not marry at all) and then have very few children. This pattern has continued more or less up to the present; for instance in 1940 as many as 80 per cent of Irish men aged between 25 and 29 were not yet married; in 1960, of men between 25 and 34, 70 per cent were not married; and in 1970 the population of Eire was less than half its 1840 population — only 3 million. The same tendencies occurred, though not quite so strongly, in Protestant Ulster, which in 1970 had a population of 1.6 million, only fractionally larger than it had been in 1840.

Some students of population have raised the possibility — often with a tone of wistful longing in their phrases — that other parts of the world would 'do an Irish' on their population problems. Given a catastrophe as drastic as the collapse of the potato economy in Ireland, when the population dropped by about a quarter in ten years and went on dropping for some time thereafter, it cannot be ruled out that other people would behave in a somewhat similar fashion, but it seems unlikely. As an example on the other side, when about half a million people were drowned by a storm and tidal wave in Bangladesh in 1970, it only took five or six *weeks* before they had been replaced by new births, and the population of the country was as great as it had been before.

4. *The United States*[11]

The rest of the world may perhaps be forgiven if it feels that the United States doesn't have any very threatening population problem on its hands. For the country as a whole the density of people is only 54 per square mile, which compares very favourably with European countries such as France (231 per square mile), West Germany (618 per square mile), the UK, England (583 per square mile). Moreover, much of the country is very fertile, so that the United States along with Canada has become the major food-exporting region of the world, without whose produce great masses of people would starve to death. Finally, although

Figure 1.14: United States, Age Distribution Projection, Year 2000

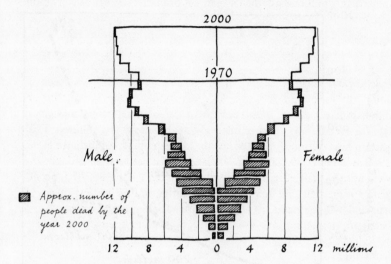

Source: *Population Bulletin*, February 1971, p. 19.

the medical services in the United States are of course sufficient to ensure a very low mortality-rate the country also has a very low fertility-rate, so that its rate of population growth is fairly slow. The population has actually increased from about 100 million in 1915 to 200 million around 1970, but quite a considerable proportion of this increase is due to immigration.

However, that simple view of the situation is by no means the whole picture. In the first place population is continuing to grow by natural increase apart from any effects of immigration. Within the last ten years the total fertility-rate in the United States has varied from little over 3.5 at the beginning of the period, to a little under 2.5 towards the end of it. If it stayed high enough to give a total of three children per family the US population would double to about 400 million in about 40 years; even if there were only a two-child family on the average, the population would gradually increase to 300 million in the same period. Many people in the United States feel that this would produce too severe crowding, and that something needs to be done about the situation.

These fluctuations in fertility are not at all fully understood. They are affected by fashions. For instance, immediately after World War II most countries underwent a 'baby boom' in which there was high

Figure 1.15: US Population Growth and Family Size

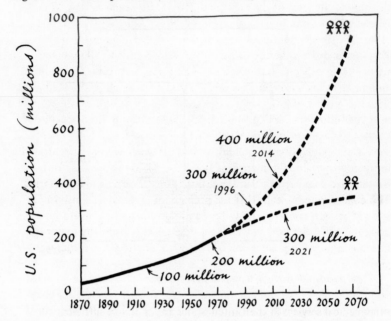

Source: *Population Bulletin*, June 1971, p. 9.

fertility. In the United States this went on until the late 'fifties
or early 'sixties. Another factor is the usual age of marriage. In
general this has been falling for women in Europe; in the last quarter
of a century it has remained more or less stationary (somewhat less
than in Europe) in the United States during this period. Another
element is the availability of jobs for women. Finally, a factor which
raises a good many moral problems is the number of births which are
unwanted. Recent studies in the States show that in the period of
1960–65 nearly a fifth of all births were unwanted. As might be
expected, the percentage of unwanted births rose steeply for the
third or later ones. If the percentage of unwanted births were
reduced by better birth control, this would not only help to reduce
the rate of population increase, but would presumably increase the
general sum of happiness by reducing the number of unwilling
mothers and unwanted children.

    The two major factors which complicate the simple picture
obtained by dividing the land area by the number of people are

the following. In the first place, the population is extremely unevenly distributed. In some of the major industrial states, such as New York, Pennsylvania, Ohio, Indiana and Illinois, population density is as high as in any ordinary European state such as France. In a few of the Eastern sea-board states it is as high as in the most densely populated parts of Europe, such as the Netherlands. This concentration of more and more people into relatively small parts of the area is connected with the process of urbanisation, and is leading to these areas developing into 'Megalopolises', which we shall discuss in Chapter 5. The best guesses (*Population Bulletin*, October 1971) seem to be that 70 per cent of the population growth in the next 20 years will be concentrated in the four megalopolitan areas of Boswash (Boston to Washington), Sansan (San Francisco to San Diego), the Great Lakes area, and Florida. This concentration means that the problem of population density is already being very considerably felt, and is producing a demand for a definite population policy, which would at least prevent any major increase in population, and possibly bringing about 'zero population growth'.

There is considerable discussion whether one can have a 'no growth' population policy, without at the same time being forced into a policy of no economic growth in any sphere. There are few people who can happily contemplate an over-all zero-growth policy, since it is clear that, for instance, a great many cities require considerable rebuilding and improvement, and there are very large pockets of poverty in the United States which can only be remedied by some degree of economic development. This point will be discussed further in Chapter 5.

It also touches on one of the most sensitive and difficult problems in the whole field of the United States population policy. Many people in the United States realise, and many people in the developing nations are happy to remind them, that a United States citizen will, if he continues to live in the style of his immediate parents, make far greater demands on the world's natural resources than a citizen in a developing country. From the point of view of the economy of the world as a whole, it is not at all sensible to count people in different regions as though they were all equivalent.

The right basis of comparison is in fact rather difficult to discover. If all the world's resources were fully known, were easily exploited, and were non-renewable, it would be sufficient to say, in the words of a recent meeting sponsored by the United Nations[12] that 'A north American or a European child on average consumes outrageously more than his Indian or African counterpart'; and that in the international system the powerful nations have secured the poor countries' raw materials at low prices . . . At the same time, the very cheapness of the materials was one element in encouraging the industrialised nations to indulge in careless and extravagant use of the imported materials. Once again, energy is the best example. Oil at just over a dollar a barrel, stimulated a growth in energy use of between 6 and 11 per cent a year. In Europe the annual increase in car registrations reach 20 per cent.

This is undoubtedly one aspect of the situation, and one of which the developed and rich countries should feel thoroughly ashamed. They have indeed considerably misused their powers, failed to show a proper responsibility to the world as a whole, and in particular to the poorer parts of it. However, the situation is not really quite so simple. Many of the important world resources are renewable. Food production by agriculture is the most obvious example, and it is the rich developed countries that have improved the efficiency of agriculture so that it at least nearly keeps pace with the increase in population, and the level of nutrition of the world's people has not (yet) fallen drastically short of requirements. Then supplies of many other raw materials, such as metal ores, rubber, and indeed oil itself, have been very greatly increased as a result of the explorations and technological innovations made by the rich countries. It is argued by many economists that the only hope that the poor countries have of getting their hands on the capital required to equip themselves for producing a good life for their own citizens is by the sale of raw materials to the present industrialised nations. Clearly there is here a very complicated balance to be struck. It is no use pretending that this problem has been fully solved as yet. The best answers are likely to be different according to which part of the world one is considering.

To end on a more hilarious note, it is worth mentioning that the case history of the USA population provides a wonderful example of the persistence of a national tradition. One of the American's favourite ways of solving a problem has always been to say 'This place is becoming a mess, let's go some place else' – from Europe to North America, in the first place, and then 'Go West, young man'. Now that North America is filled up, the only way of playing this gambit is to take off into space. Twice within this year, two of my best and most trusted friends, both of whom I consider to have made important contributions to the well-being of mankind – Margaret Mead and John Platt – have spoken seriously to me of the possibility of transferring the human population into space, not as a last desperate resort to escape from a totally polluted planet, but as a practical way of finding a new frontier.

There are some positions in space in which there is a balance between the gravitational fields of the moon and the earth. The idea would be first to set up a space station in the form of a thin cylinder, with dimensions possibly a kilometre long and four hundred metres in diameter, and a thickness of a few metres. This would spin round its axis at the right rate to produce a centrifugal force equivalent to the earth's gravity. It would use solar energy for power and for growing foodstuffs, and the first colonists would employ themselves by mining materials from the moon to build a second much bigger space-island. Within a generation or two, they might have got up to space islands large enough to be inhabited by millions, or even hundreds of millions. The plan has been worked out in considerable detail, for instance by Gerard O'Neill, a leading high-energy particle physicist at the University of Princeton. It is described in as much detail as most people are likely to need in the *New Scientist* of 24 October 1974.[13]

I am willing to accept the judgement of such an expert physicist that the project is technologically feasible, but I regard it as a wishful continuation of 'The American Dream' rather than something which is likely to come about.

Further Reading

A. Jack Parsons, *Population versus Liberty* (Pemberton Books, 1971, paperback Prometheus Books, Buffalo, NY) is a good general account, particularly Parts 1, 4 and Summary.

B. *Scientific American*, Special Number on The Human Population, September 1974, also has select bibliography.

C. *The Population Bulletin*, bi-monthly publication of the Population Reference Bureau, Inc., 1755 Massachusetts Avenue, NW, Washington, DC, USA, presents useful well-digested summaries.

D. *In Search of Population Policies*: (US Nat.Acad.Sci., Washington, 1974).

E. Garrett Hardin (ed.), *Population, Evolution and Birth Control* (2nd edn., paperback, Freeman, 1969) makes available a wide range of historical and recent ideas.

F. Paul Ehrlich, *The Population Bomb* (Ballantine, 1968), is perhaps the 'classical' (and very extreme) statement of the case against population increase.

G. Paul and Anne Ehrlich, John Holdren, *Human Ecology: Problems and Solutions* (Freeman, 1973).

Notes

1. For recent figures, see D.
2. See D. Many varieties of opinion were also expressed at the UN Population Conference at Bucharest in August 1974; a concise summary of them is in *People*, Vol. 1, No. 5, International Planned Parenthood Federation, 1974, and see *Bulletin of the Atomic Scientists*, June 1974.
3. For the special case of China, see Jon Wray, 'China's Achievement', *People*, Vol. 1, No. 4, 1974, and C. Djerassi, *Bulletin of the Atomic Scientists*, June 1974, p. 17.
4. See *Population Bulletin*, November 1970, and *Demography, Development and Ecology*, report *India: a case study* by S. Chandrasekhar, to Commonwealth Human Ecology Council meeting at Malta, 1970.
5. See ref. 4.
6. See A, p. 206.
7. George Borrow, *Lavengro*, Everyman, reprint Dutton, 1972, p. 407.
8. Letter from Professor E.N. Willmer to *The Times*, 3 June 1972.
9. E. Goldsmith ed., 'Blueprint for Survival', *The Ecologist*, January 1972 and Houghton Mifflin, 1972.
10. See *Population Bulletin*, April 1971, pp. 37–8.
11. *Population Bulletins*, February, June, August, October 1971, give a good summary.
12. *The Cocoyoc Declaration* issued by UNEP/UNCTAD Symposium on 'Patterns of Resource Use, Environment and Development Strategies', held at Cocoyoc, Mexico, October 1974. *Bulletin of the Atomic Scientists*, March 1975, p. 6.
13. Gerard K. O'Neill, 'The Colonization of Space', in *Physics Today*, September 1974, p. 32, and Graham Chedd, 'Colonization of Lagrangea', in *New Scientist*, 24 October 1974.

2 THE NATURAL ENVIRONMENT

Man does not live (fully) by bread alone; but he does not live at all without bread or something equivalent. It might therefore seem logical to go on from a chapter on population to the next chapter on food. But food is produced either directly by hunters or gatherers, from the living organisms in the natural environment, or by farmers altering that environment so that it yields more to satisfy man's wants. It is only on the basis of some understanding of how the natural environment works that one can profitably discuss how man has changed, or could in the future change, the situation to his advantage.

Our environment of course provides us with much more than food for the belly. It is the general setting in which man has evolved, and in which most of mankind still lives. Recently even rich city dwellers in the 'advanced' countries have begun to realise more vividly what one may call the non-food-producing values of nature. These are not only sensuous qualities, the beauties of sky and landscape. There is a strong appeal to the intellect in the way in which all the parts of nature in one region fit together to make an 'ecosystem' which has some quality of integral unity. We shall also come across many cases in which some action fails to produce as great a change in the natural environment as would be expected. For instance, the percentage of carbon dioxide in the atmosphere is not increased as one would anticipate from all the present-day burning of fossil fuel. Environmental systems, in fact, are full of examples of 'buffering', or homeostasis and homeorhesis.

The Biosphere

It is usual to make a distinction between the man-made or built environment and the natural environment, which many people think of as owing nothing to man. In fact, of course, there is very little of the terrestrial surface of the globe which has not been more or less profoundly modified by human activity, and man's influence is already beginning to have quite a noticeable impact on the parts of the earth's surface most resistant to his methods, namely the ocean.

Living things are found within a shallow layer — a thin skin, as it were, stretched over the surface of the globe. This is known as the biosphere. Most of it lies between moderate depths in the seas and permanent snow lying on mountains, and it shades off gradually below and above those limits. Within the biosphere the various forms of life are highly dependent on one another. The conditions which one living organism requires for its existence are, in general, brought into being by the activities of other living things. The biosphere is in fact not only the supporter of life, but is also the creator of life.

The most striking example of this is the presence of free oxygen which makes up about one-fifth of the whole atmosphere. All living things above the very simplest bacteria utilise it for respiration, to provide them with energy. But free oxygen is very rare among the constituents of earth which has not been affected by life, such as the very earliest rocks before the first fossils appeared, or in the materials and gases emitted by volcanoes. The oxygen in such places is always combined with other molecules, to form compounds like carbon dioxide or oxides of iron, silicon and many other elements, including that most important of all the kinds of oxide, namely water, in which oxygen is combined with hydrogen. The early atmosphere of the earth before the origin of life must have contained exceedingly little free oxygen. One of the first achievements of living systems was the development of certain chemical reactions which use solar energy to build up carbon dioxide into more complex substances (carbohydrates, starches, sugar and the like), and this process involves the breakdown of water, with the liberation of free oxygen. It is this primitive life-process which has provided the biosphere with its present supplies of free oxygen on which all higher life is now so totally dependent.

The Biosphere Cycles

The living things in the biosphere are continually growing and reproducing, respiring, excreting and dying, so that materials are continually being moved into and out of living organisms, and built up into complex compounds which are then broken down again. These to-and-fro movements of materials are all linked together in a common system, but it is convenient to analyse this in terms of about six cycles; those of energy, water, oxygen, carbon, nitrogen, and a mixed bag of other elements which one may call 'minerals', of which the two most important are phosphorus and sulphur. We will look at each of these in turn.

Energy

By far the main source of energy for the biosphere is provided by the sun's radiation. There is a minute addition from the terrestrial heat

Figure 2.1: Atmospheric Heat Engine[a]

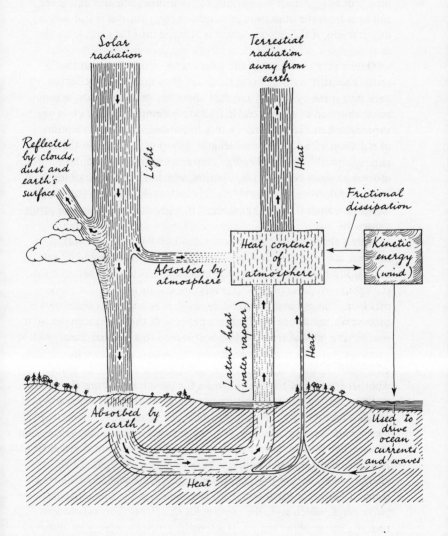

[a]The width of each channel of flow is proportional to the amounts of heat in it.

Source: Redrawn from *Scientific American*, September 1970, p. 57.

available from volcanoes etc., and some people have speculated that this might have been more important in a few particular places in the very early stages of evolution of life. Recently man is adding a new supply of energy from the burning of fossil fuel, such as coal and oil and now from the utilisation of atomic energy, but this is still only a tiny fraction of the amount which is pumped into the earth from the sun.

Only a very small part of the solar energy which arrives at the earth is actually used by living things. A good deal of it is reflected back into space by clouds, and dust above the earth's surface, without being absorbed at all. A sizeable fraction is absorbed by the gases of the atmosphere. This includes a very important selective absorption of radiation with shorter wave-lengths (short ultra-violet) in the upper atmosphere; this absorbed energy converts oxygen into ozone and the process prevents most of this radiation, which is harmful to nearly all living things, from reaching the earth's surface. If anything (e.g. very high flying aircraft) upset the system, it might have very harmful consequences.

Unless all the energy which is absorbed by the earth is finally radiated out from the earth again into space, the earth would be getting continually hotter. It is during the processes which occur between the absorption by the earth of solar radiation and its re-radiation away that living things can make some use of it. However, their share of it is quite small, about one-tenth of one per cent of the total incoming solar energy. The bulk of the absorbed heat is used to evaporate water, which, when it eventually falls as rain, gives out the heat again into the atmosphere, from which it may be radiated direct away into space. Another fraction of the heat provides the power which runs the winds, and through them the ocean currents and waves. Most of the fraction which is absorbed by the earth's surface just raises the temperature of the top few inches during the day, and gets radiated out into space again at night. However, it is on a subfraction of this portion of the heat flow that life eventually puts its finger.

The main process by which this energy is made available for living things is known as photosynthesis. It depends on the coloured substance chlorophyll, which gives the green colour to plants. This plays a key role in a remarkable chemical reaction, in which the energy of absorbed light is used to drive a series of chemical processes by which carbon dioxide and water are converted into carbohydrates (starches, sugars etc.) and into free oxygen which is liberated into the earth's atmosphere.

Figure 2.2: The Carbon Dioxide (CO$_2$) Cycle[a]

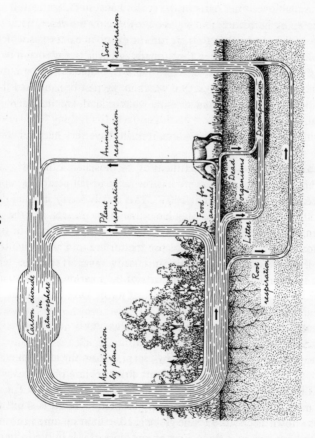

[a]The volumes of the cubes are proportional to the quantities of water.
Source: Redrawn from *Scientific American*, September 1970, p. 126.

However, a plant which absorbs carbon dioxide from the atmosphere and builds this up into complex substances by photosynthesis, giving out oxygen in the process, has also to produce energy for its own operations, and to do this must absorb some oxygen and combine it with some of the substances it has just made. This is a process of respiration and it produces carbon dioxide. The net production by the plant is the difference between its gross production and the amount of this used up in its own respiration. It is the net production which is available to other parts of the ecological system. Some of it may be eaten by herbivores grazing and browsing on the vegetation, and some of those may then in their turn be eaten by carnivores which prey on them. Some will fall to the grounds as leaves or fruits, and be destroyed by scavenging organisms like bacteria, moulds and so on. An important item for man is a fraction which in the past became buried under sediments in the seas and swampy areas of land, and has been turned into coal and oil.

Water

The second most important constituent of the biosphere is liquid water. This can only exist in a very narrow range of temperatures, since water freezes at $0°C$ and boils at $100°C$. This is only a tiny slice between the low temperatures of some of the other planets and the hot interior of the earth, let alone the temperature of the sun. Life as we know it would only be possible on the surface of a planet which had temperatures somewhere within this narrow range. If there is anything that can be called living on parts of the solar or other systems of the universe at a different temperature, it would have to be of an entirely different character.

The earth's supply of water probably remains fairly constant in quantity. A certain number of hydrogen atoms, which are one of the main constituents of water, are lost by escaping from the atmosphere to outer space, but they are probably just about replaced by new water brought up from the depths of the earth during volcanic action. The total quantity of water is not known very accurately, but it is about enough to cover the surface of the globe (510 million sq. km) to a depth of about two and three-quarter km. Most of it is in the form of the salt waters of the oceans — about 97 per cent. The rest is fresh, but three-quarters of this is in the form of ice at the Poles and on mountains, and cannot be used by living systems until melted. Of the remaining fraction, which is somewhat less than one per cent of the whole, there is 10—20 times as much stored as underground water as is actually on

Figure 2.3: The World's Water Supplies

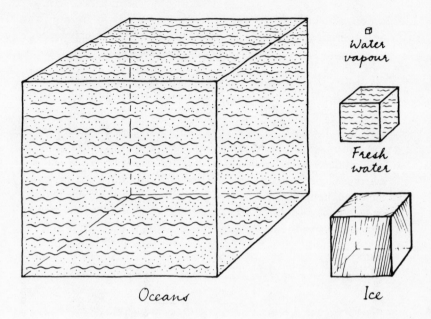

Source: Redrawn from *Scientific American*, September 1970, p. 100.

the surface. There is also a minute, but extremely important, fraction of the water supply which is present as water vapour in the atmosphere.

This tiny fraction of the water supply, existing as water vapour in the atmosphere, is the channel through which the whole water circulation of the biosphere has to pass. Water evaporated from the surface of the oceans, from lakes and rivers and from moist earth is added to it; so is the small amount from volcanoes. From it the water comes out again as rain or snow, falling on either the sea or the land. There is, as might be expected, a more intensive evaporation per unit area over the sea and oceans than over the land, but there is more precipitation over the land than over the ocean, and the balance is restored by the runoff from the land in the form of rivers.

Oxygen

The reactions living things actually employ to produce energy from oxygen are much more complex than would be suggested by the analogy of burning. Burning, which requires high temperatures, is too

Figure 2.4: The Water Cycle through the Atmosphere

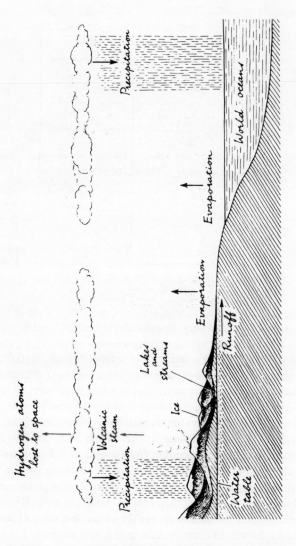

Source: Redrawn from *Scientific American*, September 1970, p. 102.

crude to be carried out in living things. Instead they make use of a series of reactions in which oxidation is carried out as it were surreptitiously, for instance by removing hydrogen from a compound rather than adding oxygen to it. However, even for these reactions the presence of free oxygen somewhere in the system is essential.

It is important to note that the great majority of the oxygen present in the biosphere is not in a free form. Most of it is combined, the greatest amount in the form of calcium carbonate, that is to say lime and chalk. Another large amount is in the form of sulphates, either dissolved in the sea or deposited in ancient sediments. There is also a large amount combined with iron in beds of iron ore. There is about 14—15 times as much oxygen tied up in these ways as there is free in the atmosphere.

Carbon

This is another element in the biosphere of which the greater part is locked away in sedimentary rocks, such as limestone. Although much of this may once have been part of living systems, it is now no longer accessible to them until it becomes dissolved, when it might be liberated to take part in living cycles. The workings of the biosphere depend on a small proportion of carbon which is more freely circulated.

The basic form of this cycle is simple. Carbon dioxide from the atmosphere is absorbed by green plants. With the aid of their photo-synthetic mechanisms they form carbohydrates by combining the carbon dioxide with water, with a net release of free oxygen as they do so (see p. 51). The organic compounds formed in the plants in this way either finish up as litter which is eventually broken down into carbon dioxide by decay organisms; or it is eaten by animals which use some of it to obtain energy by respiration (producing carbon dioxide); and the animals also eventually contribute to the general debris which the decay organisms convert back to carbon dioxide. Thus the whole supply of carbon dioxide, initially assimilated in the plants from the atmosphere, eventually gets back there again over these two or three different pathways.

A similar system goes on in the sea, only here much of the cycle takes place within the water, without any of the carbon dioxide passing out of the sea into the atmosphere. Minute floating plants (phyto-plankton) absorb carbon dioxide dissolved in sea water. The carbon dioxide finally formed by the decay of these organisms, by their respiration, and by the respiration and decay of fish and other creatures living on them, mostly passes back into the sea water to be re-used and go round the cycle again. However, in some regions of the seas some of it gets removed as calcium carbonate in the shells of various organisms, which fall to the bottom and form rocks like limestone and chalk. This loss from the carbon dioxide formed in the sea water is made good by absorption from the atmosphere at the sea surface.

Although the general character of these cycles is well known, the actual amounts of materials involved over the earth as a whole is still very uncertain. This is unfortunate in several ways. For instance, man has recently interfered with the natural carbon economy of the biosphere by producing a large amount of a type of radioactive carbon, known as carbon-14, during the atmospheric tests of nuclear explosives. It is a highly dangerous substance which retains its activity for a very long time. However, it was observed that its concentration in the atmosphere fell off much faster than could be explained by the decay of the radioactivity through processes internal to the carbon atoms. The explanation must be that there is a much more rapid turnover or interchange of carbon dioxide between the oceans and the atmosphere than had been suspected.

Again, man is changing the carbon system of the planet to a considerable extent by burning fossil fuels and thus releasing large quantities of carbon dioxide. The long-term effects of this would be much easier to estimate if we had more reliable data about quantities of carbon dioxide involved in the natural cycles. So far few people have been bold enough to claim that we can do much more than make reasonably plausible guesses. According to one of these 'guesstimates', the burning of fossil fuel at present rates should be increasing the carbon dioxide content in the atmosphere by about 0.7 per cent per year, but the increase actually observed is only about a third of this. This again appears to suggest that surplus carbon dioxide in the atmosphere is being absorbed by the sea (and possibly by the increased volume of plants being grown on the earth's surface with improved agricultural production). For discussion on the effect of CO_2 pollution on the climate see p. 273.

Nitrogen

Nitrogen is a central component of the proteins which are the enzymes on which all living things rely for carrying out their biochemical processes, and they also make up the tissue or flesh of animals. There is an abundant supply of molecular nitrogen in the atmosphere, and small amounts of nitrogen are always being added to this by volcanic action. However, molecular nitrogen is a very inert substance, and it is inaccessible to plants and animals until it has been combined, either with hydrogen to form ammonia, or with oxygen to make nitrite or nitrate salts.

Under natural conditions this so-called 'fixation' of nitrogen is carried out by a number of types of bacteria and other micro-organisms which live in the soil, usually in association with the roots of certain plants, such as clovers, peas or beans, or a few kinds of trees. These convert the atmosphere nitrogens into ammonia, and this is usually then converted into one of the nitrate salts. Both these products can be absorbed by the roots of plants of all kinds, and the nitrogen then becomes incorporated into the plant tissues. Animals obtain their usable nitrogen either by eating plants, or by eating other animals who have themselves eaten plants. Waste nitrogen excreted by the animals contributes to the store in the soil and thus encourages growth. This is the well-known principle of manuring. However, there are also other

Figure 2.5: The Nitrogen Cycle

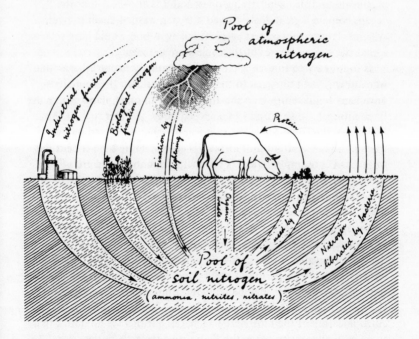

Source: Redrawn from *Scientific American*, September 1970, p. 139.

types of bacteria in soil which convert compounds such as ammonia or nitrates, derived from excretions or from dead animals or plants, back into molecular nitrogen which is released again into the atmosphere. This completes the last link in the nitrogen cycle.

Man has modified the natural cycle in two important ways. Firstly, by extensive cultivation of those plants the roots of which play host to the nitrogen-fixing bacteria. Even in relatively primitive agriculture, it was common to improve the fertility of the soil by growing a crop of one of the plants of the pea family, which are some of the best in bringing about nitrogen fixation. The second method has been by 'fixing' nitrogen in industrial plants, and thus making artificial fertilisers. These methods are used on an immense scale, and together they probably produce as much, or even a little more, fixed nitrogen as that achieved by natural vegetation before the introduction of agriculture.

Surprisingly little is known in precise terms about the nitrogen cycle in the ocean. There are certainly nitrogen-fixing micro-organisms, and also denitrifying ones; and it is also clear that the oceans contain a great deal of fixed nitrogen washed down in river systems. Presumably in past ages natural evolution would have seen to it that the various phases of the cycle were in balance.

Is it not easy to foresee what would eventually happen if mankind were adding fixed nitrogen to the oceans faster than the denitrifying organisms could return it to the atmosphere. In some places where the fixed nitrogen finishes up in an enclosed body of water such as the Baltic Sea, the Great Lakes of America, or other protected inland waters, the concentration of nitrates is already more than is desirable for human consumption, and is producing an unbalanced growth of those types of vegetation which respond readily to the increased availability of nitrogen. This is the phenomenon known as 'eutrophication'. Unfortunately the water plants whose growth is encouraged by increased availability of fixed nitrogen are usually kinds which are of very little use to mankind. Moreover their growth depletes the water of other essential nutrients, such as phosphates and oxygen, and, after a period of rapid growth of some rather undesirable water plants the water may be rendered almost sterile by depletion of these other materials. We are probably very far away from the eutrophication of the biosphere in general, but there is no doubt that some particular regions (e.g. the Baltic, and some claim the Mediterranean) are already in danger. However, there is no reason to doubt that proper management of man's effects on the natural nitrogen cycle can be achieved, although provision of the necessary sewage works etc. will be expensive.

Mineral Cycles – Sulphur and Phosphorus

There are, of course, many other substances which play essential roles in the biosphere. This general survey will mention only two of them, sulphur and phosphorus. Sulphur is very important in proteins, where it forms many of the links by which the string-like proteins are knotted into the complex shapes essential for the performance of their enzymatic functions. Phosphorus is an essential component, both of the nucleic acids (in which the information of heredity is coded) and of many of the compounds involved in energy exchanges in biochemical processes.

The sulphur cycle has some similarity to the nitrogen cycle, in that the only agents which can make it available to other living things are certain specialised types of bacteria. The process by which they do this begins with sulphur-containing salts, sulphates, which occur in rocks from which they get washed out by water. The sulphur-fixing bacteria, which are mainly found in the seas or in lakes or swamps, reduce the sulphates and combine the sulphur with hydrogen to form hydrogen sulphide. This is a gas, and much of it escapes into the atmosphere from which it is washed out by rain and thus brought on to the land surface where it can be absorbed by plants and taken up from them into animals.

Phosphorus has a different type of behaviour since there is no compound of it which is gaseous and can pass through the atmosphere. The only way in which it can move around (other than in the body of an animal) is as a salt carried in solution in water. This means that it is essentially non-renewable under natural conditions, and does not pass round a cycle at all. It is dissolved out of the rocks by rain and runs down rivers into the sea, and from there has no way to get back on to the land again. The living creatures that use phosphorus simply borrow it for a time during its one-way flow. This borrowing can in fact involve several stages and this can lead to a temporary return of phosphorus from the sea to the land; sea birds eat fish, absorb their phosphorus and may excrete some of it as guano when they return to a terrestrial environment to nest. The islands favoured by fish-eating sea birds have in fact provided some of the richest phosphate-containing deposits which man has been able to mine and use for phosphate fertilisers, but the supply is not being renewed as fast as the mining is depleting it, and these resources are rapidly running out.

Figure 2.6: Phosphorus Movements

Source: H.A. Regier and W.L. Hartman, 'Lake Erie's Fish Community; 150 years of cultural stress', *Science*, 1973, 180, pp. 1248–55.

Phosphate rock of good quality is also becoming in short supply.

In the meantime, however, man is adding large quantities of phosphate to places where they would not naturally arrive on the land's surface and in the fresh waters which drain them. Additional phosphates are added not only as agricultural fertilisers, but recently in phosphate-containing detergents. In most rivers and lakes it has been the scarcity of phosphate which was the limiting factor in controlling the growth of water plants. When extra phosphate is added, the limiting factor may be the availability of nitrates. However, some kinds of plants fix nitrogen. These can make their own nitrogen in quantities sufficient to exploit the enriched supplies of phosphate. The commonest of these are microscopic plants known as blue-green algae, and they therefore tend to grow in massive quantities, possibly depleting the water of oxygen, and having many undesirable effects in competition with other plants. Often the whole ecological set-up is changed, usually towards predominance of less useful or desirable species.

Linkage of the Cycles

The effects of phosphates in eutrophication is an example of how the various cycles are linked together. The degree to which living organisms can make use of one cycle is usually dependent on one or more of the other cycles. On land, and at the very surface of the oceans, oxygen and energy are always abundant but the extent to which organisms can use them depends on the availability of nitrogen, phosphorus and sulphur, and for land plants of water.

Plants need a great deal more water than might be expected. They absorb water from the soil through their roots, and give this off again into the atmosphere as water vapour, evaporated from the surface of their leaves; this process is known as transpiration. It is absolutely essential to plant growth, because it is the water passing up the stem from the roots to the leaves which carries into the upper parts of the plant all the minerals, nitrates, phosphates, and other nutrient materials which the roots have absorbed from the soil. The plant uses much more water for this essential transport function than it does for combining with carbon dioxide in photosynthesis. In an ordinary crop of 20 tons of fresh vegetable matter probably 15 tons will consist of water contained in the tissues of the plants; and of the 5 tons of the dry weight of the crop, about 3 tons consist of hydrogen atoms originally taken from water but now combined with carbon dioxide to form the starches, sugars and other materials; but to produce this result, something of the order of 2,000 tons of water will have passed through the plant from roots to leaves and thus into the atmosphere, from which it will eventually fall as rain and go through the cycle again, but perhaps in some other part of the earth's surface.

Thus on land, water is certainly one of the most important limiting factors on the extent to which plants can use the other cycles for their growth. And plants are the basic limitation on animals, because ultimately animals can only derive their energy from eating plants. In the sea, the availability of minerals (mainly phosphates) is usually the main limiting factor near the surface. In deeper waters to which sunlight cannot penetrate in appreciable quantities, the limiting factor may be energy.

The essential cycles are therefore not independent. They are like a set of cog wheels enmeshed with each other in a gear box, and, in different circumstances, some of them may be running free, while one of the others (in short supply) is fixed to its axle and controlling the motion of the whole set-up.

Ecosystems

These linked cycles provide the basic support for the life of communities of plants and animals. The word 'ecosystem' is commonly used to refer to such communities; it is intended to emphasise that all the members of a plant-animal community are linked together and that such communities contain many members, all important for its survival, but not all obvious at first sight.

The essential constituents of an ecosystem are of two basic kinds: (1) producers, or synthesisers, whose global effect is to operate on relatively simple compounds and produce from them something more complex, and (2) decomposers, whose effect is the opposite, to act on complex compounds and break them down into simpler ones. Clearly one could not have a system capable of continuing for a long time, unless both types of organisms were present, so that they could constitute a cycle; building up must be balanced by breaking down. But while the synthesisers are quite obvious to the naked eye, in the form of large plants or animals, the decomposers are small, inconspicuous, or even microscopic, and easily overlooked.

Producers can be arranged in some sort of hierarchical order. In the first place, there are primary producers, which can take the inorganic materials of the cycles described above and turn them directly into complex organic materials. Apart from a few special, but very important types, such as the nitrogen and sulphur-fixing bacteria, practically all the primary producers in the present-day world are

Figure 2.7: The Major Components of an Ecosystem

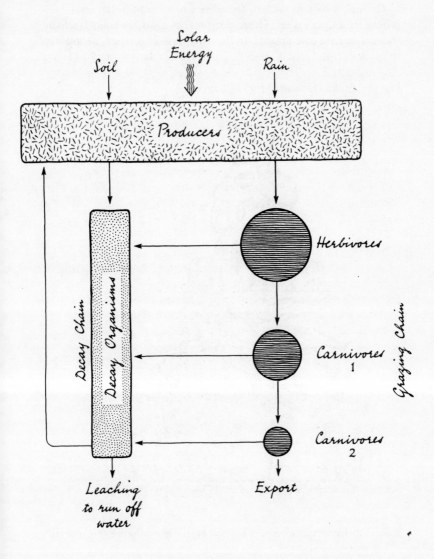

Note: The primary procedures, converting soil, rain and solar energy into vegetation (at the top); secondary, tertiary, etc. producers, who eat the vegetation, or eat those who eat the vegetation, and so on (right side); the decay organisms, who break down the dead bodies, and recycle the materials back to the soil (at the left).
Source: Redrawn from *Scientific American*, September 1970, p. 167.

plants which operate on solar energy to carry out photosynthesis with the aid of chlorophyll.

On the primary producers, there live a number of higher-level producers, animals which either eat plants or eat other animals which themselves have eaten plants. In the early days of ecology, people used to speak of 'food chains', implying that it was relatively easy to arrange

Figure 2.8: An (Idealised) Food Chain

Source: Redrawn from a figure in Marston Bates's *Man in Nature* (Prentice Hall, 1961).

these higher-level producers into an orderly hierarchy, with a secondary level above the primary producers, then a tertiary level that fed on the secondary organisms and so on. In a few very simple ecosystems, in very

Figure 2.9: Food Web

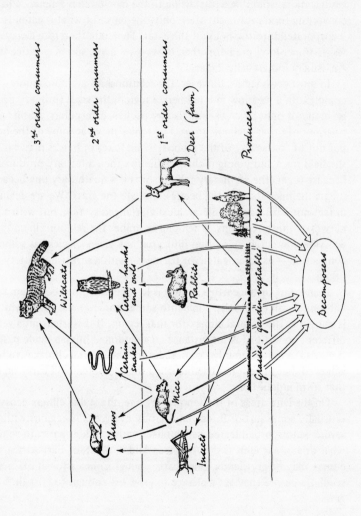

3rd order consumers

2nd order consumers

1st order consumers

Deer (fawn)

Producers

Wildcats

Certain hawks
and owls

Rabbits

Certain
snakes

Mice

Shrews

Insects

Grasses, garden vegetables & trees

Decomposers

inhospitable places such as the polar regions or the edges of deserts, where only a few types of organism are present, it may be reasonably possible to arrange them in such a clear-cut chain. At each step up the ladder, there would be a loss owing to the inevitable inefficiency in converting food into flesh; often only one-tenth of what is eaten is incorporated into the body of the eater. There are therefore always fewer upper-level predators than lower-level ones; and in practice they are usually individually larger.

In most ecosystems, however, the relationships are much more complex. In a meadow in a temperate region, the grass (primary producer) is eaten not only by cows, but also by beetles, caterpillars, rabbits and a variety of other such creatures. Field mice may eat some of the beetles, but not of course any of the rabbits, while foxes or hawks may eat both the field mice and young rabbits. Is the fox then a tertiary producer because it eats the secondary rabbits, or is it a quaternary one because it eats the mice that ate the beetles, that ate the grass? We are dealing in fact not with a neatly hierarchically-arranged system, but with a network of interrelations. When one examines the relations in an ecosystem in detail, one often finds that any given species has some connection — as eater, eaten, or partner — with a surprising variety of others.

If any part of the earth's surface is left to itself, the ecosystem in-habiting it will eventually come into some characteristic form, which is known as the natural climax for that region. If it starts from a very different condition, as for instance an abandoned human-made pasture, it may take quite a number of decades for the natural climaxes to be achieved, but once it has been reached the ecosystem will carry on in that form indefinitely.

On the land areas of the temperate zone, the stable climax ecosystem is usually some sort of forest; coniferous evergreen in regions with a severe winter; broad-leafed deciduous in rather milder parts. In some-what drier areas such as the American Middle West, or East Africa, the climax may be grasslands which carry enough animals to eat off tree seedlings before they get a chance to grow big enough to oust the grass.

Humanised Ecosystems

The main snag with these natural climaxes from the human point of view is that, although some of them are quite attractive aesthetically, they are mostly of very little economic use and are uncomfortable to live in. Almost without exception what we refer to as 'nature' in

Figure 2.10: Some of the Main Ecological Connections of One Plant Species (a Wild Cabbage) in a Certain Area

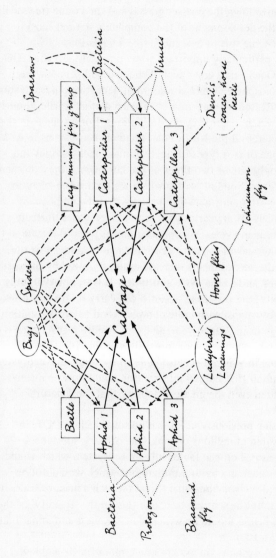

Herbivores who eat cabbage
Predators who attack herbivores
Parasites or disease organisms

Source: David Pimentel, 'Complexity of Ecological Systems', in Kenneth E.F. Watt ed., *Systems Analysis in Ecology* (Academic Press, 1966).

regions which man has inhabited for any length of time has been affected by human activities; it is a 'humanised-natural' ecosystem. For instance the smooth turf of the South Downs in England would not be there without the influence of man-controlled sheep and the man-introduced rabbit. These mow down the coarser grasses and the young tree seedlings, and so prevent the development of the completely natural ecosystem, which would be some sort of deciduous tree association.

· This point is particularly important when one considers the stability of ecosystems. One hears a great deal of rhetoric today about the fragility of the biosphere. This is a somewhat deceptive phrase. Natural ecosystems unaffected by man are not in general at all fragile, though there are some which undergo cyclic oscillations. For instance, in the northern tundra around the North Pole, there are ecosystems in which there are only one or two types of small animals, such as voles and lemmings, and only one or two types of predator which prey on them, such as Arctic foxes. Food networks which are reduced to such very simple terms are often 'unstable' in the sense that the numbers of animals vary widely from year to year or in longer cycles. Initially the foxes eat too many voles, but the year comes when there are so few that the foxes themselves starve to death in large numbers. For the next few years the vole numbers increase again, followed by increasing numbers of foxes, and so the cycle continues. This is, however, only a cyclic instability; the system as a whole can carry on for centuries. Most natural ecosystems, with more complex food networks, exhibit very little change from year to year, and very rapidly recover even after large disasters, such as major forest fires or floods.

The only sense in which it is reasonable to speak of such ecosystems as fragile is to admit that human intervention could now be massive enough to threaten even the greatest stability that these natural systems have.

Man is releasing previously unknown poisons, such as DDT, in quantities measured in millions of tons. One of these substances might introduce some crucial factor into an ecosystem which would be very stable against any natural mishap but which would not be able to withstand such an abnormal threat on such a massive scale. It would, however, not be sensible to blame this on the 'fragility' of the ecosystem. The blame should lie with the massiveness and unnaturalness of the human intrusion.

Humanised ecosystems are usually much more fragile and less stable than natural ones. This is partly because they usually contain many fewer species of plants and animals. By encouraging the expansion of those species useful to himself, man tends to reduce the variety of the ecosystem, and a lack of variety often produces a lack of stability. But man has also made many definite mistakes, when he humanised ecosystems by a process of trial and error. For instance, in the cradle of civilisation, the region between the great rivers of Mesopotamia, too enthusiastic clearing of the land for agriculture led to the soil being gradually washed away, silting up the rivers and leaving the land as infertile desert. Again the whole coastal region of North Africa and much of the near East, which used to be the main region for growing wheat for the Roman Empire, was largely wrecked by too intense agriculture, the use of its timber for houses, ships and fuel, and the uncontrolled grazing of goats.

When the South Western United States was first explored by 'improving' western man, the Spanish missionaries found an ecosystem of rough grassland which supported large numbers of buffaloes and small numbers of hunting Indians. There was very little land which they marked as deserts on their maps. The white man tried to improve it by killing off the buffalo, cutting down many of the trees, and stocking it with domestic animals like cattle. But this overstrained even the richer prairie areas, and within two or three hundred years, the usefulness of the newly introduced humanised ecosystem had practically disappeared. Large fractions of the southern part of the area relapsed into the great deserts of Arizona and New Mexico — very beautiful, very 'wild'; but this is a wildness for which man must take ultimate responsibility. In the more northern parts of the area, badly managed ploughing and cultivation of the richer soils turned them for a time into dust-bowls, from which much of the best soil was blown away by winds. But this region is sufficiently promising for a massive effort to be made to prevent it remaining useless to man, and to convert it into a better-managed humanised ecosystem.

Man has spent the whole of his evolutionary history changing natural ecosystems, since our ancestors cut down the aboriginal forests with their flint axes, or with fire. But it is only astonishingly recently — in the last few decades at most — that we have seriously tried to find our way about the spiders' webs of cause and effect, in which we have been gaily snipping connections here and there, or pulling on some strand harder than it could withstand.

Further Reading

A. Nigel Calder ed., *Nature in the Round: A Guide to Environmental Science* (Weidenfeld & Nicolson, 1973).

B. Paul and Anne Ehrlich and John Holdren, *Human Ecology :
    Problems and Solutions* (Freeman, 1973).

Rather more than ten years ago, in 1961, a major study on the various
ecologies of the world, considered as systems which use the sun's
energy to produce plants and animals, was organised by the non-
governmental scientists of the world. It was known as the International
Biological Programme. Over 50 countries took part. After running for
rather more than 10 years, at an average expenditure of about $50
million a year, it is now being wound up and the results published in
two series of handbooks; of methods (Blackwells, many already
published); and of results (Cambridge University Press). For the latter
series, 31 volumes are planned so far. Of those ready or nearly ready,
probably the most appropriate in the context of this book are:
C. *The Evolution of IBP*, and summary by E.B. Worthington.
D. O.H. Frankel and J.G. Hawkes, *Crop Genetic Resources for Today
    and Tomorrow.*
E. N.W. Pirie, *Food Protein Resources.*
    The IBP is being followed by another programme organised by un-
official scientists (SCOPE, the Scientific Committee on Problems of
the Environment, set up by ICSU, the International Council of Scientific
Unions); and by two official programmes — MAB, the Man and the
Biosphere programme of UNESCO, and UNEP, the United Nations
Environment Programme, which was launched at a Congress held in
Stockholm in 1972.

Simple general accounts of ecology will be found in:
F. Eugene P. Odum, *Ecology* (Holt, Rinehart & Winston, 1966).
G. 'The Biosphere', *Scientific American*, September 1970 (Freeman
    1971). Specially for chemical cycles, poor on animal and plant
    networks.
H. Paul R. Ehrlich ed., *Man and the Ecosphere* (Freeman, 1971).
    For more advanced treatments see:
I. Eugene P. Odum, *Fundamentals of Ecology* (Saunders, 3rd ed.,
    1972).
J. Charles S. Elton, *The Pattern of Animal Communities* (Methuen,
    1966).
K. Max Nicholson, *The Environmental Revolution* (Hodder &
    Stoughton, 1969, Penguin, 1972).

For semi-popular accounts of particular habitats, the following are
recommended:

L. Marston Bates, *The Forest and the Sea* (Random House, 1960);
R.B. Lee and I. de Vore eds., *Man the Hunter* (Chicago, 1968);
Michael Graham, *The Fish Gate* (Faber & Faber, 1943) (out of
date about the hardware, but still one of the best short scientific
accounts of deep sea fishing); Gunnar Thorson, *Life in the Sea*
(Weidenfeld & Nicolson, 1971); C.M. Yonge, *The Sea Shore*
(Collins, 1949); T.T. Macan and E.B. Worthington, *Life in Lakes
and Rivers* (Collins, 1951).

3   FOOD

Society has so concentrated its efforts in applied science on those fields which look like producing profits that we have no more than rough ideas about how much food is actually produced and how much of this finally gets eaten. We have no full understanding of how much of various types of food is essential, or even good for us, but it is certain that the world as a whole does not have enough food at present, and it is extremely difficult to see how it will succeed in producing enough for its still rapidly growing total population.

Essential Requirements

The bulk of man's food is made up of three major constituents; carbohydrates such as sugar, starches, etc.; fats and oils; and proteins. In addition, there are many minor but important constituents. There are mineral salts, which are the form in which we take in such things as calcium to be deposited in bone, the sodium and potassium required in the fluid parts of the blood, the iron necessary for the red blood pigment haemoglobin, and many other elements. There are also more complicated molecules, synthesised in other animals and plants, which are necessary for the running of the human body, but which it cannot make for itself and must acquire from its food. The vitamins are the most obvious of these, but new vitamin-like substances are continually being discovered, and there are probably quite a lot more that have not yet been identified. In particular regions, where man has to rely excessively on one kind of foodstuff (e.g. places where there is almost nothing to eat but maize), some of these minor factors may have real importance. In most of the world, however, mankind still lives on a mixed diet which gives an adequate supply of the minor constituents provided there is sufficient of the three major substances, and therefore I shall not here say anything more about the minor constituents.

Only quite a small fraction of the food man eats is retained in the body. The rest is essentially fuel. This provides energy for movements, both of the body as a whole and of its internal machinery, such as the heart beat, movement of the lungs in respiration, and so on, and for the chemical processes by which food is first broken down into simpler compounds and then rebuilt into the substances of the human body. The amount of food which a man processes during a lifetime is rather

Figure 3.1: Man's Lifetime Food Intake

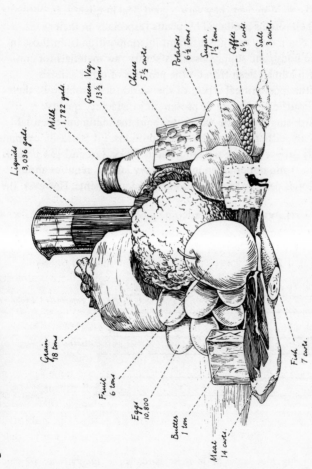

Liquids
3,036 galls.

Milk
1,782 galls.

Green Veg.
13½ tons

Cheese
5½ cwts.

Potatoes
6½ tons

Sugar
1½ tons

Coffee
6½ cwts.

Salt
3 cwts.

Grain
18 tons

Fruit
6 tons

Eggs
10,800

Butter
1 ton

Meat
14 cwts.

Fish
7 cwts.

Source: After a picture by Hans Bauer, originally made for an exhibition 'Wunder des Lebens' held in Berlin, 1931. Based on the life-style of a German peasant of that date.

impressive when compared to his own bulk (Figure 3.1). The quantities of food used for producing energy are usually measured in terms of calories which is a measure of the energy produced. One normal calorie is rather too small a unit to be convenient in this connection, so human diet is usually reckoned in Calories with a capital C, which stands for 1,000 calories and can also be called one kilo-calorie.

All the main components — carbohydrates, fats, proteins — can be used by the body to provide energy, but it is only from the proteins in the food that the body can make its own proteins, and they are, therefore, a specially important constituent of diet. Unfortunately, they are the most costly of the three classes in terms of the energy required to produce them. Moreover they vary a great deal in quality. In particular, most of the proteins produced by plants (especially in their seeds, which we commonly eat) are different in composition from those in the human body, and supply less satisfactory raw materials for conversion into human flesh than do the proteins of other animals. Probably the most critical aspect of the world food problem is, therefore, the insufficient supply of protein of satisfactory quality.

It is surprising how little we know about the minimum essential requirements, either for Calories or for proteins.[1] It is usually estimated that a fully grown person, weighing about 70 kg (around 154 pounds or 11 stones) and not engaged in very heavy labour, requires about 3,000 Calories per day to meet his energy requirements. However, the

Figure 3.2: The Sharing of the World's Food

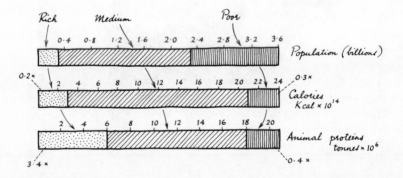

Source: Drawing from figures in Georg Borgstrom's *The Hungry Planet* (Macmillan, N.Y., 1967).

Figure 3.3: Calorie and Protein Supply, Selected Areas

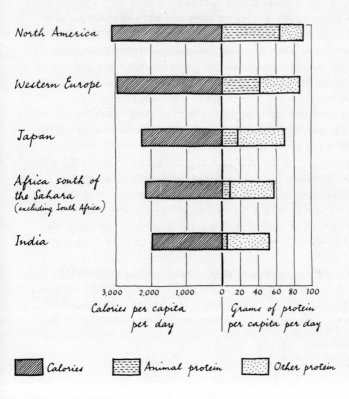

Calories per capita per day

Grams of protein per capita per day

- ▨ Calories
- ▨ Animal protein
- ▨ Other protein

Source: *Population Bulletin*, vol. 24, no. 1, February 1968.

world's food is very unequally shared between the rich and the poor countries (Figure 3.2), and there are many of the world's inhabitants, perhaps as many as one-third, who do not get as much as this. The average Calorie intake of the Indian peasant is calculated to be about 1,800–2,000 per day per person (Figure 3.3). If this is adjusted to cover the numbers of children and people of small stature, this would correspond to 2,500 Calories for our standard 11 stone person, which would still leave a gap of about 500 Calories. One would think that such people must either behave in a rather lethargic way, which uses up little energy, or starve to death quite soon. However, the minimum of 3,000 was worked out for people from the rich countries of Europe and America who are accustomed to dealing with much more than 3,000 Calories per day, and it is possible that their physiology has become rather wasteful and inefficient; if they had to live on a smaller Calorie intake they might learn to digest and make use of a greater proportion of what they put into their mouths. Indeed experiments with some laboratory animals, particularly rats, have shown that restriction of the diet to a very low level may produce an increase in the life span. It has been argued that, in those regions of the world where people tend to live to unusually late ages, a contributory factor has been the low level of their Calorie intake throughout their life.[2] (Another even more important factor may be unreliability of the records!)

The estimates for the minimum requirements for protein are also uncertain. Protein is not only required to make the new proteins which constitute the main part of the body's growth during early life; it is also necessary for the renewal of some proteins which wear out and have to be discarded during the working of the body. The digestion of the food in the gut, the formation of urine and sweat and

Figure 3.4: Minimum Protein Requirement per Day (FAO/WHO)

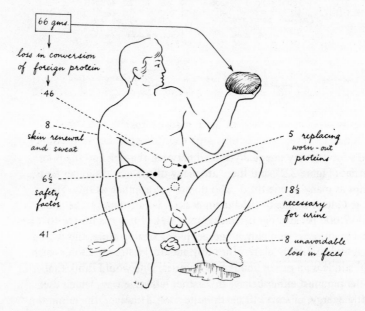

Source: *Energy and Protein Requirements*, Joint FAO/WHO Ad Hoc Expert Committee, publ. FAO, Rome, 1965.

various other functions require the nitrogen from broken-down proteins as an essential part of their machinery (Figure 3.4). It is not certain, however, just how little would suffice, but the main international organisations (The Food and Agricultural Organisation (FAO) and the World Health Organisation (WHO) of the United Nations) have quoted a minimum requirement of about 66 g of protein per day for a 65 kg person. This is regarded as an absolute minimum, below which damage would soon become serious; a safely adequate diet would require about half as much again.

In view of the difficulties and uncertainties of trying to fix these theoretical minima, it is probably more sensible to approach the problem by enquiring whether a lack of protein or of Calories is producing harmful effects on the health of a population.

In many of the poorer countries of the world, particularly in the tropics, the clinical evidence of under-nourishment is often obvious. The best-known example is the disease of children known as Kwashiokor, which produces a swollen belly, spindly arms and legs, lethargy and eventually death. One of its major precipitating factors is certainly a deficiency of protein in the diet, although some doctors think other factors may also be involved. It is also common to find a pattern of ill health known as marasmus, which is brought about by deficiency in energy-producing foods. Dr J.C. Waterlow[3] of the London School of Hygiene and Tropical Medicine has recently written that

broadly speaking Kwashiokor may perhaps be regarded as a disease of rural communities, marasmus of urban ones. With rapidly increasing urbanisation in most developing countries, marasmus is becoming an ever more serious problem. Since it tends to occur at an earlier age than Kwashiokor, permanent effects on development are more likely.

It is, of course, more difficult to recognise definite medical signs when the diet is only slightly inadequate. However, in nearly all countries, the richer citizens, who may be expected to provide themselves with a better diet than those at the other end of the scale, are healthier and usually larger and more muscular than the poor. It is worth remembering, also, the remarkable increase in the average height of the Japanese population, or of the children of Japanese who emigrated to America, when they started eating richer, more adequate diets.

Producing and Using the World's Food

As we saw in the chapter on ecology, all the natural foodstuffs in the
world are ultimately based on the use by plants of the sun's energy.
Through the mechanism of photosynthesis, water is combined with
carbon dioxide to produce starches and sugars. Some of these are
eaten directly by man, whereas other parts may be processed through
animals, to form animal proteins and fats. Borgstrom has made
estimates of the total amount of energy fixed by plants, and of the
amount of this which is used, either directly or after processing by
animals, to produce the world's food. His estimates are shown in
Figure 3.5. Apparently we are already converting into food about

Figure 3.5: Use of Primary Photosynthesis Calories

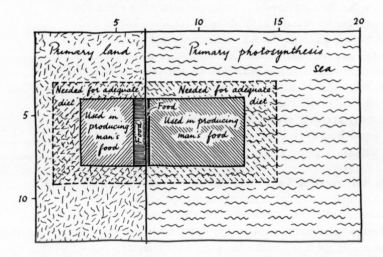

Source: Based on data given in Georg Borgstrom's *The Hungry Planet* (Macmillan,
NY, 1967).

one-fifth of the Calories produced on land, but only somewhat under
15 per cent of that fixed in the seas. Borgstrom reckons, however,
that if everybody alive today had a really adequate diet we should
need to double both these figures. If the population then doubled, we
should have to double them again, which would mean we would have
to use 80 per cent of all the sun's energy fixed by plants anywhere on
the land's surface for converting into food. This certainly sounds a very

formidable, and perhaps impossible, undertaking.

It is characteristic of man's dietary habits, at least since his remote hunting ancestors, that he derives much of his food from animals. These animals themselves have to live on plants, and the burden which man's food places on the plant world must therefore be assessed not only in terms of the numbers of men but of their domestic food-producing animals as well. The magnitude of this extra load is shown in Figure 3.6, in which the world totals of sheep, pigs, cattle, etc. have been converted into 'man equivalents' in respect of their protein requirements. That is to say the areas in Figure 3.6 indicate the relative demand made by that variety of animal on plant proteins. The world's cattle, for instance, consume about three times as much protein (all of it vegetable protein) as does the human population.

One might ask whether it is necessary for man to have this enormous

Figure 3.6: Man and Livestock — Total Protein Requirements

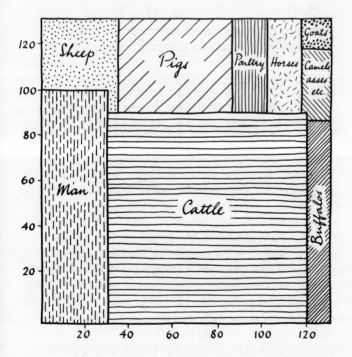

Source: Based on data given in Georg Borgstrom's *The Hungry Planet* (Macmillan, NY, 1967).

entourage of domestic animals. Undoubtedly some of the animal protein man eats can be regarded as a luxury. This comes out if one compares, as in Figure 3.7, the contributions which the animal and

Figure 3.7: Reliance on Animal and Vegetable Foods

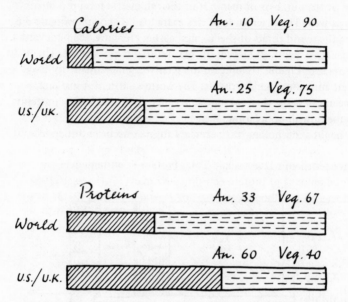

Source: Based on data given in Georg Borgstrom's *The Hungry Planet* (Macmillan, NY, 1967).

vegetable world make to the diets of the rich countries, such as the USA and UK, and to the world as a whole. For both calories and protein, the rich countries make disproportionate use of animal sources. However, even the average world citizen gets about one-third of his protein from animal material, and animal sources are not entirely luxuries which could be got rid of without doing much harm. Domestic animals can harvest vegetation, such as grass, which would be very difficult for man to collect himself, and can then digest this material, with which man's stomach is not able to cope. We finish up with proteins of high quality and good digestibility, starting from vegetable material which it would be impractical or impossible for man to use himself.

Thus some sorts of domestic animals like cattle, sheep, buffaloes and goats certainly perform a very valuable function. On the other hand, two quite important categories of livestock, pigs and poultry, are often fed on material which is closely similar to human food. It is true that they also can deal with food which is below normal human standard, such as inferior grains, or slightly spoilt or inadequately cleaned materials. So long as they are used as scavengers, to consume the more or less inevitable wastes of the human food production processes, they can be regarded as earning their keep. But quite often nowadays, particularly in the industrialised agriculture of the developed world, they are fed protein – rich materials which with a little further care could have been made quite suitable for direct human consumption. Even though pigs are reasonably, and poultry extraordinarily, efficient converters of second-rate foodstuffs into bacon and eggs, these must really be considered as luxury products which the world as a whole may not be able or willing to go on producing in large quantities.

Another way of looking at the budget of man's protein foodstuffs is shown in Figure 3.8. Again the figures are taken from Borgstrom, but I have set them out in visual form. On the left we have estimates of the total amount of protein consumed by man (for the years 1958–9). That was 60.1 million metric tons of vegetable protein, 21.3 million metric tons of terrestrial animal protein and 3 mmt of fish protein. To the right and below are shown the quantities of protein in

Figure 3.8: Man's Protein Budget

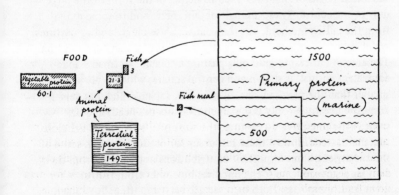

Note: The large squares (right and below) show the primary production of protein by the photosyntheses. That used for human food is indicated in the small rectangles at the top left. The figures (corresponding to the areas of the rectangles) are in million metric tonnes: years 1958–9.

Source: Based on data given in Georg Borgstrom's *The Hungry Planet* (Macmillan, NY, 1967).

plants (including the minute marine phyto-plankton) which had to be processed to produce the animal and fish proteins which man has eaten. As this diagram shows, it took about 7 units of primary terrestrial protein to produce one unit of animal meat for human consumption and as much as 500 units of primary protein in the sea to be processed into one unit which man could use.

There is in general a very clear-cut relationship between the wealth of a country, measured by GNP per head and the amount of animal protein which its population consumes. Some typical figures are shown in Figure 3.9. Notice that on this figure the horizontal lines for a minimum, and for a fully adequate intake refer to total protein, including vegetable as well as animal. Many of the countries which fall below this line are actually getting enough protein because of the additional vegetable material they eat. Meat-producing states, such as Argentina or Australia, eat considerably more animal protein than would be expected solely on the base of their monetary income.

Different countries get their food by remarkably different arrangements of the basic processes. Three contrasting examples are shown in Figure 3.10; the Indian, American and Japanese. In each of these figures, there is a large square which shows the relative areas of cultivated land available per head of the population. However, in each country there are also a number of domestic animals, and these are shown, in terms of 'man-sized' equivalents, in the form of the large dots in the centre. These animals obtain their food to some extent from the cultivated land, but they can also use range land or pastures, which do not give any crops directly suited for human consumption. The area of cultivated land plus pasture available per 'man + man-equivalent animal' is shown as a central square, which is always smaller than the previous one, although in Japan, which has very few domestic livestock (only 0.6 man-equivalents per head) and also rather little uncultivated pasture, the sizes of the two areas are close together. In addition to these resources for producing food, some of the countries obtain important contributions not derived from their own land surface. One such contribution comes from fish, another from trade (imports). Both of these are very important for Japan, and make some, but rather less, impact on India. They are expressed here by being translated into terms of land areas which would yield the same amount of protein.[4]

The Costs of Food Production

The industrialised countries differ enormously from the unindustrialised

Figure 3.9: Animal Protein per Head Plotted against GNP

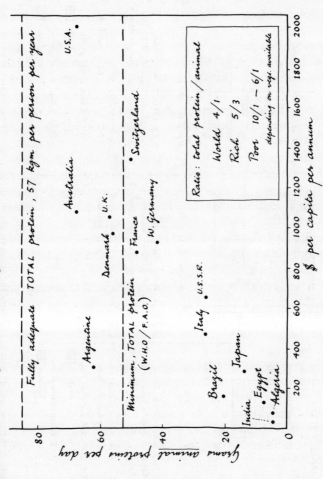

Source: For the particular case of Britain, see Kenneth Mellanby, *Can Britain Feed Herself?* (Merlin Press, 1975); and *Agricultural Productivity in the 1980s*, Phil. Trans. Roy. Soc. London, B267, 1973, 1–172.

Figure 3.10: Three Ways of Obtaining a Diet

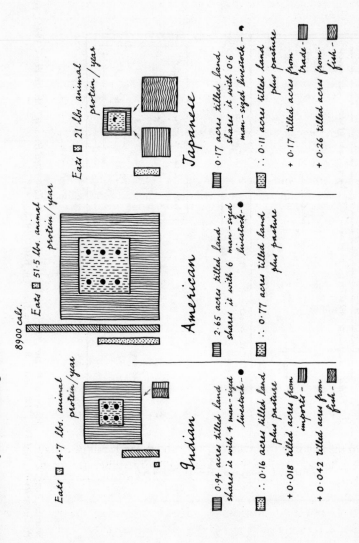

Note: In each diagram, the two upright bars at left show the amounts of protein and carbohydrate eaten per year (carbohydrates for Japan not shown). The lined squares show amounts of tilled land available per head, or tilled-land-plus-pasture per man-plus-livestock. India and Japan both have imports of food and important fisheries.

Source: Based on data given in Georg Borgstrom's *The Hungry Planet* (Macmillan, NY, 1967).

majority of mankind in the proportion of their labour force which is
employed in food production, in the quantity of energy devoted to
getting a meal ready to eat on the table, and in the productivity per
year of one agricultural worker or one acre of cultivated land. The
most publicised of these differences are the last two; America probably
heads the world league for greatest production per year per farm
worker, and England produces most per acre. But that is not the whole
story.[5]

Modern methods of agriculture, which industrial societies regard as
so 'efficient', do indeed require not too much human labour, though a
good deal more is involved than most people think — up to 20 per cent
of the whole labour force, when one takes into account all the ancillary
services. But there is one thing they undoubtedly do require in large
quantities, and that is energy. It is only in the last few years that anyone has tried to estimate the energy inputs into growing a crop. Table
3.1[6] is concerned with producing an acre of corn (maize) and transporting
it to the point of bulk sale (not of later processing, storing, selling etc.).

Table 3.1: Inputs into an Acre of Corn (Maize)

	1945	1970
Labour	23	9 hours
Manufacturing machinery	180	420 K. cals
Gasoline	15	22 gals
Nitrogen fertiliser	7	112 lb
Phosphorus	7	31 lb
Potassium	5	60 lb
Insecticides and herbicides	0	2 lb
Irrigation	19	34 K.cals
Drying	10	120 K.cals
Transportation	20	70 K.cals
Electricity	32	310 K.cals

In 1970 the inputs per year amounted to about 954 K.cals of energy,
plus 22 gallons of gasoline, about 200 pounds of fertilisers (nitrogen,
phosphorus and potassium), a couple of pounds of pesticides and weed-
killers, and only 9 hours of human labour. For this the average return
in 1970 was 81 bushels of harvested corn. For comparison the figures for
a quarter of a century earlier (1945) were 260 K.cals, plus 15 gallons
gasoline, about 19 pounds fertilisers, no pesticides or weed-killers, but
23 hours of human labour, with an over-all return of 34 bushels (Table
3.1). Thus US agriculture has increased output per acre almost two and

a half times, at the same time cutting down labour per acre in about the same proportion, so that the output per hour of human work on the land has been increased by a factor of about 2½ times 2½, i.e. about 6¾, but this has been at the cost of reducing the number of jobs available by 2½ and of using a bit over 3½ times as much energy, increasing the fertilisers by more than ten times, and using new poisons – and both fertilisers and sophisticated selective pest- and weed-killers cost a great deal of energy and labour to produce. Another recent estimate is that the energy input into US food production was increased over ten times between 1920 and 1970, but output was only doubled: if so, the process is at the upper end of an S-shaped curve.[7]

Slessor and Leach[8] have made similar estimates for a wider range of crops, including animal produce, using figures for the UK, which has in some ways (in terms of acreage, for example) the most efficient agriculture in the world. They sum up their figures in terms of an Energy Ratio, E, which is Output of Food divided by Input of Energy. Most vegetable crops have an Energy Ratio between 1 (potatoes about 1.1) and 2 (wheat, farm gate 2.2, and bread 1.4). But animal products have usually much worse ratios, except for stock like hill sheep, which are kept under almost wild conditions. Intense dairying, and still more pig and poultry production, which rely heavily on other agricultural crops (maize, barley, etc.) for food, have strikingly low ratios (milk 0.33, battery eggs 0.16, freezer trawler fish as low as 0.05 even if one takes account only of the oil fuel loaded at the docks).

Of course, the mere fact that industrialised farming needs great inputs of energy does not necessarily imply that it isn't a good buy. It does greatly reduce the demands for labour in farming, and thus the number of farmworkers to be fed, and makes it possible to produce food for greatly increased urban populations on a smaller acreage than would otherwise be required. However, the world is certainly moving into a period in which energy will not be available on such easy terms as in the past, so the food/energy equation is likely to be a major concern of industrialised countries for the next few decades at least; in developing countries with great reserves of manpower, it may really be wasteful.[9]

One solution may be a more sensible recycling of farm wastes. Cereal crops, for instance, produce great masses of straw. It is difficult to use these as animal food-stuffs and they are often just burnt in the fields where they make a smoke nuisance. They could be burnt in a con-trolled way, to produce power; or fermented and turned into methane gas or alcohol, which are quite useful fuels. Leach calculates that on an

ordinary mixed farm of the type common in Europe (though not so
widespread in the US where farms tend to be more specialised) the
cereal straw contains as much energy as the present fuel input per acre
for all farms except the most intense pig and poultry outfits. Again,
nearly all the fertilisers required are there in the wastes and animal
manure of a mixed farm, which are nowadays treated mainly as a
nuisance, the disposal of which often uses considerable energy and
which would require even more if pollution were to be properly
controlled. The manufacture of the fertilisers used on a modern farm,
particularly the nitrogen fertilisers, accounts for around a quarter of
the energy inputs. It would cost some energy to spread the animal
manures back over the surface of the land, but certainly nothing like
that amount, if suitable equipment were developed.

The figures discussed above give the energy costs of farm produce
'at the farm gate'; but of course a great deal more goes on before it
appears as a cooked meal at anyone's dinner table. So far even fewer
attempts have been made to estimate quantitatively the energy
inputs 'downstream from the farm gate'. One analysis of data for the
whole US in 1963, by Hirst,[10] produced results summarised in the
Table below, with the figures rounded out, and shown as a diagram in
Figure 3.11.

Table 3.2

	Energy use (trillion Btu)	Electricity use (billion-kw-hr)
Farm produce (at farm gate)		
to personal consumption	230	4
to processing plants	860	16
Food processing	2000	36
Transport	170	1
Trading (wholesaling, retailing)	980	26
Home (cooking, refrigeration, shopping)	1870	104
Totals	6110	187

Thus, roughly speaking, the actual production of the food on the
farm takes about one-sixth of the total energy; processing it takes
another two-sixths; transport and selling it, slightly over one-sixth,
and buying it and dealing with it at home nearly the last two-sixths.

Figure 3.11: Energy Inputs into Producing and Preparing Food

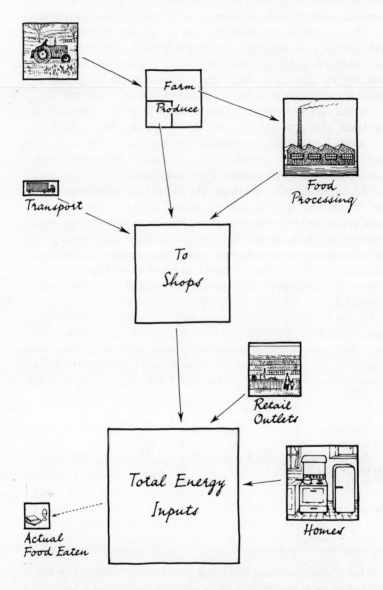

Note: The area of the squares are proportional to the energy quantities.

Source: Eric Hirst, 'Food-Related Energy Requirements', *Science 184*, 12 April 1974, 132.

The whole operation uses about 12 per cent of the total US energy budget, and 22 per cent of the electricity budget; its day-to-day operations absorb nearly a quarter of the disposable personal income of US citizens (plus the long-term investment costs of building the mines, refining plants, car factories, generating plants etc., which have not been included in the above costings).

It is alarming to realise the degree to which we have allowed the production of man's basic biological necessity, food, to become dependent on inputs of energy from such fundamentally unreliable or dangerous sources as imported fossil fuel (e.g. oil) or nuclear energy.

The food/energy equation is of course very different indeed in the Third World. Roughly speaking, the more primitive the agricultural practices, the higher their energy ratio, as Leach defines it. For simple agriculture, with hardly any energy input except direct human labour, the ER is around 30 to 50. These systems typically require both great areas of land and large labour forces. In the future large labour forces may be available in the developing world, but there is not enough reasonably fertile land to support the increased numbers of people in this way. On the other hand, it is almost inconceivable that sufficient energy could be made available to enable the Third World to run its agriculture on an American or even European pattern.

Clearly, the Third World has to look for a sensible path between the two extremes. With present techniques, the poor countries would give a better return for the investment of some more energy into farms than would the rich countries, which are getting into a situation of diminishing returns. They should certainly get a bigger share, but they should not squander it as thoughtlessly as industrialised agriculture has been doing.

Producing More Food

It is usually claimed that, as a result of improvements in agriculture, the food supplies per head in the world as a whole are gradually improving. This of course is not claimed as anything more than an average figure, which can conceal very large local deficiencies (or gluts). But it also fails to reflect geographical differences which are too large to be dismissed as merely local. It is the (relatively small) richer part of the world population whose food supplies have been increasing; in the much more populous developing countries food production has been barely keeping pace with population increase. In the future, as populations grow still greater, the amount of food per head will diminish unless something can be done to increase production.

Figure 3.12: Food Production and Population Increase

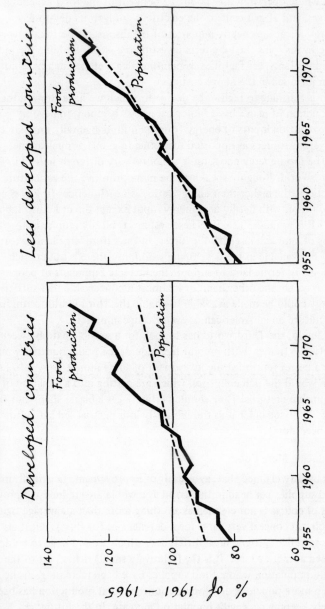

Source: Redrawn from *Ceres*, May/June 1974, no. 39, p. 33.

New Land

It was mainly by exploiting the then virgin lands of North America, Australia and New Zealand, that Europe was able to feed the enormous increase in its population which accompanied the Industrial Revolution of the last century. By now, however, there is very little unused but usable land left in most parts of the world (see Figure 3.13); and what there is requires rather expensive treatment to bring it into use. The Soviet Union has been making quite intense efforts to increase its cultivated area, and still has a good deal of not unpromising space in which this might be done, but the experience of its Virgin Lands Programmes has shown that the job is not an easy one. Most other parts of the world are worse off.

Some of the poor and ill-fed countries might try converting some of their agricultural land from growing export crops to producing food for their own use. The problems here are twofold. Would it really pay a country to forego the foreign exchange it earns with some export crop, say coffee, which it can use to buy grain from the regions of the world where grain can be grown most easily? It would clearly depend on the exact prices reigning. Sometimes it might be sensible to do so and sometimes not. Secondly, there is the enormous size of the problem. Borgstrom[11] calculates that to bring the Brazilian diet up to the standard of Italy requires an increase of acreage (or increase in yield) of about 60 per cent, which is equivalent to about twice the area in Brazil at present devoted to coffee. However, it seems quite likely that, as the pressure of population on foodstuffs increases, there will be some diversion of agricultural land from relatively luxury crops to more directly food-producing ones, and although this alone cannot solve the problem it might provide a useful amount of help.

Fertilisers

Crop yields per acre in intensively cultivated areas such as north-western Europe, Japan and certain parts of the United States are often several times as great as those of similar crops grown under average conditions. This is mainly due to the use of greater quantities of fertiliser, together with chemical control of pests and weeds. There are still enormous areas in the grain-growing regions of the US Midwest and in Canada, whose yields could be much increased by extra fertiliser. What are the difficulties? The fertilisers containing nitrogen require a great deal of power both for production and for transport. The other main type of fertiliser, phosphate, is already beginning to be in short supply; it has to be produced from rocks containing phosphate, and

Figure 3.13: Use of Potentially Arable Soils in Tropics

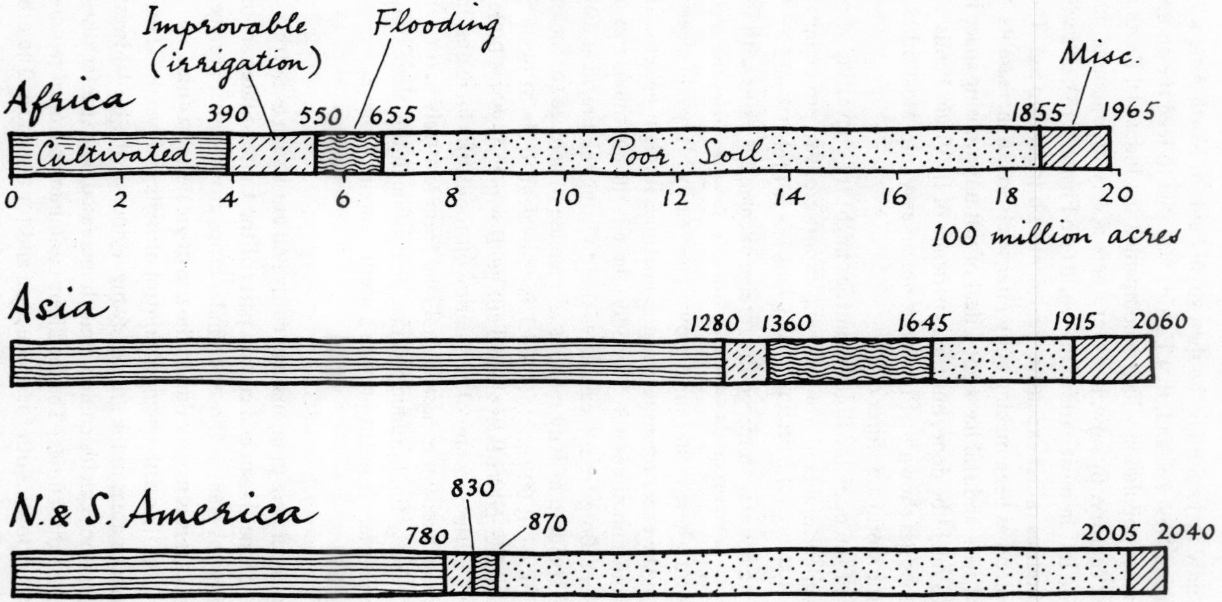

Source: *The World's Food Problem*, Report of President's Science Advisory Committee, vol. 2 (Government Printing Office, Washington, DC, 1972).

the richer sources are beginning to become worked out.

However, there is an enormous waste of valuable fertilisers involved in our present treatment of sewage. In traditional agriculture in most parts of the world, human excrements have been returned directly to the soil, while manure from animals, usually mixed with straw, collected into a great open dung heap, was one of the most valuable properties a farmer could possess. But scattering untreated human excrement about the place is a wonderful way to disseminate diseases such as cholera, enteritis and intestinal worms, and spreading manure is extremely labour-consuming.

It is, however, very unsatisfactory to allow good fertilising sewage from high concentrations of human beings or their domestic animals simply to run into rivers and lakes, which they over-fertilise to such an extent that they produce degenerative eutrophication. One relatively simple procedure for handling small quantities would be to pipe it into ponds managed for the production of algal protein or fish. It is urgently necessary to develop methods to extract the valuable constituents from larger quantities of sewage from intense animal-production locations and from big cities. Probably the most important substances are the phosphates, since good mineral sources are rapidly being used up. Some of the mined phosphate is used as fertiliser in food production, which gives it at least one turn through the human digestive system, but some of it goes into the manufacture of detergents and appears in the sewage effluent before it has added anything to man's food supply. How to capture and recycle this raw material at costs which are economically acceptable is still a largely unsolved problem. One development might be high intensity production of vegetable crops indoors, in buildings perhaps something like multi-storey car-parks, with artificial lighting and artificial atmosphere control, located in some of the semi-urban areas by which most cities are surrounded. Here they would be quite near the sewage works, so that the problems of transporting and spreading the fertiliser would be minimised.

Another improvement would be more control over where the fertiliser is put. At present fertilisers are usually spread over the whole land surface and a great deal is washed away before it actually gets to the the roots of the plants. In the early stages of plant growth, before the roots have spread widely, the fertiliser should be applied only in the immediate vicinity of the seed, and should be in a form in which the valuable nutrients go on being released gradually over a long period, rather like the drugs in the 24-hour cold cures.

Much of the nitrogen used by our crops has been converted out of the atmosphere into usable form by naturally occurring bacteria and little has so far been done to improve their efficiency. They are just beginning to be accessible to geneticists, who are trying to breed and disseminate more efficient forms of them.[12] Moreover, as we learn more about how these organisms work, we should be able to discover why they are at present only associated with the roots of certain types of plants. One of the great biological Utopian daydreams — which does not look quite impossible — is to arrange an intimate liaison between nitrogen-fixing micro-organisms and the major cereal crop plants such as wheat and rice or even root crops, such as carrots.[13]

We should, in fact, be able to find much better chemical ways of producing nitrate fertiliser out of the atmosphere. The present methods require very large amounts of energy at high temperatures, but if bacteria can do it at soil temperatures, with very little energy input, it should not be beyond the wit of man to find out how to do it under those circumstances too. Chemists have already found some substances ('catalysts') which can bring about the essential step of causing nitrogen to combine with hydrogen to form ammonia at fairly low temperatures, but they have not yet discovered anything very efficient. Another possibility is to extract, out of the nitrogen-fixing organisms, the substances (biological catalysts or enzymes) which they use for this purpose. A new technology is developing, by which such enzymes can be absorbed on to pellets of plastic, and still go on performing their extraordinary chemical feats.[14] Carl Heden, the Director of the most important Applied Microbial Laboratory in Sweden, once listed,[15] only half jokingly,

> the three gifts I would ask from a good fairy, if I met one. The *first* was a solid-phase enzyme reactor, small and simple enough to do the job of making a nitrogen fertiliser directly from the air, in any small Indian town.

I guess that with about one week's expenditure on Concorde you would have at least a 50:50 chance of getting it within ten years (we will come on to Heden's other two wishes in the section on 'Single Cell Protein').

Water Control

The growth of vegetation requires enormous quantities of water, from about 400 tons (wheat) to 4,000 tons (vegetables), to yield one ton of

Figure 3.14: Water Transpired by a Growing Plant

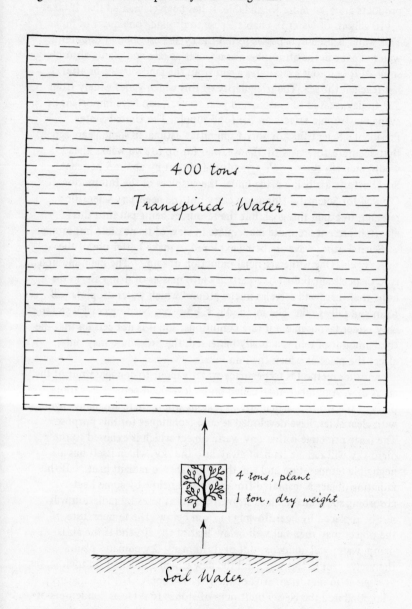

Source: Redrawn from *Ceres*, May/June 1974, no. 39, p. 33.

dry vegetable matter (Figure 3.14). The water costs of animal products are even more formidable. It has been calculated that it takes 1,110 gallons of water to enable a cow to produce one quart of milk. This water is used as it passes round the cycle described in Chapter 2; water vapour in the atmosphere condenses as rain and plants absorb some of it before it evaporates again from the land surface or after it has reached the sea. The irregularity of this which varies widely from day to day, season to season, and year to year, can have important or even catastrophic effects on the food supply. The United States President's Scientific Advisory Committee estimated some years ago that accurate forecasts of the weather for up to two weeks ahead would increase the world's agricultural output by about 5 per cent. Some efforts are being made under the auspices of the International Council for Scientific Unions to carry out the necessary scientific research to attain this goal, but the resources being put into this effort at present are quite inadequate in view of its possible importance.

Several other ways are being explored to make better use of the water cycle. One is the artificial induction of rain.[16] The main method is to disperse small dust-like particles into masses of damp air, in the hope that these will serve as nuclei around which water droplets will form and fall as rain. The method has, however, been successful so far only under favourable but rare conditions, and it is not certain that the total amount of rain is actually increased; the procedure may only affect the place at which the rain falls.

Another method is to persuade water vapour to condense out of the air as dew. A number of so-called underdeveloped peoples in various parts of the world, particularly in regions where there are many nights with clear skies, have developed several techniques for this purpose. The basic principle is that any warm object which is exposed to the night sky will radiate its heat away into the sky, which itself has a negligible temperature and can therefore absorb radiant heat.[17] If the radiating object is insulated from the earth below by some heat-absorbing substance such as straw, the heat it loses by radiation will not be replaced by heat flowing in from below. The temperature of the object may then fall well below that of the air, and if the air is damp, water will condense out of it. In many dry climates plants themselves act in this way, and the dew which condenses on their leaves at night is an important part of their water supply. The Nebataeans who inhabited the Negev built piles of stones to serve as condensers of dew. In Persia, most of which is a high plateau with very clear skies, long walls were built running east and west, so as to make an area of shade, which was heated by the sun during the day, and could also lose heat by radiation at night. In this way they were even able to make ice in sufficient quantities to market it regularly. The ancient skills of handling such devices are being studied again in places like Israel, North Queensland and Arizona, and they could probably be of real use in some of the dry desert areas.

Much more important effects on the world's food supply should come from better handling of existing lakes and rivers. Perhaps the biggest effect to be achieved in the next 10 or 20 years will be by putting to use the enormous quantities of fresh water which now flow northwards to finish up in the Arctic sea. The Soviet Union is actively working on projects to reverse the flow of some of the enormous Siberian rivers by opening canals which will conduct the water southwards instead, into the arid regions of central Asia. In America there are equally ambitious plans to bring water from the northern Canadian 'wet desert' southwards into such hot dry states as Nevada and California. Plans of this kind will probably be achieved and should produce a very substantial increase in food supplies, though it is difficult to calculate how much; and nobody yet knows what effects they might have on the general climate.

Unfortunately there are no such unused supplies of water available for Africa and southern Asia. On the other hand it would probably be possible to make much better use of what water they do have. Methods for doing this have been worked out in greatest detail in Israel, which is exceedingly short of water, and gets rather little rain-fall, and that only in the north of the country.[18] It is claimed that of the rain which falls over Israel, only 2 per cent is allowed to escape back into the sea without being used. The rest is either used to water the plants in the region where it falls or is collected, stored and dis-tributed to places where it is needed.

Each of these processes – collection, storage and distribution – involves a certain sophistication. In the desert areas, for instance, when the rare rain does fall it comes down exceedingly heavily and sweeps almost as a continuous sheet down the hillsides and disappears into deep gullies which lead it out into the sand where it does nobody any good. Another of the ancient water-handling techniques which the Israelis are reviving is to lay out the fields on the hillsides in such a way that perhaps nine-tenths of a valley merely collects water, which is directed into an underground storage tank, for use on the one-tenth on which crops are grown. Water storage should, in fact, always be underground where possible and distributed by pipes, to avoid the enormous loss involved in evaporation from the surface of a lake in hot climates. Papanek[19] has argued that one of the simple inventions the world is really waiting for is a tool, suitable to be built by a village blacksmith, which would enable ordinary peasants to form satisfactory pipes out of local material, such as clay or stabilised earth.

Control of evaporation, and particularly of transpiration of water through plants, is obviously of crucial importance in all regions of the world where water is scarce. It is being investigated most thoroughly in connection with the use of sea water for agriculture. Sea water can actually be used as such for watering certain plants, on certain soils.[20] But it seems unlikely that it can be at all widely used for growing plants useful for food, and it is not at all certain how long it can be carried on before the accumulation of salt in the lower parts of the soil makes it unusable.

Most attempts to use sea water for agriculture depend on first removing the excess salt. There are two basic methods of desalination. One depends on using a membrane which will allow the water to pass, but will hold back the salts (reversed osmosis). The other is distillation, that is to say water vapour or steam is produced and this, which does not contain salts, forms fresh water when it is condensed. The production of steam can be done by actually boiling the sea water or, more gently, by encouraging evaporation from the surface of sea water which is warmed but not raised to boiling point. Both the membrane-filtering techniques and the boiling technique require large amounts of concentrated energy. They are essentially industrial processes of a very energy-consuming kind. The evaporation methods are much less demanding, and I will discuss them first.

The cheapest way of evaporating sea water is to use the heat of the sun. The sea water is run into shallow tanks of concrete or plastic, preferably with a black bottom which absorbs the sun's heat. The tanks, which are usually built long and narrow, are covered with a transparent roof with curved or sloping sides. The water in the tanks is warmed, evaporates, and the water vapour condenses again on the cooler glass roof and runs down the sides to be collected in a trough at the bottom. Installations of this kind are already in use in many arid regions near the sea, from the coasts of Chile to the Aegean islands. It is a very satisfactory process provided one does not want too much water. It has mostly been used to provide drinking water. The quantities required for agricultural irrigation would require enormous areas of tanks.

A much more sophisticated low temperature evaporation scheme

Figure 3.15: Low Temperature Desalination of Sea Water

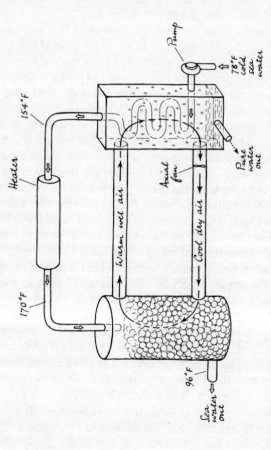

Note: Low temperature desalination of seawater. There are two circulations: (i) cold seawater is pumped in on the right, and up through a coiled tube where it is heated by warm wet air (out of which fresh water condenses); then it is heated further and passes down through a pile of stones, and evaporates some of it; the warm wet air produced is condensed by the incoming cold seawater; and the resultant fresh water is drawn off.

Source: Robert J. Bazell, 'Arid Land Agriculture', *Science*, 12 March 1971.

is being developed in Arizona.[21] The scheme involves using cold sea water which is pumped into the installation to aid the condensation of the water vapour which has been produced by hot sea water. Originally solar energy was used to heat the sea water, but since any place that wanted to run such a scheme would certainly be generating its own electricity, probably with a diesel engine, use was later made of the 'waste heat' in the cooling water of the engine.

They also introduced another improvement which is of very general application. The fresh water was used on plants grown in plastic green-houses. A large sheet of plastic is attached to a low brick or stone wall, and a small pump keeps the air pressure inside the plastic at about half a pound per square foot, above the air pressure outside, so the plastic is inflated, in the form of a long low sausage. The plastic is transparent to the sunlight which the plants need, while the water, led to the plant roots and transpired through their leaves, is trapped inside and not allowed to escape back into the general atmosphere; it can be used again and again. Experimental plants of this kind are working in Arizona and Mexico, and a quite big one, planned to provide food for a sizeable population, is being built in the oil-rich Persian Gulf state of Abu Dhabi. There are quite a large number of areas in the world, in which arid deserts come near enough to the sea coast for developments of this kind to make important contributions to the world's food supply.

The desalination systems which depend on large inputs of energy have so far also been used mainly for the provision of drinking water. They have relied on conventional fuels, such as coal, oil and elec-tricity. The possibility of organising desalination for agricultural purposes in connection with nuclear electricity generating plants is now being seriously considered. Such integrated plants have been referred to as agro-industrial complexes, or 'Nuplexes'.[22] The Food and Agricultural Organisation of the United Nations has sketched a complex centred around a nuclear power station of 1—2,000 Megawatts, with a plant to desalinate about 3 million cubic metres of sea water per day, serving a cultivable area of several thousand hectares, capable of feeding several million persons. These would, of course, involve the dangers of all nuclear power plants, particularly in the disposal of waste products. In any case, they are more a way in which the twenty-first century could solve its problem, if it wishes to, than something which will rescue us from the dangers of the next 30 years.

New Varieties of Crop Plants

The greatest improvement in the food situation of the undernourished tropical countries in recent years has been by the introduction of new varieties of important crops, such as wheat and rice, which have been bred specifically to suit the conditions in the different countries. With several of the most important crops, there has been extraordinary success in raising yields per acre. This has been hailed as the Green Revolution.[23] To give a concrete example of what this does, and does not, mean I will take the instance of India.[24]

Throughout the first half of the 1960s the Indian crop of food grains was about 83 million tons and was hardly increasing at all. In fact there was a bad drought in 1966–7 when it fell to 73 million. Meanwhile the population was growing at the rate of about 2.5 per cent (roughly a million more people each month). India was having to import 10–12 million tons of grain annually. The new high-yielding varieties were introduced in 1967, though at first there was only enough seed to plant about one-tenth of the total cultivated area. However, the total yield immediately jumped up to about 95 million tons. By 1971 the area growing the improved varieties had about doubled, and the yield was up to 108 million tons. India was for a time looking for export markets to which it could sell some of its surplus.

This looks, and is, too good to be true. In the first place, these are global figures, which do not reveal the very great differences within the rural population. The 'surplus' grain is surplus to what can be sold locally, rather than to what is needed by the country as a whole. Active discussion is now going on in India about how best to spread the benefits of the increased productivity more widely. One school of thought maintains that it is essential to take rapid and effective steps to re-distribute the land more fairly, cutting up the larger farms. According to Roy,[25] at present about 44 per cent of farmers own less than an acre of land per household, and about a quarter of these own no land at all. The argument is that all the benefits of the improved yields are going to the rich and middle-sized farmers, while this great body of poor ones gets no benefit at all. The opposite argument is that as the richer farmers get richer, they will be willing to pay wages for the extra labour required in intensive farming, and will also have money to spend on general amenities which were previously out of their reach. Thapar cites the example of Ludhiana:[26]

Nowhere is their impact more pronounced than in Ludhiana, the highly progressive district in Punjab State, whose 45,000 farmers are among the highest producers of wheat per acre in the world. Their gross incomes have shot up by well over 300 per cent in the last decade. This has brought a better deal for landless labour too. Intensive cultivation means more work. Wages have been jacked up by over 250 per cent, and because the new short-duration varieties permit double-cropping, the busy season is no longer a matter of days; it spans almost five months of the year.

He goes on to claim that the prosperity of the agriculturalists has brought new economic life to a whole set of ancillary enterprises, such as shops, rural crafts, repair works, etc., in the villages and market towns.

What 'the Green Revolution' has done for the non-farm population of these districts is perhaps even more remarkable than what it has done for their agriculturalists. In the case of Ludhiana, a population of 1.2 million is now enjoying an economic boom as the result of the prosperity of just 45,000 farmers.

Other difficulties and dangers arise from the way in which the new varieties have to be grown. Although they usually do somewhat better than most of the previous varieties even when grown by the old methods of husbandry, the really startling increases in yield are only achieved when the plants get not only plenty of water, but in particular plenty of fertiliser. Water is, of course, a limiting factor in many parts of the world. India is fortunate in that there is a considerable store of underground water all over the great Ganges plain; but the great successes of the past few years have demanded enormous quantities of fertiliser. Most of this has had to be imported. As Ashola Thapar points out, 'in a single year the (Indian) government was forced to set apart more money for the import of chemical fertilisers than the foreign exchange component of the entire first Five Year Plan.' In fact, in energy terms, the amount of power which has to be put into the manufacture and transport of the fertilisers is greater than the power equivalent of the extra grain harvested; but, of course, the grain can be eaten and that is the main point. Moreover India cannot build her own fertiliser plants at a sufficient rate to keep up with the demand. At the present time one of her largest plants, at Sindri, which took several years to build, produces about 350,000 metric tons of nitrogen fertiliser every year. This is only enough to feed the 10–12 million annual increase of population. One new plant of this size would have to be brought into operation every year merely to keep up with population increase if this goes on at the present rate. Finally, there is a danger from the fact that these great yields are only achieved when the crops are grown in large fields which can be planted and cultivated and harvested mechanically. In such large acreages of single varieties there is always the danger that some new pest or virus disease to which the variety is susceptible will appear and then it might wipe out a much larger proportion of the total than would be at risk when farmers were using many different varieties with different disease susceptibilities. Most people closely connected with it conclude that the Green Revolution will, in many parts of the world at least, buy us a little time, say 20–30 years, provided we have reasonably good luck in controlling disease problems, and can organise the provision of sufficient fertiliser. But if, during that time, the world has not succeeded in controlling its rate of population growth, the Green Revolution would eventually be swamped.

The main staple grain crops, such as wheat and rice, the yields of which have been so greatly improved by the Green Revolution, normally supply a considerable fraction of the protein in the diets of the poorer parts of the world. These same people usually get a good deal more protein from vegetables belonging to the pea family, such as beans, peas, lentils, pulses, etc. These other main protein-yielding vegetables have not yet been much improved by the plant breeders. Plant breeding is inherently a fairly slow process, but some methods have been found recently for speeding it up, for instance by the use of tissue cultures and we can expect much increased yields of vegetable proteins in not too many years.

Vegetable Proteins

Vegetable seed proteins are inferior to animal proteins because they lack some of the amino acids, and have them in a proportion different from that characteristic of human proteins. The nutritive value of vegetable proteins can be greatly improved, either by mixing together those from different plants, so as to get the proportions of amino acids right, or by actually adding the particular amino acids which are deficient. The necessary amino acids can either be synthesised in a chemical factory, or in some cases one can persuade a micro-organism, such as a yeast, alga, or even bacterium, to synthesise them for us. This fortification of natural, but not quite adequate, foods is still rather expensive, but the cost of synthesising or otherwise producing the necessary amino acids (or vitamins or minerals) is being rapidly reduced.

A more drastic proposal is to enlarge the variety of plants from which we take protein.[27] Man has selected for his diet mainly seeds and a few rather juicy plants. This is because the majority of plant tissues contain so much cellulose, which forms a coat round the really living substance of the plant cell, that it cannot be coped with by the human digestive system. N.W. Pirie, of the Rothamstead Experiment Station, England, has for many years been urging that we should develop methods of separating the living substance of the plant cell, which contains the proteins, from the cellulose coats, and then use the protein directly for human nutrition. It would probably never be worth while to try to imitate the gathering of scattered vegetation over a wide area which cattle and sheep can do, but there are many situations in which large quantities of leafy material are gathered together but not used, for instance, the leaves of sugar cane or sugar beet; and we could grow special crops of particularly protein rich vegetation if we had a way of getting at their protein.

There are also some places where good juicy leaves, suitable for protein production, occur as unwanted weeds in vast quantities. In the recently man-made lakes of the tropics, built as water reservoirs and for hydro-electric power, the water usually gets a good supply of mineral nutrients from the soil. It was hoped that this would give rise to a useful fish crop, but in many cases the first result has been an enormous crop of floating water weeds, such as water hyacinths. These are almost useless for any ordinary purposes and they encourage loss of water from the surface by transpiration of it through their leaves. It would be attractive if they could be managed as a controlled crop used for extraction of leaf protein, but the problem is so new that good methods have not yet been worked out.

Another problem is to make leaf protein palatable enough to appeal to the human consumer. Similar problems arise with all the other unconventional proteins, such as those from algae, yeasts, and bacteria, which we shall discuss later. The proteins emerge from the production process as a gooey or creamy liquid, which can be dried to a cheese-like consistency or even to a powder, without harming its nutritive qualities. The dark colour (from the green chlorophyll) can be removed if necessary. It usually does not have a great deal of taste, and can be used by adding it to conventional foods which are normally prepared outside the home, such as sausages, meat pies, dried milk powders, and so on. More adventurous ways of using it are also being developed which involve changing not only the colour and flavour of the product but its texture, so as to make it feel more like meat when it is chewed.

Vegetable protein materials — mostly made from the protein of soya beans — are already being sold to the food industry, in a form corresponding to coarsely minced meat, and there are slices of a similar substance which could be passed off as one of the more featureless conventional meats, such as turkey. But these procedures use a good deal of energy for what are essentially only cosmetic improvement; a good cook could probably produce something nicer than any factory (cf. Chinese or Japanese handling of soya protein in the form of 'bean curd').

Improved Breeds of Animals

What are the possibilities of bringing about a 'Green Revolution' among animals? It is not likely that animal geneticists can achieve such spectacular successes as the plant breeders, and if they are to have any chance at all of doing so, they will have to use unconventional methods.

A first possibility is to domesticate a few more species of animals.[28] Nearly all the animals that man commonly uses were brought into domestication several thousand years ago, before the beginning of the Bronze Age. They provide quite a good range of services, and by this time they have been so improved by selective breeding that it is unlikely that we could at all quickly produce anything more efficient to suit the circumstances and tasks for which they have been adapted. There are, however, large parts of the earth's surface, not wholly unproductive, for which we still have no very suitable domestic animals. In Australia, for instance, the original inhabitants did not use domestic animals. When the white man arrived he stocked it mainly with sheep, and also with cattle in certain regions. These are very different from the types of native animal which live on the local vegetation, which are kangaroos, wallabies and the like, and these might do better in the long run. Certainly the cattle have to be specially bred to stand much hotter climates than their European ancestors were used to, but this problem is being tackled in all sorts of parts of the sub-tropical world fairly successfully. The sheep have so far on the whole been a success, largely because of their production of wool as well as meat. If the world demand for wool is reduced by synthetic fibres, it might well turn out that in parts of the continent some sorts of kangaroo might be better meat producers than sheep.

There are probably more opportunities for new domestications in Africa. Large parts of the continent are open scrub and grassland, famous for carrying enormous herds of grazing animals, such as zebra, wildebeeste, antelopes, buck, etc. Many of these can eat leaves of bushes

as well as grass, so using a greater proportion of vegetation than conventional cattle or sheep. Moreover, much of the continent is afflicted
with serious animal diseases to which the native fauna have in the course
of evolution become immune, while introduced cattle and horses etc.
are very susceptible: in great tracts the presence of the tse-tse fly makes
it impossible to keep cattle. In some regions, which are run as game
parks, there is already some organised cropping of the wild game to
supply the local butchers, and of course the African population has
always relied heavily on game as part of its normal diet and continues to
do so even if it has to get the meat by poaching. Very little has been
done, however, to domesticate the animals in a true sense, involving
controlling their movements and grazing, and selectively breeding them
to increase their efficiency as meat producers. (One of the few recent
domestications has been that of the ostrich to produce feathers for
the fashion trade.)

This is one of the fields in which some of the far-out modern
techniques of cell biology might perhaps be able to play a useful role.
For many decades one of the standard procedures of plant breeders has
been to transfer, into a good cultivated variety of a crop plant, one or
more of the chomosomes from a related wild species, which has
acquired an immunity or resistance to a disease. It is not too difficult
to do this in plants, partly because plant species cross with one another
much more readily than animal species and partly because plants
usually produce such a vast number of seeds that even if the hybrid is
nearly sterile it usually produces just enough seeds to carry on.

Animal breeders have so far not been able to do anything similar.
However, two recent techniques in handling animal cells might come
to the rescue. In the first place, we have discovered how to fuse together
the body cells of animals, even if they belong to different species, by
treating the cells with a killed virus, which injures their outer surfaces
so that they tend to stick together. Reconstituted cells are formed
which contain one nucleus from each of the two parents, say a rat and
mouse, or even a mouse and man. These cells grow and divide; but they
often do this irregularly, so that the daughter cells contain a mixture of
various numbers of chromosomes from the two parents. With patience
and ingenuity, one could pick out the cells which contain whatever
mixture of the parental chromosomes one wished. These would, of
course, still be body cells, incapable of growing up into a new organism.
But there is another method, which consists in removing or inactivating
the nucleus from an egg of one species and injecting into it some other
nucleus under whose influence it is capable of developing into a fully-

formed adult creature.[29]

These methods have been developed in the last few years, and so far they can be applied only to a few types of animals. However, if sufficient effort were put into developing them one should be able to produce, say, a horse with one or two zebra chromosomes, or cattle with a chromosome from some antelope immune to the tse-tse flies' attacks. It would be foolish to suppose that success in this sort of effort would come next year or the one after, but with a reasonable amount of effort one might be able, in say ten years, to make new meat producing strains of animals much better suited to disease-ridden tropical environments than anything we have at present.

There is another allied method which some people (e.g. John Platt[30]) believe could have a very important effect on animal meat supplies. There are enormous differences between individual cattle in the efficiency with which they put on flesh. Careful breeding over centuries in the temperate zone has produced breeds in which the best animals are probably as efficient as one is likely to get for those conditions. Even so, there were many sub-standard animals until the use of artificial insemination made it easier to spread the influence of the best strains more widely. But improvement of the mass of cattle or other animals by normal methods of breeding is bound to be slow, because although a superior male produces a large number of sperm, which can be used to fertilise many females, the offspring will get the other half of their hereditary qualities from their mothers, which will be average, not above it.

One could improve the general run of the animals much faster if one could use only the very superior females as mothers, as one now uses only the very superior males as fathers. Recently this has begun to be a practical possibility. We can, by suitable hormone injections, induce a female to produce large numbers of eggs and after they have been fertilised these can be introduced into the genital tract of foster mothers, and allowed to develop. There is an even further refinement which would be even better. One can imagine taking the body cells of a superior individual and implanting their nuclei into a series of eggs, to substitute for the egg's own original nucleus, and then transplanting these eggs into a foster mother. This would give rise to a whole set of identical twins (known as a 'clone'), all very superior creatures with the characteristics of the individual with whose cells one started.

Both these methods are beginning to be tested in experimental herds.

Figure 3.16: 'Cloning'

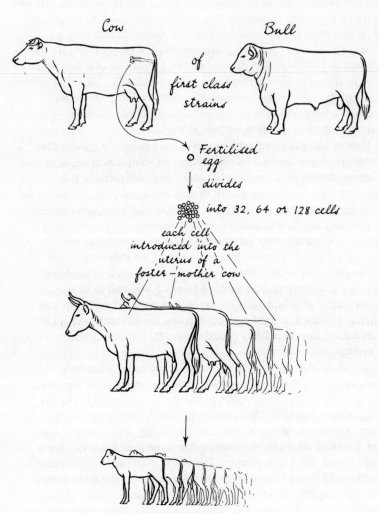

Cow   of   Bull

first class
strains

Fertilised
egg

divides

into 32, 64 or 128 cells

each cell
introduced into the
uterus of a
foster-mother cow

30 or more identical calves

Fish and Fish Farming[31]

At first sight, the figures for the total fish catch compared with the area of the ocean, indicated for instance in Figures 3.5 and 3.8, suggest that there must be more potential to be exploited. However, in practice a great deal of the ocean is almost a desert as far as life is concerned. The limiting factor is the availability of suitable mineral salts, particularly phosphates and nitrates. The minute floating plants capable of photosynthesis, on which the whole productivity of the seas depend, are always so thin on the ground (or rather in the water) as to make non-sense of the suggestion, which has sometimes been made, that we should filter them directly out of the water and convert them into something palatable to eat. In most regions it would be necessary to filter 1,000 million litres of water to get 1 ton of plankton; and it would need 100 plants filtering this quantity every minute to equal the present fish catch.[32] There are a few places where rather larger planktonic animals may be concentrated enough to be worth catching, but whales (if we do not kill them all off) can do this job better than us. For human consumption we need quite sizeable fish. Each step upwards from the plankton is carried out with an average efficiency of about 20 per cent (one-fifth), so that the losses as we go up the ladder are considerable. They vary according to the kind of fish. The herring is fairly efficient, since it is only two steps up the food chain, but the cod is about five steps up. The average over the whole fish crop in the North Atlantic is probably about three steps.

Attempts have been made to calculate the total possible crop from the North Atlantic, an ocean which is relatively well known. The total amount of photosynthesis in it can be calculated with reasonable accuracy. The total quantity of fish now landed would allow for about 3.7 steps up the food chain, whereas the average for the fish we actually catch is probably about 3. This argument suggests that there really are some fish there which we are not at present catching. Most experts seem to think that the fish catch could be increased by perhaps two to three times. In fact certain countries, particularly the Soviet Union and Japan, are investing heavily in deep-sea trawlers and fishing vessels to try to do just this. The poor countries of course, cannot afford such expensive methods of exploitation, but even they are increasing their catch gradually as more boats are fitted with motors instead of relying on sails. From a world point of view, it would be more beneficial to improve this labour-intensive, low capital, peasant fishing in poor countries than to pour more resources into building bigger and better trawlers to get a small improvement in the rich man's diet, or in landings of fish used as animal foodstuffs.

Fish is only a moderately important fraction of the world's supply of animal protein. If the whole of the world's fish were consumed in India it would provide each Indian with about one herring per day. It is a much more important element in the diet in some countries, like Norway, Portugal and Japan, than in other regions, so fish supply can be locally a major factor.

But it is not only the consumption of fish which is different in different regions. Their actual production in the sea is very localised. By far the greater proportion of the fish are found, either in inshore waters which are enriched by runoff from nearby land, or in a few parts of the deep ocean, where there are currents which bring up to the surface water from the depths where there is very little light and life, so that the minerals have accumulated in it (Figure 3.17). One of the most famous of these upswellings is off the coast of Peru, and conjures up enormous swarms of small herring-like fish called anchoveta. The droppings from the sea birds which fed on these fish formed great deposits of guano along the sea coast where they nested, and these have been extensively mined for phosphate fertilisers. Recently the anchovetas themselves have been fished very heavily by the Peruvians. Most of them are turned into fish meal, which was exported to feed livestock in North America and Europe. Only a few years ago there was a spectacular fall in the anchoveta catches.[33] It looked as though man had broken another of the ecological laws which governs his acquisition of food. If too many fish are caught and removed before they have time to lay eggs, the next year's crop will obviously suffer. The Peruvian fisheries seemed to have been devastated by over-fishing, but there has been an unexpected revival already. This is still not fully understood, but it is now thought that it was a change in ocean currents, rather than over-fishing, which caused the sudden drop in production.

There is another great area of upswelling of deep ocean water in the belt around the Antarctic continent. The main animal which man utilised here was the whale, and here over-exploitation has ruined the production. Some species of whale are extinct, or almost extinct, and all the remaining species are in danger; however there is some indication that recent international agreements to limit catches are beginning to be effective.[34]

Fish Farming

Fishing is still carried out mainly by hunting — basically a neolithic way of getting food, even although our fish-hunting methods are vastly

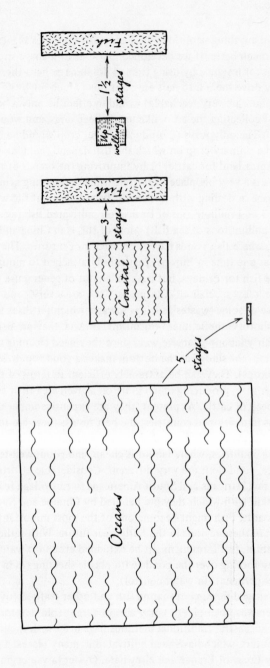

Figure 3.17: Comparisons of Areas of Different Types of Ocean and their Yield of Fish

Source: Based on article by Ryther, *Science*, October 1969.

better than anything neolithic man had. It is sometimes suggested we could do much better if we developed methods to manage shoals of fish at sea, for instance by using trained dolphins to herd them and eventually drive them into nets etc.; but this (which might be possible, since dolphins are very teachable) would in effect be only a better method of collecting the crop, like using sheep dogs, and would not increase it. The only ways to produce a larger crop would be by producing more of the primary crop on which the fish depend (comparable to fertilising grassland for cattle) or by improving the breeds of the fish.

The sea is a very big place to try fertilising or applying genetics. There is more hope in dealing with freshwater fish. At present the world produces 3 or 4 million tons of freshwater cultivated fish (as against about 60 million tons of sea fish). Most of this is in China and South East Asia, where fish ponds have been used for centuries. They were common at one time in Europe, particularly attached to monasteries to provide fish for Fridays, but have fallen out of general use there, except for a few specialised enterprises. They are a very good way of making use of some 'wastes', such as sewage, which fertilises the primary photosynthetic micro-organisms. In Asia, they are usually run in a fairly labour-intensive way, since they need cleaning out from time to time (the sludge at the bottom makes a good top dressing for ordinary crops). They can be extremely efficient in terms of tons of protein per acre, producing much more on a given area than animals such as sheep or cattle. At present, they are expensive under the conditions in developed countries; the best results there are for trout, which can be produced at a cost about twice that of chicken. But in developing countries, where labour is cheap, and good, well-fertilised land scarce, conditions are very different. Considerable efforts are being made to train Africans and South Americans to run village fish ponds with the skill with which they are handled by Chinese and South East Asian peasants. Fish might become one of the most important sources of protein in these regions in the fairly near future. With rather more sophistication, fish farming might be extended even into water-poor regions, by roofing over the ponds with plastic sheeting (as in the Arizona experiments in water control).

The managed farming of marine fish and other seafood (oysters, mussels, prawns, scampi, etc.) may also undergo rapid development. The most successful traditional methods have been with shellfish, such as oysters, which have been cultivated in many places, e.g. Japan, the Biscay Coast of France and elsewhere. Oyster larvae begin their life drifting free in the water, and then settle down and fix themselves to something solid. They can be persuaded to do this not on the sea bed, but on ropes, which can then be hung from floats. In this way enormous numbers of shellfish can be packed into a small area. If this is fertilised to encourage the growth of primary producers, and if there are adequate currents to remove the waste products, enormous crops can be grown. It is claimed that up to 300,000 kilos of mollusc can be produced per hectare per year (the average annual yield of fish from continental shelf seas is about 50 kilos of fish per hectare). But these huge yields are only achieved under ideal conditions, and there are very few places where these occur naturally. There may be other places where ideal or nearly ideal conditions could be produced artificially, but they would require some expenditure on engineering works to control currents.

There has been much less work on the farming of sea fish, but experiments are now being made in several parts of the world to develop suitable methods. One of these regions is Scotland. Attempts to fertilise sea lochs on the West Coast were made as long ago as before World War II, but they were not successful; the fertiliser simply went out to sea with the tide. The most promising method is to grow fish (such as sole) in cages submerged in the water, and to feed them artificially on such things as ground wastes from fish markets. The results are good, if one is content to produce a luxury article, and perhaps that is the way to begin. But we need to find methods of 'mixed farming', for instance stacks of cages containing different species, so that the lower ones pick up the food which drops through the floors of the upper cages and is now wasted. Also, there is as yet little genetics and applied breeding of the kind which has produced our cattle and sheep from their wild ancestors.

Above all, we have not yet learnt how to handle the whole food chain from primary photosynthetic procedures to fish. The importance of this is that the growth of the primary producers could almost certainly be assisted by low temperature heat, which is available in vast quantities in the warmed cooling water from electricity-generating plants. It is one of the great scandals of modern technology that this is looked on as 'waste heat', to be got rid of as cheaply as possible. Small-scale experiments in using it to improve the productivity of fish farming have been made, but the heat was used in such a way that it only prolongs the growing season for a month or two without increasing the food supplies of the fish. Attempts to make use of warm 'cooling' water to irrigate crops in the northwestern United States also have not had much success so far.[35] But underground soil heating has proved its value in the intensive production of vegetables in places with chancy climates (e.g. Scotland). Some way of using this 'waste' energy in food production, either in fish farming or more conventional cultivations, seems certain to be developed fairly soon.

Single Cell Proteins

There are quite a large variety of very primitive organisms, mostly living as isolated single cells, which unlike man can take in very simple materials such as nitrates and phosphates and something containing carbon, and build these up into a protein. One group are the algae, the microscopic single cells floating about in the upper layers of fresh or salt water where they receive energy from the sun's radiation and use this to produce all the constituents of a living organism, including starches, fats and proteins. There are other single-celled organisms, such as yeasts and bacteria which, given fairly simple raw materials, can build up their living substance without the sun's energy. We are only just beginning to learn how to cultivate these things and reap the harvests.

The algae have perhaps been the most thoroughly explored. One of these, known by the name *Spirulina platensis*, is in fact already a traditional human food. It grows in certain lakes around the edges of the Sahara, and at some seasons of the year forms quite a thick green scum, which the local people skim off and cook and eat. It is only in the last few years that outsiders have discovered this peculiar crop and have started to see how it could be more widely used. Most of the work on cultivating algae has been with other species which nobody has used before. Several quite large pilot-plant installations to grow concentrated crops of algae have been erected. Essentially one needs to supply the algae with a continuous input of nitrates and phosphates, and possibly additional carbon dioxide, though they can usually get enough of this out of the air; they need a strong source of light. One place I have visited in Czechoslovakia grows them in water which is pumped round a circuit, one part of which involves sliding as a thin layer down a sloping surface exposed to the sun. Other installations, for instance in California, grow them in large shallow tanks, in which there is much less movement of the water, but just enough to ensure that all the algae get their ration of sunlight. Then there is the problem of harvesting these minute organisms out of the water. *Spirulina* is particularly favourable because it spontaneously rises to the surface and clumps together in quite large mats, which it is easy to skim off. The others have to be separated by more elaborate techniques of centrifuging or filtering. The eventual product is a protein-rich pasty material. When I ate some of the Czechoslovak product, it seemed to me to resemble blood sausage or 'black pudding' more than anything else; it was not very nice, but then nobody had spent much time finding out how to prepare it. In any case, it would be very useful to feed to animals like pigs, poultry or cattle, even if we did not want to eat it outselves.

The yeasts mostly need fairly complicated carbon-containing substances to grow on. However, there are large supplies of these for which we have no good use at present. For instance, the production of sugar also yields large quantities of molasses, the crude material left when the sugar has been extracted – like the old-fashioned 'black treacle', only more so. It is not always easy to get rid of this; in some places it is used instead of tar to bind sand on the roads. But yeasts can turn it into quite good protein. Similarly they can live on certain parts of crude oil, particularly on the waxy constituents which have to be removed when oil is refined for most of its important uses.

Bacteria can grow and multiply – which implies producing protein – in many raw materials much simpler and more widespread than waste carbohydrates such as molasses or crude oil. There are bacteria that can get their main energy from methane; this gas, made up only of carbon and hydrogen, is the major product from the treatment of sewage, and also the main constituent of 'natural gas'. There are others which get their energy from combining hydrogen with oxygen – and hydrogen is another gas that can be produced from sewage, or of course from water with a certain input of energy. Here is a collection of methods, which are only just beginning to be explored, of making protein when we start to run out of fertile land. They are the basis of Carl Heden's second wish to his good fairy:[36]

The *second* would be a sewage convector, with the methane oxidised and the carbon dioxide photosynthetically bound, that would turn out an undenatured protein, suitable for making meat analogues, or for coagulation to make cheese.

So far all these processes, using algae, yeasts or bacteria, are more expensive (in money) per pound of protein than high-efficiency conventional agriculture or good land treated with plenty of fertiliser. But these methods of food production are still only taking their first faltering steps, and are certain to become much cheaper, in money and probably in energy input also.

There is one further way of utilising these little biological protein-factories. In many undernourished parts of the world there is a good deal of purely starchy foods, cassava, sago, yams and the like, but there is little protein. There are many bacteria and/or yeasts that could grow in such substances and turn part of them into proteins. In several regions there are traditional practices based on such principles. For instance in Africa, a thin porridge of grain and water is allowed to get infected with micro-organisms which ferment it into native 'beer', which not only has some alcohol, but,more importantly from the nutritional point of view, also contains a fair quantity of protein derived from the bodies of the cells which have fermented it. Much could be done to make these traditional practices give higher yields of protein. This was the basis of Carl Heden's last wish:

> The *third* would be a starter pill (micro-encapsulated bacteria resistant to a heat-labile antibiotic included for controlling con-tamination, together with growth factors and minerals) which could be centrally manufactured, and could be used in small protein-starved communities, to turn a brew of cassava or other cheap starch into a protein-rich soup.

Further Reading

A. N.W. Pirie, *Food Resources; Conventional and Novel* (Penguin, 1969).
B. Lester Brown, *By Bread Alone* (Praeger, 1974).
C. *Ceres*, Journal of the UN Food and Agriculture Organisation, is a good way of keeping up to date.
D. *Food*, special number of *Science*, 9 May 1975 (with Bibliography of articles in *Science*) is good but fairly technical.

Notes

1. *Energy and Protein Requirements*, joint FAO/WHO Ad Hoc Expert Committee (FAO, Rome, 1965); H.N. Munro, 'The Nature of Protein Needs', in C. Mateles and P. Tannenbaum eds., *Single Cell Protein* (MIT Press, 1968).
2. Recent work is summarised in M.H. Ross, *Am. J. Clin. Nutrit. 25,* 834, 1972, and 25.
3. J.C. Waterlow in *Nature*, 28 April 1972.
4. Based on data given in Georg Borgstrom, *The Hungry Planet,*(Macmillan, NY, 1967).
5. David Pimental *et al.*, 'Food Production and the Energy Crisis', *Science*, 3 November 1973, *182*, 443; Gerald Leach, 'The Energy Costs of Food

Production', in Arthur Bourne ed., *The Man-Food Equation* (Acad. Press, 1973); Malcolm Slessor, 'Energy Subsidy as a Criterion in Food Policy Planning', *J.Sci.Fd.Agric.*, 1973, *24*: 1193; K.L. Blaxter, 'The Energetics of British Agriculture', *J.Sci.Fd.Agric.* 1975, *26*, 1055.

6. Simplified from Pimental *et al*. above.
7. Ibid.
8. See note 5.
9. Arjan Makhijami and Alan Poole, *Energy and Agriculture in the Third World* (Energy Project, Ford Foundation, Ballinger, 1975).
10. John S. and Carol E. Steinhart, 'Energy Use in the US Food System', *Science* (Energy no.), 19 April 1974; Eric Hirst, 'Food-Related Energy Requirements', *Science*, 12 April 1974, *184*, 132. Fig. 11 from Hirst.
11. See Borgstrom, note 4 above.
12. Nitrogen fixers. IBP synthesis volume will appear shortly. For a recent summary, see Jean L. Mava, 'Nitrogen Fixation', in *Science*, 12 July 1974, and 'A Discussion on Nitrogen Fixation', organised by J. Chatt and G.E. Fogg, *Proc.Roy.Soc.Lond.* B, 1972.
13. See Borgstrom, note 4 above.
14. Carl-Göran Heden, *Socio-economic and ethical implications of enzyme engineering*, Int.Fed.Institute Adv.Study, Study no. 1 (Nobel House, Stockholm, 1974).
15. In C.H. Waddington ed., *Biology and the History of the Future* (Edinburgh Univ. Press, 1971).
16. Landsberg, H.E., in *Science*, 18 December 1970, p. 1269.
17. Peter Bunyard, 'Will the Desert Bloom?', *The Ecologist*, September 1973.
18. Nicholas Valery, 'Water mining to make the deserts bloom', *New Scientist*, no. v, 1972. Walter C. Lowdermilk, 'The Reclamation of a man-made Desert', *Scientific American*, March 1960 (and in Ehrlich, P. ed., *Man and the Ecosphere*, Freeman, 1971).
19. I. Papanek, *Design for the Real World* (Thames and Hudson, 1972).
20. H. Boyko ed., *Salinity and Acidity — New Approaches to Old Problems* (Junk, the Hague, 1965).
21. A simple account is given in Robert J. Bazell, 'Arid Land Agriculture', *Science*, 12 March 1971.
22. J.M. Martin, 'The Rise of the Agro-industrial Complex', *Ceres*, November/ December 1972, no. 30, p. 39, and Richard L. Meier, 'The Social Impact of a Nuplex', *Bulletin of the Atomic Scientists*, March 1969.
23. See Lester Brown, *Seeds of Change* (Praeger, 1970).
24. See for instance the articles by Ashola Thapar and Probhat Roy in *Ceres*, September/October 1972, no. 29, pp. 37—43. A more recent account of the general effects is Nicholas Wade, 'Green Revolution', *Science*, 20 and 27 December 1974, and David Spurgeon, 'Updating the Green Revolution', *Nature*, 24 April 1975.
25. See note 24.
26. See note 24.
27. For a summary of recent work on new supplies of protein, from all manner of sources, see N.W. Pirie ed., *Food Protein Resources* (IBP Monog. 4), (Cambridge Univ. Press, 1975).
28. F.B. Golley and H.K. Buechener ed., *A Practical Guide to the Study of the Productivity of Large Herbivores* (IBP Handbook 7) (Blackwell Scientific Publications, 1968).
29. C.H. Waddington, 'Genetic Engineering', *J.Roy.Soc.Arts*, April 1975, p. 262.
30. John R. Platt, 'Life Where Science Flows', in W.R. Ewald ed., *Environment and Change; the next 50 years* (Indiana Univ. Press, 1968), pp. 69—80.

31. S.J. Holt, 'The Food Resources of the Ocean', *Scientific American*, September 1969. Proc. of conferences on 'Development of Fish Farming', *J.Roy.Soc. Arts*, in press.
32. See Ian Morris, *New Scientist*, 3 December 1970. There may, however, be a few limited areas, e.g. near the coast of Antarctica, where the concentration of fairly large planktonic species is considerably greater, and where direct harvesting might be possible.
33. C.P. Idyll, 'The Anchovy Crisis', *Scientific American*, June 1973.
34. J.Z. Young, 'Save the Whales', *NY Review of Books*, 17 July 1975.
35. A comprehensive account is John E. Bardock and John H. Ryther and William O. McLarney, *Aquaculture* (Wiley, Interscience, NY, 1972). For British experience see *Roy.Soc.Arts*, June 1975.
36. See note 15.

4 NATURAL RESOURCES AND ENERGY

Nothing can continue to grow exponentially if it is confined within non-expanding boundaries. The photographs of the earth recently taken from space remind us forcefully that the human species lives on a finite planet, which is not growing any bigger. The growth of the human population, which for some periods of history has been exponential, or even accelerated exponential, must eventually slow down; it must over a long period of time take the form of an S-shaped curve. Among the factors which tend to produce a slowing down of growth in later stages are the supplies of energy and natural resources such as metals.

In the last few decades, the quantities of these materials, and of energy, which have been used by the richer countries, have been growing at ever-increasing rates. This is really a secondary reflection of the dynamics of the populations of the rich countries and their social and productive systems. The process of discovering and exploiting a natural resource contains no internal drive pushing it forward; it has to be powered by human forces. In fact, the only inherent factor is a negative one, namely that some resources, which do not spontaneously renew themselves, become harder and harder to obtain.

One of the most important distinctions among the materials used by man is the division into two great classes: those derived from *sources which renew themselves*, that is, essentially, plants which yield paper, cotton, etc., and animals which yield wool, leather and other such products; and on the other hand, materials derived from sources which *are not renewed* at any appreciable rate, such as fossil fuels, metals, etc. It is the latter which are the more difficult to deal with. The next section will discuss some of the most important, namely metals; fossil fuels will be considered in connection with energy in general.

Non-renewing Resources: Metals

It is quite difficult to reach a balanced view about the seriousness of the situation about non-renewable resources in the short and medium term. On the one hand, the monetary value of the mineral resources used in the world are only a small fraction of the monetary wealth created in one year, as measured by the GNP (Table 4.1[1]).

Table 4.1

| | (billions of 1973 dollars)* | | | | | |
	US	% of US GNP	Rest of World	World GNP (ex US)	Total	** % of GNP
Energy	24.3	2.3	40.0	1.6	64.3	1.9
Ferrous	7.3	0.7	28.0	1.1	35.3	1.0
Non-ferrous	6.3	0.6	17.9	0.8	24.2	0.7
Non-metallic	7.5	0.7	30.9	1.2	38.4	1.1
Total	45.4	4.3	116.8	4.7	162.2	4.6

* Billion = $1,000m
**Commodities Research Unit estimate
Source: US Bureau of Mines, *Mineral Facts and Problems*, 1970 (adjusted to include value of pig iron production).

Some economists conclude that the world's economic system can easily handle anything so relatively trivial. The industrial nations always have found sources of raw materials when they wanted them and, these economists claim, will be able to do so again, even if they have to pay slightly more for them. Many scientists and others, however, argue that a pound spent on raw materials has real importance to industrial production quite different from one spent, say, on advertising or making minor alterations to particular products. Raw materials may cost a small fraction of total wealth, but may be of overwhelming importance for it. The turmoil caused by the rise in oil prices is one example of this. It also shows how the availability and price of important raw materials, and their location in particular regions, may have profound effects on political power and influence. It seems unlikely that the Christian West will ever again dominate the Mohammedan Persian-Arab world as completely as it has done in the last four centuries or so.

It is possible that the distribution of natural resources will cause equally great shifts in the balance of political power, but on the whole this seems rather unlikely. It depends on the concentration of a resource within one geographical region, or in the hands of one culturally unified group, on the possibilities of finding substitutes, or using lower-grade sources for the material. There do not seem to be many candidates for resources which fulfil these conditions; phosphorus (for fertilisers) is perhaps the most 'promising' (from the producers' point of view) but the main suppliers of that also belong to the Mohammedan world, though they are located at the other end of the Mediterranean to the oil producers, in Morocco and the West African coast just to the south.

Several estimates have been made of the length of time available stock of the various materials are likely to last. They are based on the assumption that the world demand for a given material, such as copper, goes on increasing in the future at much the same rate as it has been doing in the past, that new ore deposits are discovered at a similar rate as in the past, and that man exploits deposits of about the same richness as he now uses; on these bases one can calculate how long it will be before the supplies are exhausted. As an example one set of

Figure 4.1: Lifetime of Metal Reserves

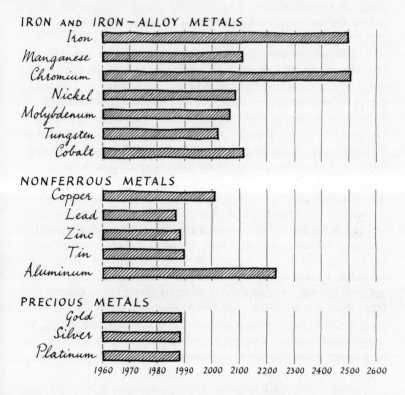

Source: After Figure in Harrison Brown, 'Human Materials Production as a Process in the Biosphere', *Scientific American*, September 1970, p. 195.

estimates is shown in Figure 4.1. The important point to note is that
for some items the forecasted lifetime is quite short, to be measured in
a few decades or a century or so. Clearly the situation calls for some
hard thinking.

Some of the metals used in the greatest bulk, such as iron and
aluminium, are available in enormous quantities in ores only slightly
less rich than those being exploited at present. The same is true of
some of the less widely used minerals, such as copper, nickel and lead.
When the richest deposits of these materials have been used, further
supplies will be obtainable at not too drastically increased cost.[2] But
some metals important for special purposes are mined from rich mineral
veins, which are rapidly being exhausted. It is difficult to decide how
fast we may expect to discover new bodies of ore. On the one hand,
it could be argued that most of the earth's surface has by now been
pretty thoroughly searched, and that there cannot be very much more
to find. On the other, mining techniques are becoming more powerful,
so that we can go deeper, or even mine on the continental shelves. Both
such developments make the technique of recovery more expensive, but
they at least open up the possibility of finding new sources of supply.
But it may turn out that there are no other deposits of some metals,
except for their general presence in exceedingly low concentrations.
These include mercury, wolfram, silver, tin, manganese, molybdenum.
The only way to deal with this will be to be much more conservative in
the use of these metals, to go in for intensive recycling, and to develop
substitute technologies, using carbon fibres or special plastics in
place of some of the special alloys which call for these metals as
constituents.

One very crucial and difficult material is phosphorus, which is
required in the form of phosphate as a fertiliser.[3] The richest deposits,
such as guano and rocks with a high phosphate content, are fairly
rapidly being exhausted. The price of phosphate rock was recently
trebled by a group of major producers (Morocco, Tunisia, Algeria
and neighbouring countries) and doubled by another producer, the
USA. There is considerable uncertainty about how much lower-grade
ore is available, but it seems almost certain that within fairly few
decades phosphate fertiliser will become scarce enough for it to be
really worth while taking very energetic steps to re-use the phosphate
now discarded in sewage.

Another factor which may become very important over a large
range of resources is the organisation of producing countries to raise the
price of raw materials. This has, of course, recently happened with oil,

whose producers, tightly knit into OPEC, the Organisation of
Petroleum Exporting Countries, were able to impose a threefold
increase in price on the much richer, but in this connection almost
powerless, importing industrial countries. Some people argue that this
is a special case, since the oil-producers — mostly Arab and Muslim —
are unusually coherent in culture. But others do not share that optimism.
Other commodities which look to be candidates for similar actions
are bauxite, now one of the main ores used for aluminium (though
others are possible at greater expense), mercury, and natural rubber
(which is making a come-back, particularly since the increase in oil
prices has put up the cost of synthetic rubber). However, many poor
countries which export minerals to the industrial world are themselves
dependent on importing fertilisers or foodstuffs from that world,
particularly from the United States and Canada, and this limits their
freedom to impose massive price increases as the Arab oil exporters
did.[4]

Nearly all estimates of the impact of shortages or price increases of
raw materials assume that the world's demands will increase with
trends similar to those of the recent past. Many people have hoped
that, on the contrary, the next few decades would see a rapid increase
in the wealth of developing countries; and if these were to run their
lives in ways similar to those of the present developed nations, this
would call for enormously increased quantities of material. In fact, the
amounts of material required would be so large that one must ask
whether this is really a feasible proposition at all. Harrison Brown, the
Foreign Secretary of the US National Academy of Sciences, and a
highly responsible geophysicist, has estimated the amounts of various
metals etc. which have been accumulated in the USA and are now at
the disposal of every American citizen (Table 4.2).

Is it sensible to imagine that the undeveloped three-quarters of the
world's population could equal those figures? Harrison Brown writes

> if by some magic the per capita inventory of metals in the world as
> a whole were to be brought up to the current US level, all of the
> present mines and factories in the world would have to operate for
> more than 60 years just to produce the capital, assuming no losses.
> But we know that the population of the world is increasing rapidly,
> as is the US per capita inventory of metals. If we were to assume a
> world population of 10 billion persons, and a per capita steel
> inventory of 20 tons, some 200 billion tons of iron would have to
> be extracted from the earth. At the current rate of extraction, 400

years would be required.

Table 4.2: Cost of the Average American

Accumulated steel	10 tons
Accumulated copper	160 kg
Accumulated lead	140 kg
Accumulated zinc	100 kg
Accumulated tin	18 kg
Accumulated aluminium	110 kg
Automobiles	0.4 per head
Annual travel in USA	5,000 miles
Annual transport	9,000 ton miles
Annual 'phone calls	700
Annual mail	400 items
Annual energy	10 tons coal

Source: Harrison Brown, 'The Place of Value in a World of Facts', Nobel Symposium 14 (Almquist and Wiskell, 1969, Stockholm), pp. 347–52.

Such figures suggest some very tough conclusions. The twentieth-century citizens of the developed parts of the world have had a quantity of material possessions which is quite abnormal in the whole history of mankind. To provide these they have been squandering the natural resources of the planet at a rate which cannot be spread over the whole earth's surface. Furthermore, I think we have to conclude that this rate should not, and probably cannot, be sustained even in the rich nations. Harrison Brown, at the end of the paper from which I have quoted, finishes off by offering three alternative scenarios for the future:

(1) The affluent nations get richer, and the gap between rich and poor gets wider. The world's population becomes permanently split into two groups, the larger group being inexorably poor, with no possibility of improvement; the smaller very wealthy, but highly armed and vulnerable to disruption. Tension will be great. There will be a nuclear war. The poor will inherit the earth and live miserably ever after.

(2) Before this division is complete, we shall run out of usable resources. The rich civilisations will collapse. The poor again inherit the earth; but technology survives, and develops again, giving rise to scenario one.

(3) Which I regard as highly improbable, the rich nations take a

series of rational decisions. . .

Is it possible that something like a 'material wealth transition' might occur, people deciding that they had really got enough cars, refrigerators and such things, and would prefer to transfer their interests to something else? Some authors, such as Dennis Gabor,[5] have argued that there are signs of this already, in growing rates of absenteeism from work, which amounts to foregoing money wages in favour of leisure. There are also arguments, often of a moral or spiritual kind, against the old 'world ethic' which implies the consumption of resources, and these arguments clearly have a considerable appeal particularly to the younger generation. It would probably be too optimistic to think that a 'material wealth transition' will appear spontaneously, without much discussion, as the demographic transition did; but it may be that the discussion of it, which is already taking place, will successfully act as a midwife.

Energy

Energy is such a fundamentally important resource that it needs separate consideration. In this section I will leave out of account the solar energy used by agriculture, and the animal muscle power, which has been very important for past civilisations, but can scarcely be so in the future, when man will not have enough food to spare over and above his own needs to make much use of horses, draft oxen, and so on.

As a basis with which the rich countries may be compared we can take a glance at a fairly typical (but hot) poor country. The total energy consumption of India in 1968/69 has been estimated as equivalent to 358.65 million tons of coal. This is rather less than one ton per head; the Americans use about 13 tons per head. Rather more than half the Indian energy was used privately and domestically (for cooking, perhaps running one-family workshops, etc.) and never appeared on the commercial market. The sources were completely different from those of the rich world (Table 4.3).

At present the use of industrial-type energy is very closely related to material wealth as measured by GNP (Figure 4.2). In global terms, we find that the 30 per cent of the world's population living in the industrialised countries use about 80 per cent of the world's total supplies of energy. They use this in the most capital-intensive forms, such as coal, oil and nuclear energy, while animal muscle-power still makes a sizeable contribution to the 20 per cent used in the non-industrialised countries. In the world as a whole, the amount of energy

Table 4.3

Commercial sources		Non-Commercial	
Coal	19.4	Dung	5.5
Lignite	0.6	Firewood	37.7
Oil	23.5	Vegetable waste	9.1
Hydro-electric	4.2		
Total	47.7	Total	52.3

(Total of both equivalent to 358.65 million tons of coal.)
Source: From data in *Solar Energy in Developing Countries* (US Nat.Acad.Sci., Washington, 1972).

used has been increasing very fast, and the greater part of this went into the industrialised countries. According to an article, in *The Times*,[6] the world's consumption of energy was equivalent to 16,000,000 barrels of oil a day in 1920, and had increased by nearly six times to 72,500,000 by 1971. The breakdown of sources in 1971 was oil 54 per cent, natural gas 18 per cent, solid fuel (= coal etc.) 21 per cent, hydropower 65 per cent, nuclear power 1 per cent.

Weinberg[7] estimates that man now produces energy at a rate equivalent to 1/20,000 of the energy inflow from the sun to the whole planet (1/5,000 of that to the land). He guesses that, if energy production continues to increase at the rate it has been doing — which implies little advance for the developing countries — it will be not more than 30 to 50 years before there may be important and at present quite unpredictable effects on the world's climates. This is an impressive note of caution, coming from an acknowledged advocate of 'Big Science'.

Sources and Uses

Figure 4.3 shows the general picture of energy in the United States. On the left are the fuels from which power is derived. Considerable quantities are utilised for generating electricity, the rest more directly. On the right, we see the main uses: household and commercial (which is largely space-heating); transport (about 80 per cent of it automobiles); and industry. Note the considerable inefficiency of several of these processes, which reject a great deal of the energy input as 'waste heat', which goes out as warmed cooling water, or as energy lost in various mechanical inefficiencies. The generating and transmission of electricity is particularly bad in this respect, but so is transport.

Figure 4.2: Energy Consumption and Living Standards

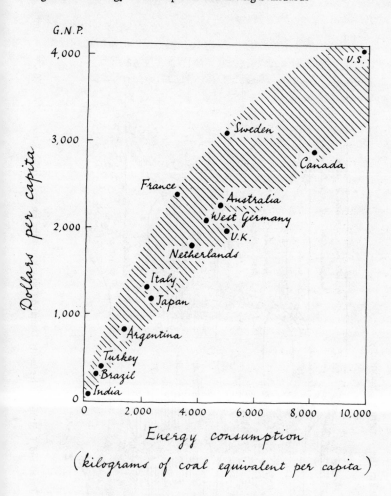

Source: John McHale, 'World Facts and Trends', *Futures*, December 1971.

Can we expect to go on obtaining energy from these same sources? There does not seem to be much difficulty about coal for at least a few thousand years. It becomes rather more expensive to mine, but there is a lot of it. The situation about oil and natural gas is very different. In the last half century the production of crude oil has been increased 20 times, but the estimates of reserves have only gone up

Figure 4.3: Uses of Fuel in the American Economy

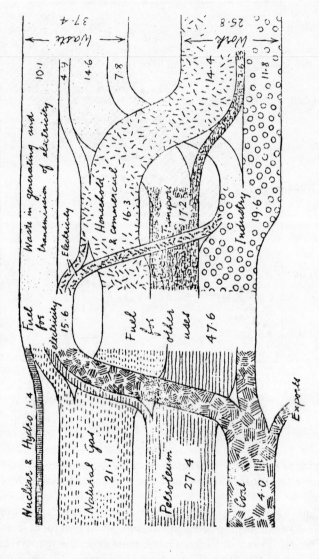

Figure 4.4: Oil Resources

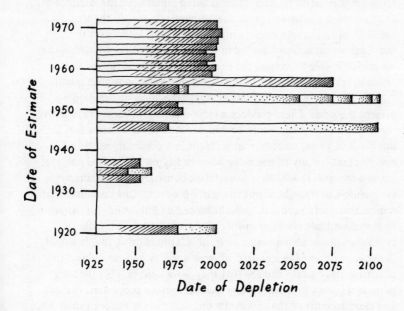

Source: Earl Cook, 'Energy Sources for the Future', *The Futurist*, August 1972.

by about 10 times. Figure 4.4 summarises a number of estimates that have been published over the last 50 years. It is remarkable that, except for a certain optimism by a few people in the early 1950s, all the changes in rates of utilisation and of new discoveries leave the over-all opinion more or less unchanged, that oil reserves will not last much into the next century. This raises one of the most basic questions for the next few decades. Even if we reduce the rate at which our energy demands have been increasing, or even the energy not put to use, we shall still have to find other sources. The most obvious is nuclear power.

Nuclear Power

There are several different sorts of nuclear power, which have to be considered separately. In present plants power is derived from a form of uranium known as U-235. This is a rare constituent of natural

uranium, of which it makes up only about 0.7 per cent. Uranium itself
is a substance which does not often appear in concentrated deposits;
they would be exhausted within a few decades. However, the
technology of uranium extraction is being rapidly improved. Since a
little uranium produces a great deal of power, to supply the world's
needs from this source would only mean dealing with about twice
the volume that is now handled in coal mining. It is even possible that
we might be able to extract the uranium from the sea, in which it
exists in very low concentration but, of course, in enormous quantities.

However, there are very considerable snags in using uranium by
present methods. These produce a large quantity of highly radioactive
waste products, which would be dangerous to living systems for
hundreds of years; moreover an accident in a conventional atomic
energy plant (or any of the more advanced types we shall be considering in a moment) could have devastating consequences.[8] There are
two schools of thought about the waste products. One considers that
radioactive waste products could be stored underground, for instance
in abandoned salt mines or in specially made bore holes, without
causing an intolerable amount of trouble. Others think that it would
demand an impossible standard of responsibility and carefulness to
put them away safely and see that they were kept safe for the long
periods required for them to lose their dangerous properties. A short
and clear account of the arguments on both sides is the correspondence
between two leading physicists, Weinberg (optimist) and Edsall
(pessimist).[9]

One of the most responsible groups of scientists from all over the
world (the Pugwash movement) decided in 1973 that present nuclear
technology is so dangerous that the building of new generating stations
should be postponed for further consideration.[10] Moreover, atom
bombs could be made fairly easily from some types of waste products,
possibly by terrorists.[11]

But there are other technologies by which we might utilise nuclear
reactions for generating power. There is, in the first place, a system
known as the 'breeder reactor', which uses the more common form of
the uranium atom, uranium-238, and also the much more plentiful
thorium-232, and which turns out less waste products in proportion
to the power produced (but still quite a lot). Finally, there is the
theoretical possibility of a 'fusion reactor', which might employ one
of the forms of hydrogen which is available in essentially unlimited
quantities. The breeder reactor is near to being a reality; the main
question is whether it can be made economically feasible, and that

appears quite possible, particularly as other sources of energy, such as oil, become more expensive. The fusion reactor is a much more doubtful proposition; nobody has yet got anything of the kind to work even on a small laboratory scale. If it can be made to work at all, it would have the great merit that it could be used in a way which would produce almost no radioactive waste; but it would be more efficient to use it along with a breeder reactor, and so the problem of radioactive wastes would not be avoided after all.

It is in the light of these considerations that another forecast of energy sources for the United States was drawn up by Earl Cook in 1971 (Figure 4.5). He supposed that natural gas and oil will run out quite fast, the rich United States sources being exhausted shortly after the year 2000, though oil imports may keep going for another 30 or 40 years, and the use of relatively poor sources such as tar sands and oil shales could continue for most of the next century. He suggests that the conventional atomic power of U-235 will be a major factor in the first half of the next century, but after that the USA will have to rely mainly on the breeder reactors using U-238 and Th.-232.

The recent actions of the oil-producing (OPEC) countries, in raising the price they demand for their oil, and the imposition of cuts and embargoes, have made it clear that those developed countries dependent on oil imports — and that means nearly all of them — have to worry not only about the physical exhaustion of reserves, but about political and economic factors as well. They are rapidly waking up to the fact that they will, relatively soon, have to develop alternative sources. These might, of course, be nuclear, but we have seen that there are many snags in that solution. There is every incentive, except the short-term economic, to explore other possibilities. This would be unlikely to be pursued with the necessary thoroughness if the price of oil once again fell to anything like its low figure before OPEC took steps to raise it. A very thorough study has been made in the United States ('Project Independence'[12]) of the whole situation as it affected that country in 1974; the domestic and foreign energy supplies, the uses made, the economies possible, the alternative sources with their technological possibilities and likely economic costs. One of its conclusions is that the basic cost of conventional energy (coal or oil) should be kept high enough to make investment in alternative but more speculative sources remain attractive.

We shall now discuss, in general outline, some of these alternatives.

Figure 4.5: A Forecast of Energy Requirements for the USA

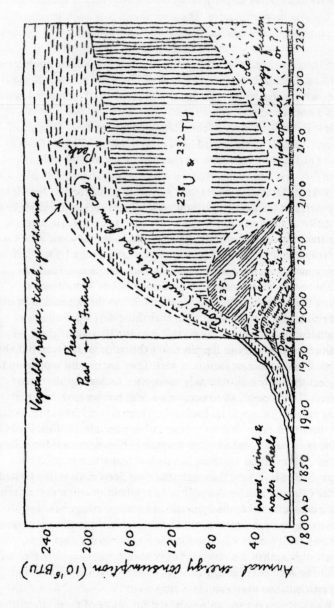

Source: Earl Cook, 'Energy Sources for the Future', *The Futurist*, August 1972.

Unconventional Sources of Energy

There is actually no shortage of energy in the world; the difficulty is to get control of it in the right form and in the right places. Broadly speaking, there are two major types of energy-source other than the fossil or nuclear fuels; geophysical sources and the solar source.

Geophysical. There is energy packed into the way in which our planet and its accompanying bodies are constructed. The main types are tidal and geothermal.

Tidal energy is produced by the attraction of the moon for the waters of the seas. It is essentially unlimited, as far as mankind is concerned, but it is difficult to harvest. It appears as the rise of the sea level by a few tens of feet over a period of some twelve hours; how can one collect the energy from such a slow process spread over such a large area? Only in a few suitable estuaries or deep inlets have reasonably effective methods of using tidal energy been worked out. One operates in Normandy. If oil-generated electricity becomes even more expensive, a similar scheme in the Bristol Channel might become economic. But there are not many suitable places; and the total energy produced in this way is never likely to be more than a small contribution to the needs of an industrial society, even one located on an island.[13]

Geothermal energy is dependent on the fact that rocks contain low levels of radioactive substances, which produce heat as they break down. This can escape only slowly by conduction through the overlying strata, so rocks deep below the surface of the earth are therefore always hot. In a few places the overlying crust is thin, and hot rocks are near the surface — or actually at the surface in volcanoes. This heat is already used to produce electricity at a few favourable places. Most of the power used in the Italian railways comes from a geothermal centre in Tuscany, which has been running since early in this century. New Zealand, Iceland and California have regions with natural geysers (escaping steam from underground) and some of these have been harnessed for power generation. The naturally favourable places are few and far between, but it is possible to foresee engineering developments which might tap this source on a much larger scale.[14] Methods of boring deep into the earth are being greatly improved (mainly in the search for more oil) and underground nuclear explosions are being used to create fractures and fissures in the deep rocks. It might become worth while to create gigantic underground boilers, with water pumped down one bore into the hot, fractured rocks, then brought up again through another bore to power electricity generators. There are still formidable engineering problems to be solved, but this looks one of the better bets for, say, fifty or more years ahead.

Solar.[15]   The difficulty in using solar energy is that, like tidal energy, it is spread rather thin, but at least it occurs overland, where people live. A good deal of power consumed at present is used in small-scale, widely scattered applications, such as domestic space-heating, cooking, refrigeration, lighting and the like. Much of the energy required to keep the climate inside a house within the comfort zone could be derived from solar energy; perhaps as much as two-thirds of the present energy expenditure on domestic and commercial space-heating could be met in this way.

Industrial processes require large concentrated energy inputs and transport also needs its energy in concentrated form. There are several options. The simplest might seem to be to concentrate the sun's rays with a lens or mirror, to produce a spot of intense heat. Some of the highest man-made temperatures (other than atomic ones) have been produced in this way, but the apparatus is costly and very cumbersome. Possibly it would be more practical to use large batteries of small mirrors instead of one large one.

There are some combinations of metals which produce electricity directly when the junction between the two components is heated. *If* the State of Arizona could be covered with a suitable fabricated sheet of such minerals, the whole of the United States' energy requirements could be met. But it is by no means certain that sufficient of the right metals actually exist. Some 'energy farms' of this kind may eventually be set up, but it is likely that they will remain of minor importance.

There are other, and more tried and trusty, means for directly capturing the sun's energy — namely plants. They use solar energy to build carbon dioxide from air into starches and sugars, from which quite convenient fuels such as methane gas or fluid alcohols can be made. Plants are not very efficient energy convertors. A good one, like sugar cane, produces only about 2½ per cent of the solar energy falling on it. That is not much, but it is a great deal better than nothing. Plants like sugar cane, which cover the ground with a dense matt of vegetation and thus protect it against the destructive effects of tropical rains, are thought by many ecologically-minded agriculturalists to be the most suitable crops to grow in the tropical rainforest areas, such as the Amazon basin and some of central Africa, which at present are almost useless to man. The production of liquid gas fuel from

vegetation in these areas may make a considerable contribution to
the world's energy budget.

But one need not be so direct in getting at the sun's energy. A small
fraction of that which falls on the earth's surface — but in our context
it is a large total amount — produces the winds, the ocean currents and
the waves. The kinetic energy in the wind and waves is estimated at 1.2
x 10^{22} joules, which is about sixty times the world's present energy
use. Harnessing the wind, with windmills (or sails for transport) is of
course a very ancient technology. It is probably due for a revival for
energy uses which can be decentralised (e.g. domestic) but there are
great difficulties in producing continuous supplies of concentrated
power. Yet it may be worth developing systems of storing low-grade
energies for short periods to give intermittent bursts of strong power
every few minutes, say to operate a power digger.

Wave power looks more promising.[16] The surface of the seas is the
collecting component of the world's largest windmill — it picks up
wind energy and turns it into quite rapid and large movements of
water, with both up-and-down and transverse components. The
average power in the North Atlantic is about 77 kilowatts per metre
of wave frontage throughout the year. There are several designs of
apparatus which can take this moving water as input and convert it
into a flow through a hydro-electric generator. This would only take a
line of 'wave interceptors' a few tens of miles long to produce as much
power as that hoped for from the most productive oil well in the
North Sea; and it is estimated that the electrical energy requirements
of the United Kingdom would be satisfied by a few hundred kilometres
of equipment to the west of the Outer Hebrides — a very stormy area.
Accurate costing for large installations has not yet been made, but the
running costs would be quite small. This looks one of the best possibilities
for some countries, including Britain.

Another proposed method of harvesting solar energy is to use the
difference in temperature between the surface and deeper oceanic
waters.[17] These tend to be greatest in the neighbourhood of strong
ocean currents, like the Gulf Stream which brings warm water from
the Gulf of Mexico across the much colder waters of the Atlantic to the
shores of Northern Europe and Britain, and gives us a pleasanter
climate than that of Labrador, which is on about the same latitude.
It is theoretically possible that this difference in temperature (about
twenty to thirty degrees Fahrenheit) could be used to generate electricity.
There are enormous quantities of energy there, because the situation
involves oceanic quantities of water; but the capital cost of equipment

to handle water in such quantities is a subject the proposers of such schemes tend to forget to discuss. I doubt if Britain is in danger of being frozen into a new Ice Age because the Gulf Stream may be used to cool American homes during the summer.

A Hydrogen-Methane-Methanol Economy? The times and places at which many of the unconventional sources of energy, particularly those which derive from solar power, are most productive tend not to be where the energy is most needed. The energy produced would have to be stored and transported. Electricity is, of course, easily transported, but not so easily stored in large quantities. Sometimes it is convenient to store energy by pumping water uphill into a reservoir, but that could not easily be done, for instance, with wave-generated energy.

We have to pay some price, in energy terms, for convenience of handling, storage and transport. Perhaps the most likely method will be to use electricity to break down water into its constituent hydrogen and oxygen. The oxygen is useful, for instance in producing iron or steel, while the hydrogen would be the main energy store, and could be burnt, with air, in many sorts of motors. It is an almost pollution-free fuel, and some people have been so impressed by this that they advocate the 'hydrogen economy' as a good thing in itself.[18] However, each step away from the primary source such as waves or tides, through electricity to hydrogen and then perhaps back to electricity again, must involve an energy loss; it is a question whether it is worth paying this price for the sake of convenience.

Hydrogen is a good material for large-scale storage and transport, but it is not so convenient for handling small quantities. Under ordinary conditions it is a gas, and for most purposes it would have to be kept under high pressure and at very low temperature. It can form temporary compounds with some metals and it can be recovered from them again fairly easily; but that way of handling it, though perhaps the most convenient, is likely to be expensive. A better material might therefore be methane or methanol. The first of these is a gas formed when four atoms of hydrogen combine with one of carbon, while the second contains an atom of oxygen in addition. Thus they are largely composed of hydrogen, but they have several properties which would make them more flexible.

In the first place, they are easier to handle; methanol is a liquid under ordinary conditions, and methane, which is a gas, can be turned into a liquid without the great pressures and very low temperatures necessary to liquify hydrogen. It is also much simpler to adapt a petrol engine to run on methane or methanol than to convert it to hydrogen fuel. Also they can be produced rather easily from a wide range of materials, without the application of the intense power which is normally used to produce hydrogen. They are in fact common materials in the natural world, formed during the decay of organic substances, as their common names suggest: methane is 'marsh gas' (and also the main constituent of 'natural gas' from underground), while the common name of methanol is 'wood alcohol'. Both could be produced in large quantities from sewage or by the controlled fermentation of farm wastes, like straw, which are today commonly wasted by burning. Development of these methods, which are becoming known as 'enzyme engineering',[19] would give us access to large new supplies of conveniently usable power, and make 'energy farms' — crops grown to serve as fuel — in many parts of the world. Methanol can also be produced from hydrogen, for instance by making it react with limestone or chalk. Hydrogen, methane and methanol are not to be regarded as alternatives for energy, but rather as complementary. The world will probably develop some mix of them, but in just what proportions no one can yet say.

Economising in the Use of Energy

The difficulty of producing enough energy raises the question of the ways in which we might be more economical in its utilisation.[20] It is only recently that serious attempts have been made to estimate the quantities of energy used in various enterprises ('energy budgeting') and there are still great uncertainties. In general it seems that the earlier estimates were on the low side. For instance, in May 1972, Berry[21] estimated that it took 5,000 kilowatt hours of energy to mine and refine the steel and other materials and to build a car; so that if it were built to last twice as long as present cars, one would save that amount per car. But a year later, Peter Chapman[22] put the cost at about 23,000 kWh. There is no doubt that in recent years energy has been so cheap that industry has made little attempt to minimise its use; it has usually been more profitable to maximise sales, for instance by rapid obsolescence. There are also many energy-squandering activities which a more rational society would probably greatly curtail or even abolish altogether. It takes about 850 acres of timber (mostly Canadian) to produce one Sunday edition of the *New York Times*, of which probably less than 5 per cent of the paper-area is ever read; and it costs the city about 10 cents a copy to clear it away and dispose of it, mostly by burning to produce waste heat and air pollution; this wood could have been converted into a convenient and useful fuel.[23]

Many energy savings could be made in the domestic field without lowering standards. Industrialised countries usually construct buildings from materials, such as steel, plastics, glass and (still worse) aluminium, which are expensive in energy to produce. There are alternatives, such as soil cement blocks, which demand much less energy. The developing countries (except the oil-rich ones) will have to use building materials of this kind, and the richer countries should move in that direction also.

The cheapness of energy has led us into profligate ways of using it in houses, and to fail to design so as to minimise energy loss. The old English open fireplaces wasted a great deal of coal; but central heating, though more economical per volume heated, is often used to heat rooms which are not in use at the time. The American practice is much more wasteful; in winter houses are kept hotter than most Europeans find comfortable, and in summer cooler than necessary. Both house-heating and house-cooling throw out considerable amounts of heat into the atmosphere. Air-conditioning plants in the summer are in some places beginning to create a nuisance outdoors. In Los Angeles, where the air is often stagnant, they are raising the outdoor temperature to the point where people are beginning to move out of town on that account.

Houses could be built from which the heat losses are much less than from the conventional designs of today. Table 4.4 shows one set of estimates for an ordinary suburban villa in Britain.[24] It has become quite fashionable to improve insulation by double glazing of windows, but in most houses losses through the walls, ceiling and floors are also very considerable. Many experiments[25] are now under way to build

Table 4.4: Effects of Adaptations

Adaptive Process	Reduced heat loss kWh
Double insulation standards	10,300
Install 38m² of solar flat plate collector	7,300
Reduce heat differential 10°C 8°C	5,300
Reduce window size to maximum of 12% of shell surface	4,400
Reduce ventilation to 1 change/hour	4,310
Total normal heat loss	20,600

houses which rely mainly or entirely on solar energy to control the internal temperature. Most are still more expensive to build, though less to run, than conventional houses, but considerable savings in energy use can be made at little capital cost and, as experience is gained, the cost/benefit ratio of such modifications will certainly improve.

Savings of this kind may substantially affect the future demand for energy. Both the estimates shown in Figure 4.5 are straight-forward 'extrapolation forecasting', carrying on the curves of demand in the recent past into the nearish future. We may have to accept a dose of 'normative forecasting' — cutting our coat according to how much cloth we look like being able to get hold of.

In a recent study, John C. Fisher[26] has tried to discover what factors were responsible for the energy demands of the United States over the past century, and considered how they are likely to operate in the future. The US has always been an extremely profligate user of energy. Even a century ago, the per capita energy corresponded to about 6 tons of coal, as the early settlers had to contend with the severe winters, but in most of the country they had very large supplies of forest timber and coal was also plentiful. The 6 tons coal equivalent they used has still not been reached in many highly-developed countries which have less bountiful natural resources and less demanding climates. In the past hundred years, the energy used per head has risen only just more than twice, to 13 tons coal equivalent. The much greater rise in total use results from the growth of the population by seven times during the period. Fisher argues that the increases in per capita use have been mainly caused by two major social changes. Between 1900 and 1920 it went up about 40 per cent due to great movements of people into cities, which meant that a man's work place had to be heated as well as his house. The next increase in energy consumption, dating from about 1960, Fisher attributes to female employment outside the home, so that a man and wife need three warmed places rather than the one which filled their needs when they both lived and worked on a farm. There have, of course, been other factors, tending to increase energy demands, such as larger and more powerful cars. But the efficiency of industrial processes is usually improved as time passes, and thus would operate to reduce energy use.

If Fisher's arguments have any substance, we should not expect the causes which brought about the increased demands of the recent past to continue in the near future. The family is now almost fully dispersed into separate warmed places for work and living; and the population increase in the energy-consuming nations is greatly slowed down. The extrapolation of Figure 4.5 probably really is unjustified. Furthermore, many people are beginning to dislike wastefulness as such; there is a movement of feeling away from conspicuous consumption towards a more harmonious, less aggressive and demanding way of life. If this tendency continues and we use our ingenuity to tap the many sources of energy the world contains, mankind should be able to look after itself quite well, at least after it has got through the next few years of painful adjustment to the greatly raised price of oil.

Further Reading

Natural Resources

A. *Resources and Man; A Study and Recommendations*, Nat.Acad.Sci. of USA (W.H. Freeman, 1970).
B. Brian J. Skinner, *Earth Resources* (Prentice-Hall, 1970).

Energy

C. 'Energy in the 1980s', A Discussion at the Royal Society, London, Phil.Trans. A., *276*: 1974, 405–620.
D. *Science*, Special Energy Number, 19 April 1974.
E. *Nature*, Special Energy Number, 21 June 1974.
F. *Energy and the Future*; 22 articles from *Science*, edited Allen Hammond and Thomas Maugh II (American Association for the Advancement of Science, 1973).
G. Amory B. Lovins, 'World Energy Strategies', *Bulletin of the Atomic Scientists*, May, June 1974, also as booklet published by Resources Research Ltd, London, 1973.
H. *Project Independence* (US Government Printing Office, Washington DC, 1974).

Notes

1. *The Times*, 27 January 1975, p. 15.
2. Report of lecture by Harvey Brooks, in *Nature*, 1 September 1972, p. 11.
3. Andrew Staines, 'Digesting the raw materials threat', *New Scientist*, 7 March 1974.
4. Ibid.
5. Dennis Gabor, *The Mature Society* (Secker & Warburg, 1972).

6. *The Times*, 21 February 1973.
7. Alvin M. Weinberg, 'Global Effects of Man's Production of Energy', *Science, 186*, 205, 18 October 1974.
8. For extensive discussions of the safety of nuclear reactors, see six articles by Robert E. Gillette in *Science*, 5 May, 28 July, 8, 15, 22 September 1972. Also articles on 'Nuclear Reactor Safety', Parts 1 and 2, *Bulletin of the Atomic Scientists*, October and November 1974.
9. Letters to the Editor, *Science*, 1 December 1972.
10. Proc. 23rd Pugwash conference on 'Science and World Affairs', Anlanko, Finland, 1973, and see E. Rabinovitch, 'Challenges of the Scientific Age', *Bulletin of the Atomic Scientists*, September 1973; on the other side Hans Bethe and others, 'No Alternative to Nuclear Power', *Bulletin of the Atomic Scientists*, March 1975.
11. See 'Radioactive malevolence', *Bulletin of the Atomic Scientists*, February 1974; 'The Strangelove Scenario', *Nature 248*, 725, 1974. Mason Willrich and Theodore Taylor, *Nuclear Thefts, Risks and Safeguards*, report to Energy Policy Project, Ford Foundation, (1974).
12. *A Time to Choose: America's Energy Future*, Ford Foundation Report (John Wiley, 1975).
13. 'Energy in the 1980s', Phil.Trans.Roy.Soc.Lond. A *276*, 1974, p. 485.
14. Ibid., p. 507; *Science*, 19 April 1974, p. 371, special number on Energy.
15. Farington Daniels, *Direct use of the sun's energy* (Ballantine 1974). *Sun in Science of Man*, UNESCO, Paris, 1973.
16. *Nature*, 21 June 1974, Special Number on Energy, article by S.H. Salter.
17. See *Science, 180*, 1266, June 1973, and *Science, 182*, 121, 12 October 1973.
18. *Nature, 248*, 628, 19 April 1974.
19. Carl Göran Heden, *Socio-economic and ethical implications of enzyme engineering*, report to International Fed.Inst.Adv.Study (Nobel House, Stockholm, 1974).
20. See Charles A. Berg, 'Energy conservation through effective utilisation', *Science*, 13 July 1973. *Energy conservation*, Central Policy Review (HMSO, 1974). Bruce Hannon, 'Energy Conservation and the Consumer', *Science*, 11 July 1975.
21. R.S. Berry, *Bulletin of the Atomic Scientists*, May 1972.
22. Peter Chapman, *New Scientist*, 1973, *58*, 408.
23. A. Papanek, *Design for the Real World* (Thames & Hudson, 1972).
24. Estimates by Andrew MacKillop in *Ecologist*, December 1972.
25. Philip Steadman, *Energy, Environment and Building* (Cambridge Univ. Press, 1975).
26. John C. Fisher, *Energy Crisis in Perspective* (Wiley, 1974) (this study was sponsored by General Electric 'with the instruction that I [the author] write as objectively as I could').

5 URBANISATION

The Rural-Urban Migration

If the population of the world doubles before the end of this century, as seems almost certain, the new people will demand the erection of a new set of buildings at least as large as that which the world possesses at present. In fact, the demand on man's capacity to build is even larger, since most of the world's existing population needs more and better buildings than it has at present. Finally, many people in all parts of the world are leaving the houses they already have — often very poor ones — in the countryside and moving into the cities where something new has to be provided for them.

The trend to move from a rural to an urban environment has been increasing all over the world for the last century or more. In the richer countries where most people already live in towns of considerable size it may already have passed its peak. In the developing countries the movement is more recent, but it is already taking place at great speed and seems to be still accelerating; the rate of growth of urban populations may be three times that of the population as a whole. It presents the growing cities of developing countries with fantastic problems. Sir Geoffrey Vickers[1] gave one example: 'The Ivory Coast is a country of only 3—4 million people, speaking 69 native tongues, none written and none mutually understandable; but the Ivory Coast capital, Abijan, has grown in 10 years from 10,000 to 300,000.' It is thought by responsible people — nobody really knows — that there are at least a million people in Calcutta whose whole life is spent on the city streets, with no roof over their heads, except perhaps a stationary cart or doorway, and nothing more comfortable to sleep on than the pavements.

The expansion of cities in the next few decades is a challenge to human welfare, as threatening as the population explosion or the need to produce adequate food. Its magnitude has only recently been recognised. In 1963 a group of people, called together by the Greek architect and planner Doxiadis, issued a 'Declaration of Delos',[2] named after the Greek island at which it was formulated, in which they drew attention as strongly as possible to the urbanisation crisis. At the time they were fairly widely considered to be making an unnecessary fuss. Eventual 'urbanisation' has not so far been taken into account as a

Figure 5.1 :Growth of Cities in Developing Areas, 1950–1970

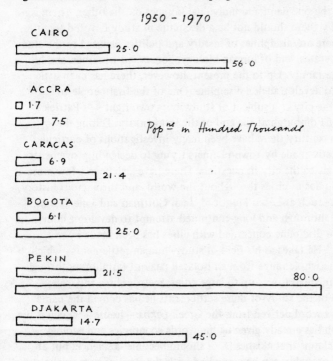

Source: *Population Bulletin*, June 1972, p. 14.

separate factor in the simulations of the world *Problematique*, but it will certainly have to be before any of those models can be regarded as adequate.

Unfortunately, no one can yet claim to understand its dynamics. It exhibits self-amplifying growth, chain reactions, and also some of the feedbacks and tendencies towards stabilisation of a terminal state (homeostasis), and running along a groove (homeorhesis); but these types of behaviour are woven together in different combinations in different cities or regions, and there is no good example in which a complete regional urbanisation process has been sufficiently analysed for anyone to feel confident that he really understands what is going on.

The Study of Human Settlement – 'Ekistics'

A city is an organisation of a certain order of complexity; its place in

the hierarchy of organised structures is somewhere between nations or
states on the one hand and individual families on the other. There is no
reason why there should not be a discipline or study devoted to cities,
just as there are disciplines of history and politics devoted to the study
of nation states, and of human biology, concerned with man and his
immediate family. Up to the present, however, there has been little
attempt to develop such a discipline. One of the first people to
consider the city as a subject of study in its own right was Patrick
Geddes of Edinburgh at the end of the last century. During the
twentieth century there have been many investigations of particular
cities, mostly made by town-planners trying to design improvements
or additions to the city in question. There have also been a few more
general studies of cities throughout the world, and throughout history,
by authors such as Lewis Mumford, Jean Gottman and Jane Jacobs.
The most thorough and long-continued attempt to develop a comprehensive discipline concerned with cities has been made by
Doxiadis.[3] He takes as his field of study 'human settlements', which
include the whole range from an isolated peasant farmhouse, through
villages and small tow:.s up to large cities, metropolises and even
beyond. For the study of these settlements he has coined the name
'ekistics', a word derived from the Greek *Oikos* — house — which is the
root which has already given us the words economics and ecology.
Doxiadis claims that ekistics is, or should become, a science; but at
present it probably can be compared with the state of botany about
the time of Linnaeus, who worked out the first system for classifying
and naming plants, rather than with any of the more highly developed
natural sciences such as physics, chemistry and biology, such as we
know them today.

Interesting attempts are being made to develop a formal, even
mathematical, theory of the structure of human settlements, in terms
of complex systems such as the hierarchical or non-hierarchical order,
the theory of programming and the like.[4] But they have not gone far
enough to provide a framework for a general discussion and we shall
have to use the conceptually simpler schemes of Doxiadis.

Classification

The first step in the development of any science is to describe the
subject matter, in all the varieties in which it presents itself. If
descriptions of varied subjects are to be comparable, they need to be
framed in terms of some system of classification, and the first steps
in the development of ekistics have been to formulate a complex

system of categories.

The classificatory system proposed by Doxiadis[5] is as follows:

(1) *The basic elements*, whose character and interactions have to be considered by ekistics, are five in number: (a) man; (b) society; (c) shells — a word used to indicate all built structures in which man encloses himself or his activities, such as hospitals, theatres, offices, etc.; (d) networks, used to cover all means of communication and transport, roads, water, electricity, gas supply lines, telephone lines, wireless links, etc.; (e) nature, usually at least partly improved or controlled by man, but still with a large element of the natural environment.

Figure 5.2: The Five Interconnected Ekistics Elements, as Proposed by Doxiadis

fourth principle: optimisation of the quality of man's relationship with his system of life

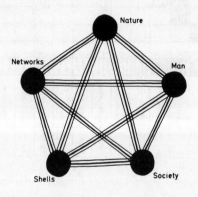

Source: C.A. Doxiadis, *Anthropopolis* (Athens Technological Centre, 1974).

(2) *The range of sizes.* These are classified into fifteen steps, on a roughly logarithmic scale, as follows: man, room, house, group of houses, small neighbourhood, small town, town, large city, metropolis, conurbation, megalopolis, urban region, urbanised continent, the world city.

(3) *Approaches.* The five main types of consideration involved are

Figure 5.3: Time Spent in Every Unit of Space in Every Phase of Life

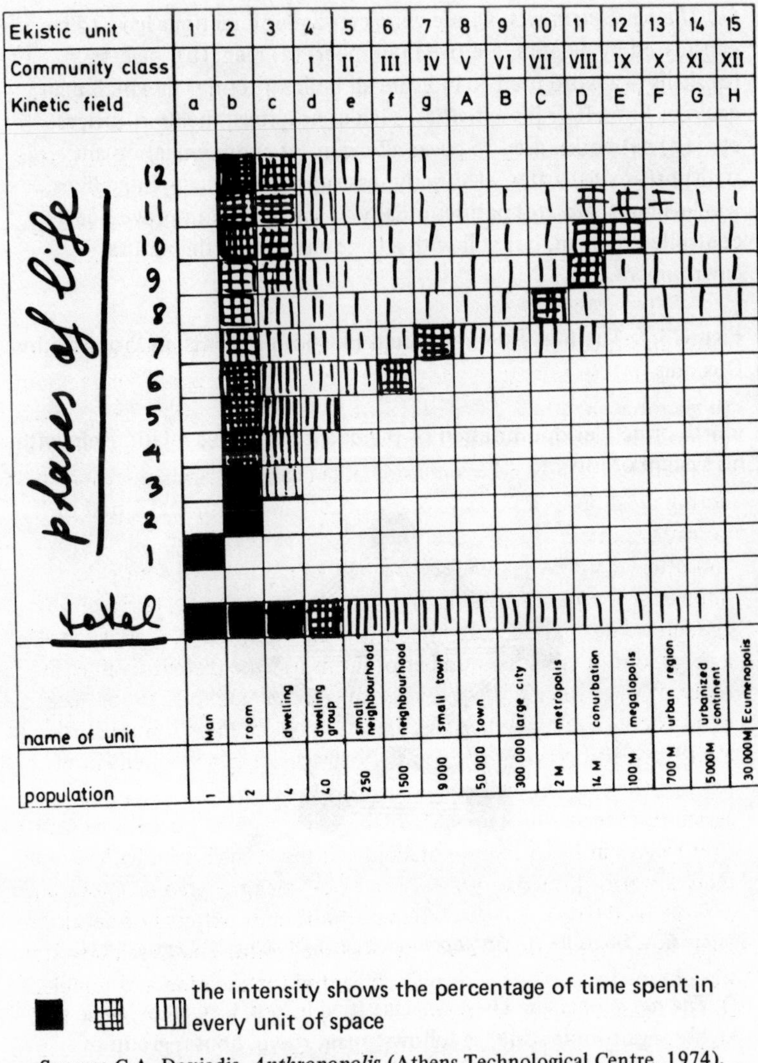

the intensity shows the percentage of time spent in every unit of space

Source: C.A. Doxiadis, *Anthropopolis* (Athens Technological Centre, 1974).

economic, social, political, technological and cultural.

With this system one can locate the area which is being considered in any particular discussion: for instance, the political effect of a railway network which connects large cities but which does not provide branches to small towns; the cultural impact of air connections between metropolises in different countries which might use different types of railway track. Perhaps the main value of the system is that its use continually draws one's attention to the narrowness of any particular discussion and forces one to remember how much is being neglected.

The Development of Cities

After classification the next step in the development of a science is to discern and describe the processes of change which are occurring in the subject matter, and the first test of a system of classification is whether or not it is satisfactory for this task.

There has clearly been a considerable change in human settlements during the course of history. The first settlements in the period of nomadic hunters of the Paleolithic Age must have been quite small and often temporary, involving probably only the first four ekistic units of size up to the dwelling group. Not until the development of agriculture in the Neolithic Period was there anything larger, such as a neighbourhood with a number of farms not too distant from each other. It was probably only at this stage that a network, in the form of a system of recognised paths, began to be developed. But shortly after the development of agriculture, towns began to be built in those parts of the earth's surface which were most fertile for the primitive agricultural techniques then available. These regions were in the great river valleys in Egypt, Mesopotamia, and the Punjab in India.[6] From then onwards throughout history one can trace the gradual appearance of larger and larger cities. A number of different patterns of development were formed in different parts of the world. The Greek city state was grouped around its Acropolis, a central fortification and temple, and its Agora, a place for marketing and social interaction. Asian and Mesopotamian cities followed different patterns, and there were also several different types of medieval European cities.

By the time of 'classical antiquity' the largest cities had populations of the order of one million, for instance in Rome and in Chang-An, the capital of classical China. This maximum size was not surpassed until the time of the Industrial Revolution, about two centuries ago. In fact, in the intermediate period the maximum size fell somewhat, particularly during the Dark Ages in Europe and the troubled periods in China's history. But from the time of the invention of new sources of power, particularly in those regions where industrial development was most advanced, the maximum sizes increased rapidly.

There are now very many cities in the world with over two million in the population, and quite a large number with over ten million. The very large cities tend to occur in groups, and as they continue to grow the members of a group tend to merge into one another, not necessarily by the coming together and fusion of the built-up areas, but by the more subtle and probably more influential process of a fusion of their networks of communication and transportation. The city of around ten million has been called a metropolis, and the complexes of interacting metropolises with high communication between them, which we see appearing in the world today, are referred to as megalopolises. Some of the best known are the conglomeration of cities stretching from Boston through New York to Washington along the eastern coast of the United States, the Detroit-Chicago-Cleveland region around the Great Lakes, and the San Francisco-Los Angeles-San Diego region of the American Pacific coast. The whole central area of the main island of Japan from Tokyo through Osaka to Kyoto is rapidly becoming another megalopolis, and so is much of industrialised north-west France, Belgium and parts of Germany and south-east England.

The trends in the recent history of cities suggest that the expected increase in urban population will largely be accommodated by expansion and further merging together of the elements in these megalopolises. What little we know about the causal processes which bring about the growth of towns tends on the whole to reinforce this conclusion. Doxiadis' group[7] argues that all the evidence at present points to the gradual emergence, over the next hundred or more years, of a world city or 'ecumenopolis'. This will extend as a web of interconnected cities throughout the continents, all parts being closely connected with all other parts by fast transport and other forms of communication, so that the whole system will have a certain functional unity, although it will, of course, incorporate many areas of open space and managed and conserved natural regions within it.

Causal Processes in City Development

The next step is to attempt to discover the causal processes which brings aboutthese changes and determine their character. Causal

Figure.5.4: The Formation of a Megalopolis along the Eastern Sea-board of the US

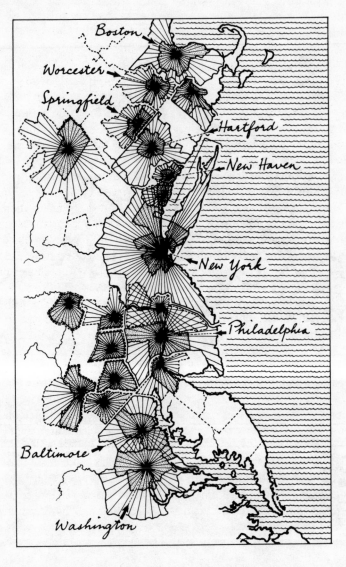

Note: Rosette round the centre of each of the cities indicates the distances over which it attracts commuters.

Source: Redrawn from article in *Architectural Design*, November 1973.

Figure 5.5a: Ecumenopolis in Europe

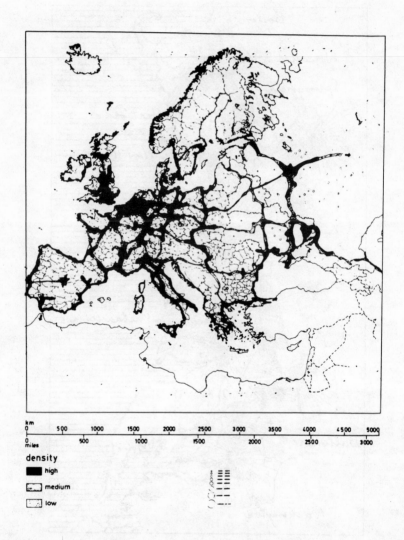

Source: *Ekistics*, February 1973, number on 'The City of the Future'. See also C.A. Doxiadis and J.G. Papaioannou, *Ecumenopolis* (Athens Center for Ekistics, 1974).

Figure 5.5b: Ecumenopolis 2060, The World

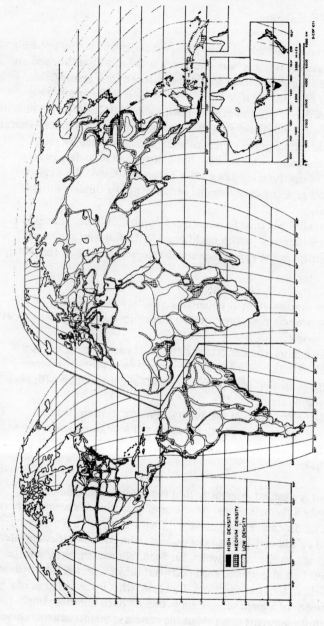

HIGH DENSITY
MEDIUM DENSITY
LOW DENSITY

Source: As for Figure 5.5a.

analyses may be made at many different levels; and it may not be, and in fact usually is not, possible to discover the most fundamental causal mechanism until a science has been developed for a considerable number of years. We now know that the basic causal mechanism of the growth and development of a living animal depends on the operations of enzymes, and that the fundamental process in its evolution is natural selection acting on the variety of individuals produced by gene mutations and recombinations; but biology had to undergo a long period of development as a science before it attained this degree of penetration. Ekistics will almost certainly need a similar period of maturation.

Doxiadis[8] has tried to formulate a number of basic 'principles of human settlements' which might provide the fundamental causal mechanisms in the appearance and development of cities. His principles are:

(1) the maximisation of potential contacts; men tend to move into positions where they can make the maximum number of contacts with other people;
(2) the minimisation of effort, in terms of energy, time and cost;
(3) the optimisation of man's protective space, giving maximum security consistent with personal contact and interaction with other people and things;
(4) the optimisation of the quality of man's relations with his environment, including both his social and his natural environment;
(5) achieving an optimum balance between the four preceding principles.

This is a gallant attempt to find general principles, but almost certainly a premature one. All the principles Doxiadis mentions have some validity and effectiveness but they are of such a general nature that they add very little to our understanding of how cities operate.

An alternative tactic, which has been followed by many sciences in their first attempts to tackle difficult subject matter, is to analyse the field in terms of functions. One asks, what is the function of a given system, or of a given sub-system within it? Such questions imply that the most important thing about the system is that its activities have some general over-all characteristic, which is the *function* of the system. When one has discovered what this function is for the system as a whole, one can enquire how the various parts of the system contribute to the over-all activity.

But in many cases it is not easy to discover what the over-all function is. One might say that the over-all activity of a man is to grow, develop and live a healthy life. On the other hand, from a longer-term point of view, one would conclude that his over-all function includes not only a healthy life for himself, but the transmitting of genetic and cultural potentialities to his offspring, and thus contributing to the long-term processes of evolution and the development of civilisation. However, even somewhat inadequate definitions of the general function of a system may be sufficient to allow one to make meaningful analyses of the way in which the parts contribute to the workings of the whole. The science of the biology of a healthy life, and of the physiological functioning of organs, was developed in a period when people were willing to accept the first of the definitions of human function given above, before they had realised the importance of the evolutionary aspects.

The functional analysis of cities is still at a very early stage. There is, in fact, an unresolved controversy about the function of the first primitive groupings of settlements, which might be called towns, in the early agricultural period of history. The orthodox view supposes that towns arose after the improvement of agricultural methods had produced surplus foodstuffs. People who did not have to cultivate their own subsistence could then gather into towns, where they acted as rulers, or priests, or merchants, or in some other service capacity. From this view, the towns were essentially parasitic on the countryside, dependent on surplus produced by the agricultural workers. The alternative view is expounded by the American historian Jane Jacobs.[9] She argues that towns are essentially places where people meet and stimulate each other to produce novelties. The more efficient agricultural methods were invented in a region where the houses were close together and the farmers met and discussed their agricultural problems. The first town was at first a mere group of neighbouring farms with houses perhaps a little nearer than average; and then, as they produced more surpluses, some people might become soldiers, rulers, lawyers, priests or traders, but the town was from the beginning itself the producer of the surpluses on which it thrived. And it is always the town which invents the innovating and more efficient technology even in agriculture.

However the town may have originated, certainly it has developed a character closer to that described by Jane Jacobs than to the orthodox view. In all more advanced civilisations, the town has been the innovator, not the parasite. Its functions have been not merely to disseminate things, and to facilitate their interchange, but also to bring about the production of novelties.

The Five Ekistic Elements

Probably the most useful approach to an understanding of cities at the present time is to turn back to a consideration of the five ekistic elements formulated by Doxiadis — man, society, shells, networks and nature — and enquire, first, what functions the city ought to be fulfilling, and secondly, what evidence there is as to how well existing cities, or foreseeable future cities, fulfil these functions.

Man

Organisms belonging to the species *homo sapiens* have certain basic physical and organic needs, without which they cannot stay alive. Their biological organisation also determines certain *desiderata*, the fulfilment of which facilitates, or even is necessary for, a complete development of the potentialities in their genetic constitutions. It is remarkable that we know rather little about these *desiderata*. Many branches of biology have been greatly expanded and deepened during this century, including of course profound studies of disease or pathological conditions of the human body; but although many people have stressed the importance of an equally profound study of the human body in health, and of the conditions which advance development (and have even proposed the name 'anthropics' for such a study), it still remains incompletely explored territory. Most of what has been written about it is founded on casual observation, guesswork and intuition, rather than on scientifically ascertained facts.

It seems to be generally agreed that large parts of modern cities provide far from ideal biological environments.[10] They are noisy, polluted and stressful (except perhaps for some of the richest suburban areas in the most favourable climates). Probably the same could have been said for almost all cities in the past. However, we now have good reason to believe that the technological know-how is available to create conditions better than those of our existing cities or of most past cities.

One of the first steps towards a rational treatment of the situation would be to learn the hard facts about the nature of the stresses imposed on man's body in different regions of cities, and in different ways of city life. The micro-miniaturisation of electronic equipment should now make it possible for people to carry with them a small piece of equipment to record such physiological variables as the heartbeat, breathing rhythm, blood pressure and galvanic skin reflex, together with the incident noise, temperature, wind speeds, accelerations, and so on. Given such records, we could get some facts about the physiological responses of various people to the conditions they meet as commuters, slum dwellers, office or factory workers and so on. So far such records have been made only of people in extremely stressful conditions, such as pilots of aircraft landing at busy airports, space travellers and the like. The ordinary man in the street has not yet been studied.

Using a more intuitive approach, Doxiadis[11] has considered the changing size and mobility of people throughout the human life history from the time of conception to real old age of 75 or above and has considered the architectural form of dwelling places that seem to be appropriate for the various stages. He points out that our tradition is to build dwellings and settlements suitable primarily for adulthood, i.e. the period from about 19–60 years old (which he divides into three sub-phases). But about 47 per cent of the world's population is younger than this, and another 7 per cent older (see Figure 1.5, p. 20). In the richer countries, which have made the demographic transition (see p. 25), there is a smaller proportion of young people, but a larger proportion of old ones, and in them also the adult population is less than half the total. Doxiadis suggests that dwelling places should be designed with much more attention to the needs of young children. This would involve, for instance, greater separation of play areas from traffic streets, with much greater emphasis on the provision of pedestrian precincts, a proposal which we shall meet again when we consider societies. The needs of young people also make it very undesirable to provide housing for families in the form of high-rise blocks of apartments, unless these can be provided as they almost never are, with extensive play verandas and internal open areas on a number of floors, so that a young mother can be not too far away from her playing children. This turns the whole project into a luxury type of building, rather than one to meet the common needs.

Doxiadis's study is primarily in terms of appropriate size of dwelling places in relation to spatial mobility. There are other biological aspects of man which change throughout his life history, which need to be considered in a similar way. An example is muscular movement. Most people of most ages like to use their muscles to a certain extent and, when they live in cities which do not encourage them to take sufficient exercise by walking, even go to the length of inventing games like tennis, football, dancing, ski-ing and golf to enable them to do so. Doxiadis in his proposals provides more opportunity for walking, and

Figure 5.6: The City Built for Adults Only

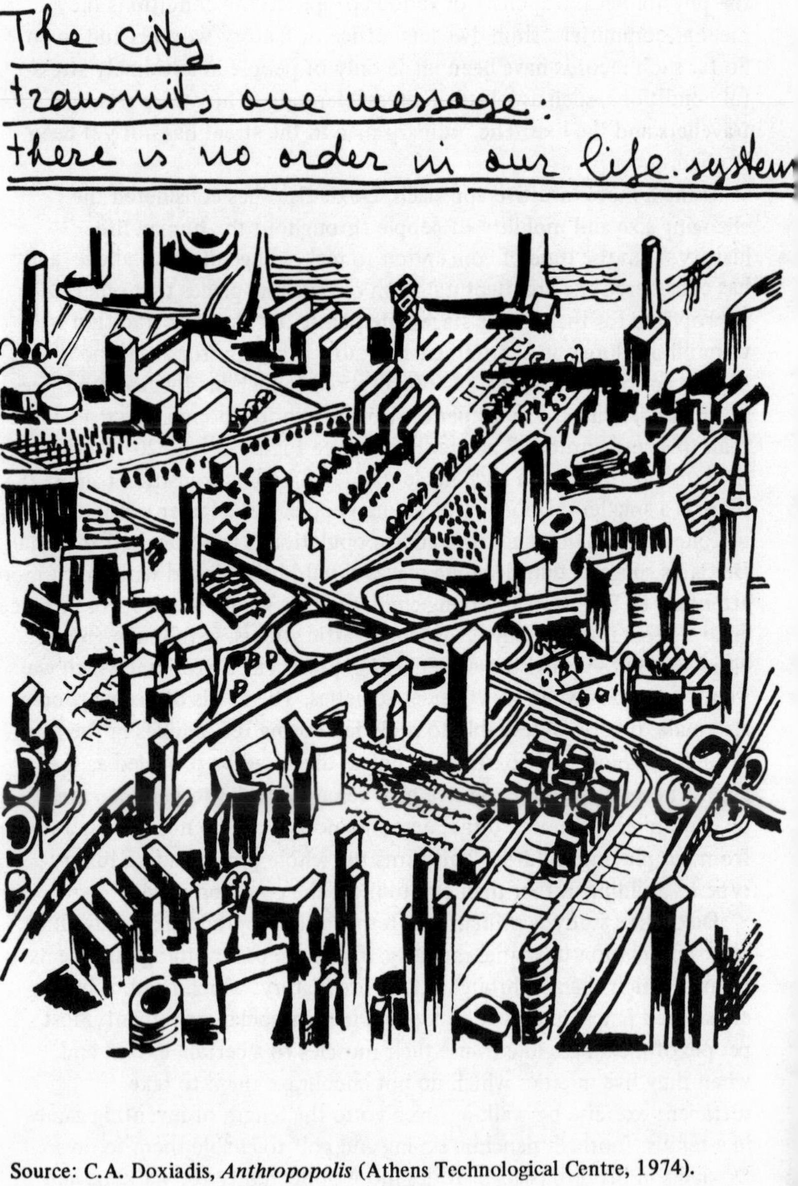

Source: C.A. Doxiadis, *Anthropopolis* (Athens Technological Centre, 1974).

even suggests making steps in pedestrian streets to provide more exercise for sedentary office workers, as a precaution against heart failure or obesity. But modern cities are so large that the most frequent journeys within them are too long for walking to be an acceptable form of transport. There might be something to be said for the revival of the bicycle, or something similar, for journeys of up to three or four miles (see p. 185).

In his 'City for Human Development' Doxiadis considers primarily dwelling places. These are certainly the most numerous and perhaps the most neglected units within a city. But there are many other types of buildings. There has been considerable study of the appropriateness of specialised buildings, such as schools and hospitals, for the biological needs of the human beings concerned, but shops, offices and factories are usually considered only in terms of efficiency in fulfilling their function — of promoting sales, producing goods, or processing information; much less attention has been paid to the biological well-being of the people inside the buildings. Is continuous enclosure in an air-conditioned windowless building for eight hours a day biologically good for a person? It is to be doubted if anybody knows.

Society

Human social relations within modern cities have been enormously extended over those possible in cities of the past. The telephone, and rapid transit by underground, bus or car, has multiplied many hundred-fold the number of people from whom it is a practical possibility to select one's friends and acquaintances.

But in spite of this many people in cities find themselves isolated and may actually be acquainted with almost nobody. This situation of great loneliness when surrounded by wonderful means of communication could almost never have happened in the past. It occurs now because a variety of developments, including improvements in communication-technology, have conspired to destroy or greatly diminish the importance of small communities based on acquaintance between neighbours. The village where everyone knows everyone else is one of the basic forms of human settlement. Early cities which depended on pedestrian transport with a little supplementation from horses preserved the essential character. It is a very recent situation when people do not know the name of their next-door neighbours and are not on speaking terms with more than a tiny fraction of the people in the next street or apartment block. Many people concerned with cities consider that this is not merely novel but harmful.

Its effects differ at different stages in life history. Children develop better if they play with other children from houses nearby, and this is likely to bring together their mothers and possibly even their youngish fathers. Young adolescents may feel a need to get well away from any neighbourhood in which they have been brought up, and to lose themselves for a time in the anonymity of the big city. Men and women, at the stage at which they are likely to be parents of pre-adolescents, at the height of their working and creative lives, may get more satisfaction in friendships with people from outside their neighbourhood, who fit better into their active lives. But in older age it becomes important again to be able to make human contact without travelling long distances.

There is, therefore, a good case for building dwelling places so as to facilitate the formation of small neighbourhood groups, during the ages at which this is a desirable part of the human experience, but there will always be a demand for areas in which people can live more private lives, more isolated from their immediate neighbours, but connected by modern means of transport and communication with people widely scattered over the whole city.

The reality of neighbourhoods as effective sub-units within towns has been thoroughly studied in some countries for at least a quarter of a century. In the mid-forties in Britain there was still considerable truth in the saying that cities are essentially collections of villages; London was really Hampstead plus Highgate plus Camden Town plus Bloomsbury and so on. But when attempts have been made in the design of new towns built after World War II to provide a series of sub-centres around which neighbours would be encouraged to develop definite local identities, the response has been on the whole discouraging. The idea of basing a new (British) town on a suitably dispersed set of 'village greens' has become a target for disparaging remarks.

Possibly the snag has been a failure to pay attention to the historical circumstances in which the old town neighbourhoods arose, and in consequence a lack of new thinking about what form of sub-unit would be appropriate to modern society, with its new technologies, particularly of transport. In other parts of the world less technologically developed than Britain, the 'Chelsea-sized' neighbourhood still has some vitality. Extensive studies have been made by the Doxiadis group on the structure of the city of Athens.[12] There the small-scale community seems to be still alive. It evolves according to a certain pattern. New communities appear first on the outskirts of the enlarging city. They grow from very low densities to higher densities with an increasing feeling of togetherness, but eventually a community becomes incorporated in the main

Figure 5.7: The City Adapted for Young and Old as Well as Adults

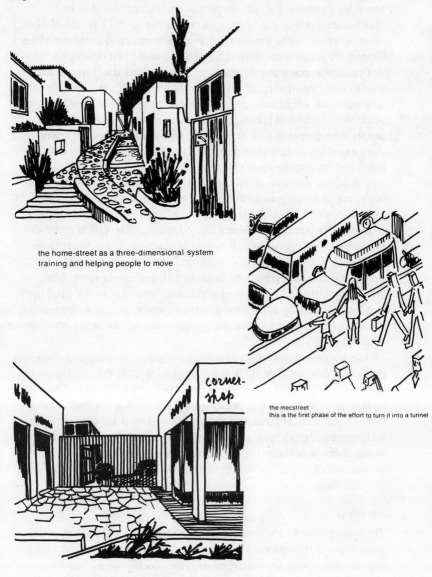

the home-street as a three-dimensional system
training and helping people to move

the mecstreet
this is the first phase of the effort to turn it into a tunnel

the exit from home-square to mechanical street

Source: C.A. Doxiadis, *Anthropopolis* (Athens Technological Centre, 1974).

part of the city and then the local developments become static, and in a way the community disintegrates again towards the end of its life. This is a temporal cycle, taking from beginning to end a period of 30, 40 or 50 years, but in a country of average economic development like Greece, the stages seem to be quite real and quite well developed.

One of the important steps taken by the Athens study was to define a series of different sorts of neighbourhoods, of different sizes. The 'Chelsea-sized' neighbourhood, or 'Greenwich Village' in New York, attained its individual cohesion in the days of horse transport, when people were prepared to walk a mile or two without thinking it anything exceptional. It is considerably larger than the effective neighbourhood for a mother with a baby in a pram, or for the child who is sent out from home on an errand to the local corner shop, or the man in the evening who goes down to the local for a pint or two. These smaller localities certainly have much to offer in richness and frequency of human contact. But in these days of high mobility within cities, the most effective stages on which human contacts occur are either these very small localities (5 to 10 minutes walking distance) or larger, less precisely bounded regions, reachable in a 10 minute car drive. And, increasingly, the factor which in practice defines an effective neighbourhood may be hardly at all mere geographic space, nor even very much the transit time in view of the traffic, but more and more the convenience of parking.

The whole conceptual framework appropriate for analysing cities in the rich developed world is in fact becoming quite different from the conventional geographical schemata we have used in the past. There is an indication of this new approach in the title of Rayner Banham's recent book *Los Angeles; the Architecture of Four Ecologies*.[13] It is no longer enough to look at the use of geographical space, the form of the shells or of the networks connecting them; what gives the city its essential character are the social behaviours for which they provide only the stage.

Networks

The main networks are the means of communication and transport of people, goods or services. All modern technologies of communications and transport, with the exception of radio and television, require physical apparatus in the form of roads, rails, pipes, cables, etc., and few people have occasion to realise just how complex the network structure of modern cities has become. A fully automobile-dominated city, such as Los Angeles, now devotes a greater total area to roads and

Figure 5.8: Networks of the Detroit Daily Urban System (1970)

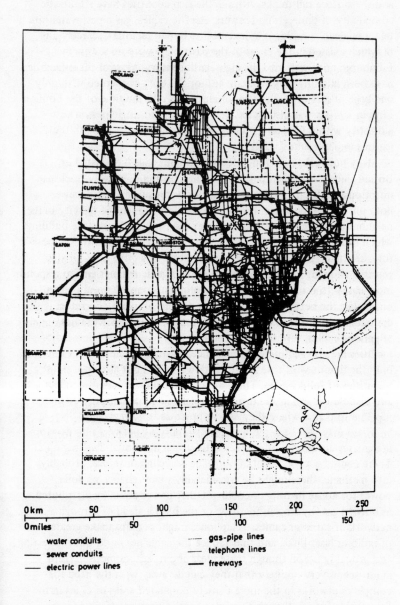

Source: C.A. Doxiadis, *Anthropopolis* (Athens Technological Centre, 1974).

parking places than it does to human habitation. And besides the roads and the surface rail tracks, cities in the rich countries have a fantastic complexity of underground sewers, electric cables, gas pipes, water pipes, telephone cables and half a dozen other buried facilities, scarcely any of which existed in the cities of the past; there were no sewers in Edinburgh until well into the eighteenth century. Most of these facilities have been laid down by separate authorities each concerned with only one type of service, such as gas or electricity. At the time of the London Blitz in 1940 it was discovered that there was no single person or authority within Greater London who knew the location of all the various underground facilities.

Many networks have long lifetimes. Some roads have lasted in Britain since the Roman period, and the position of railway tracks is notoriously difficult to change. A major water supply line or sewer not only has a powerful influence on the development of the city in its neighbourhood but tends to last longer than any of the surface buildings which become attracted into the area it serves. Service networks, therefore, are rigidifying elements in the structure of a city. A major step towards allowing cities to grow in a more organic manner and to respond more easily to the changing demands of circumstances, would be to rationalise the network systems into a pattern of 'utility corridors', containing the main roads and the gas mains, electric power lines, telephone cables, sewers, water conduits and so on. Some new major facilities are also required. For instance, waste-disposal involves not only the liquids which we now pass down sewers but also enormous quantities of solid wastes. These are now a major problem to collect and dispose of, and in the future we might wish to transport them by pipeline to plants where they can be processed and recycled.

There may also be some scope for simplifying networks by developing greater autonomy of services within each individual dwelling unit. There could be a good deal of domestic recycling of refuse, probably into methane; there might be considerably more reliance on solar power for house heating or cooling. Other power could be distributed as bottled gas (hydrogen, methane or the like) instead of through a network of tubes or cables. Telephones might perhaps make greater use of radio or laser links, and thus reduce the cable network. But interesting and probably useful though these ideas about 'autonomous housing' are, it seems very unlikely that they can do away with the need for complex networks in the more densely populated areas of cities in the foreseeable future, though they may have important effects in less dense suburban areas.

It is not only in developed cities that service networks are of paramount importance. They are probably the most fundamental of all components in the young, more rapidly expanding, cities of the poor countries. These contain a great deal of do-it-yourself housing erected by people who are going to live there, with whatever material they can lay their hands on. Until fairly recently, the orthodox response of city authorities was to regard these shanty towns as demeaning slums and to bulldoze them out of existence; but it is rapidly being realised that there is no prospect of replacing them with better built houses on an adequate scale in the future. The best that can be done in the short term is to provide a network of elementary facilities; some roads, water supply, sewage, which may give the squatters just sufficient services to encourage them to improve their own dwelling places.[14]

Shells

In the rich countries, the nature of the buildings provided for man's use does not contribute very much to the major dangers to our future, though it does give rise to two quite important problems. One arises from the harmful effects of high-rise apartments on the development of young children. The answer here is to build lower dwellings; actually high-rise apartments are more expensive than an equivalent number of low-rise ones, when account is taken of the management and other costs which are not included in the actual price of the structure. Local authorities in many parts of the world have already changed their policy from one of high-rise apartments to low-rise ones, at least in dwellings intended for families.

The other major defect of the present type of building in the rich world is the development of an almost intolerable contrast between rich, fairly pleasant suburbs and decayed older more central parts of the city, inhabited mainly by the poor and in the States disproportionately by black, Mexican and other disadvantaged groups. An enormous literature has grown up about the 'central City ghettos' and what to do about them.[15] The standard remedies have been of three types:

(1) 'Urban renewal' (i.e. knocking down and rebuilding) carried out by central government (federal) agencies. These have usually failed because they produced buildings too expensive for the population they they were trying to help.
(2) Similar programmes carried out by local agencies, with as much co-operation from the population immediately concerned as possible. The

difficulties here have been that the ghetto population usually has rather little cohesion as a community and few community organisations strong enough to be effective.

(3) Some American planners (e.g. Forrester[16]) have responded to these disappointments by going back to the old-fashioned recipe of trying to provide jobs, in the form of productive industry which should create wealth which will enable the problem to solve itself. But this does not seem so likely to be effective in the present situation of over-production of goods, and the approaching post-industrial leisured society, as it did in Victorian times.

Llewellyn Davies[17] makes the point that the first essential is the provision of more resources, both financial and in personnel. Once society has allowed the central areas of a city — one of mankind's major capital assets, accumulated over a century or more — to get badly run down, rebuilding and resuscitating it cannot be cheap in real terms. But those real terms might perhaps not take the conventional form of presently-accepted money. The areas to be improved contain many unemployed but potentially capable people; and the job to be done — building — is one which is traditionally labour-intensive and can use readily available materials, such as bricks. Can some new form of economic organisation be devised, which will make it possible for the available supply of labour and materials to satisfy the obtrusive need? Various forms of 'new money' have in fact been invented in relation to 'shell building' in recent years, such as government-guaranteed mortgages and the like but so far they have served more to facilitate the expansion of relatively well-off suburbs than to meet the needs of the poor.

The kernel of the problem is social and political rather than merely economic. Does society really wish, genuinely enough to implement its aspirations, to be egalitarian rather than hierarchical? Is there a majority in the middle, strong enough to coerce the upper crust into the flexibility and sacrifices required to get rid of the segregation of a stratum of under-dogs, and also willing themselves to accept ex-ghetto dwellers as members of the same integrated community as themselves? These, much more than technological problems, are the real issues of the present phase of urbanisation in the richest and most 'developed' country in the world.

In poor and rapidly urbanising countries many people live in conditions in comparison with which the so-called ghetto slums of America would seem like palaces. The major world problem about dwellings is to discover what to do for these millions, who live either with no shelter at all, or on the pavements of big cities such as Calcutta, or in huts made out of beaten petrol cans, cardboard cartons and the like. Can modern industry provide them with something better at prices they can afford? The answer seems to be that it probably cannot, in the short run at any rate. The industrial production of housing can never reduce the price sufficiently if it uses conventional capital and conventional materials, such as bricks, stones and mud, which may be cheaply available but are labour-intensive to work up. Modern methods can erect shelters very cheaply from raw materials, such as plastics, which require considerable investment to produce; for instance, houses can be constructed of plastic foam sprayed on to an inflated bell-shaped form which is deflated when the plastic has set and taken out and used again. Such technologically innovative and exotic housing units have been produced in demonstration quantities, enough to rehouse one or two villages in an earthquake disaster area, but the prices the shanty dwellers could pay would not finance the capital outlay.

The most helpful practical policy is to facilitate self-help housing by providing basic services and various useful hand-operated devices, such as simple means for making mud bricks. Supplies of cheap structural elements, such as beams for spanning above windows and doors for supporting roofs, and of some types of fasteners and pegs for joining corners together firmly, would also give considerable help to home builders at little cost. Moreover a home is something more than four walls and a roof. Papanek[18] has estimated that the poor regions not only need 472 million houses, but need about 2 billion 'things to sit on' — chairs, stools and so on. Suitable sacks which could be filled with straw would be a good deal better than sitting on the bare earth, and a small amount of public funds invested in making these easily available would do much more for the comfort of the population than the same amount spent on building a small number of better houses. And what about beds?

Nature

Until not much more than a century ago, the city dweller had access to reasonably varied natural communities of plants, which might even contain a certain number of animals as well. Medieval cities had many gardens and a citizen could reach open fields in an hour's walk or less. In modern cities, a dweller in the city centre has to make a considerable journey to find anything more representative of nature than a piece of scruffy grass, some carefully protected urban trees and, for animals, sparrows, pigeons and the evidence of the presence of rats and mice. The world-wide tendency for richer people to move from the centre of the city into the suburbs, where they can enjoy the artificially managed, but in some ways natural, surroundings of gardens, is evidence that inter-action with nature is something which many people desire and are willing to pay quite heavily for.

For several decades, ever since the pioneer garden cities of England, town planners have tried to make access to nature as easy as possible for everyone. One of the most fashionable schemes has been to provide a Green Belt of open countryside, protected from building, around the periphery of the city. Quite soon new towns develop along the radial transport network at points just outside the Green Belt, which eventually becomes ringed with heavily built-up areas outside as well as inside. Then its raison d'être seems to have disappeared, and various forms of building are eventually allowed within it.

At present opinion seems to be that it is more promising to allow finger-like areas of natural vegetation to reach towards the centre of the town. This can sometimes be done in a natural way, when there are features such as rivers or canals along which these areas can extend. Possibly eventually the lines of the utility corridors and transport net-works could be used in a similar way, when the actual services have been put underground or into trenches, as they probably should be.

Probably, however, the time has come for a much more radical reconsideration of the form which nature should take in relation to cities.[19] At present we have three versions of it: (1) city parks, which may be very fine, but use expensive space (so that unless they exist already it is practically impossible to make new ones of any size), and they are expensive to maintain and to police; (2) suburban areas, with a great deal of grass, bushes and trees, but usually organised on the small scale of the individual house-and-garden, so that the most valuable qualities of nature — quiet, space, a complex functioning ecosystem — are diluted out of existence; and (3) derelict or semi-derelict areas, between new factories, or on the sites of old industrial works, quarries and sandpits, etc., and farms struggling to exist in the Green Belts where there are overwhelming pressures from non-agricultural neighbours. Fairbrother, in particular, has argued that we should boldly set about *creating* a mixed 'Green-Urban' type of development, mainly from the third category above. This would have sculptured landscapes with hills and ponds, made by heavy machines either out of the derelict wastes, or around new factories, which they could shield from the neighbouring residential areas. The earth-moving feats in some of our old cities, done with pick, shovel and wheelbarrow, such as the Mound in Edinburgh, and the ancient achievements of our neolithic ancestors, in building great barrows or platforms, makes it seem ridiculous that, in the days of mechanised strip-mining and earth-moving machinery, we bring nature to our cities by nothing more daring than planting a few cherry trees.

Cities of the Next Century

At the beginning of the next century cities might be fairly evenly spread over the land surface of the globe, several thousand of them each with a population ranging from 1 to 10 million. However, the more usual prediction is that the population will be concentrated in city complexes extending through the regions most favourable in terms of climate, availability of adequate water supply, scenic attractions such as sea coasts and lakes, and position with regard to major transport net-works. These will connect up with one another to form a 'world city' or 'ecumenopolis' (p. 148). The city might be covered fairly uniformly with low-density suburban-type houses. In such areas it is usually almost impossible to distinguish one small neighbourhood from any other neighbourhood; one finds oneself in what has been called an 'urban no place'. When this extends for a few tens of miles, as it already does around some American cities, it is an environment in which few people feel themselves at home. It might be really disturbing if it is extended for hundreds or thousands of miles over the most attractive parts of the earth's surface. The alternative is the develop-ment of many individual city centres, with relatively high density, connected by facilities for rapid transport through areas of low density and extensive regions of open space and natural vegetation. This could provide a much more varied and stimulating environment and would also seem to make much more sense from a transport point of view. In the recent past people in rich countries have been moving into large areas (100 or more miles in diameter) of functionally inter-connected urban settlements. This does not imply a movement into the officially recognised metropolitan districts within those areas (10 miles in diameter). In fact, some of the oldest metropolises with the highest density have recently begun to experience a decline in population. In England,[20] the core areas of both London and Merseyside fell in population by as much as 9 per cent between 1961 and 1971. But the emigrants did not, usually, go far away, or effectively sever their links with the megalopolis. In the London region, for instance, the majority of immigrants to the central districts are quite young adults (pre-reproduction), while those who move out

Figure 5.9: Megalopolis

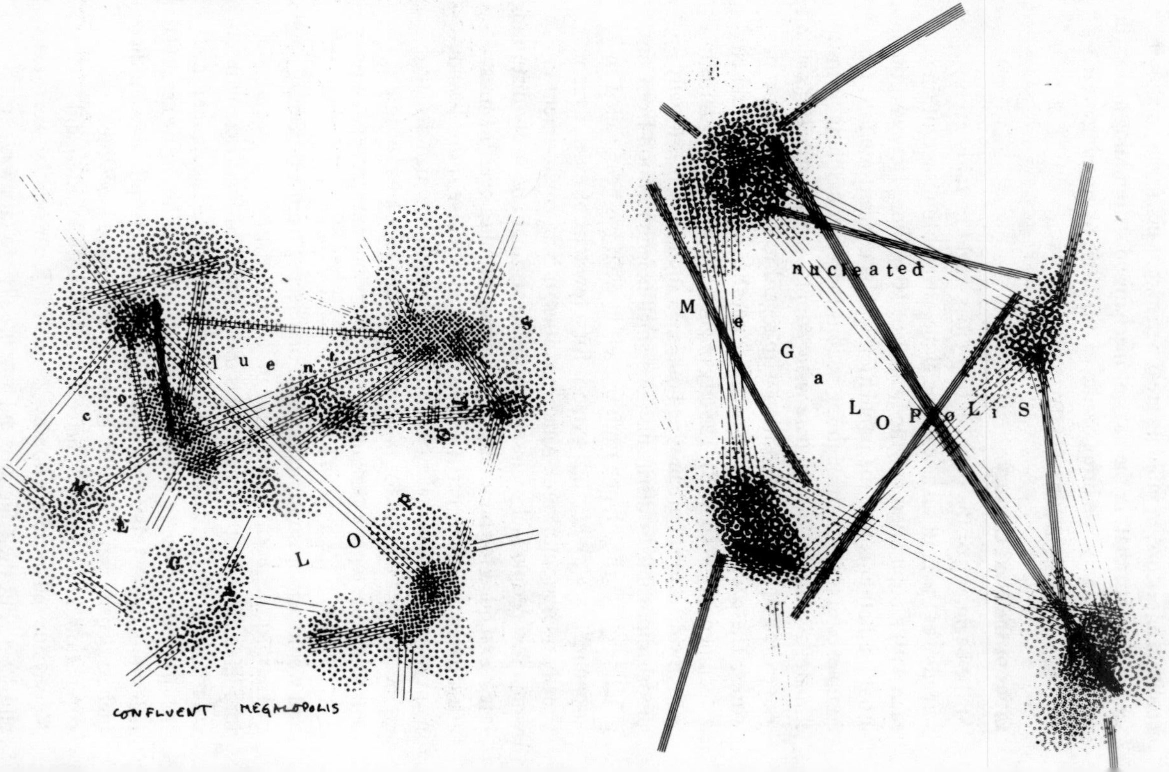

Figure 5.10: Part of the Montreal Downtown Pedestrian Underground
System

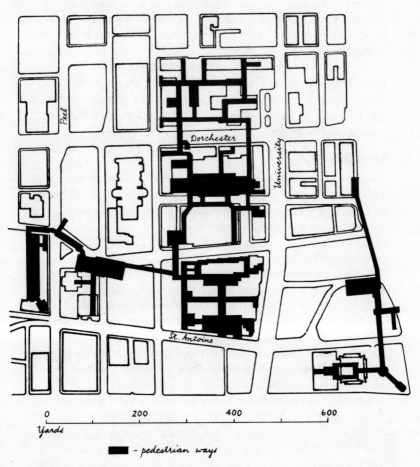

Part of the Montreal downtown pedestrian underground system

Source: *Ekistics*, 194, January 1972, p. 38.

are mostly rather older adults (often with or expecting children). Of the emigrants, about a third settle in Outer London (and a half of these still work centrally), about another third go abroad, and the final third go elsewhere in the UK. Even that last phrase does not mean that they go very far. Yet these fluctuations are of minor importance in the context of the growth of the megalopolis which stretches from the Ruhr through North East France and the Low Countries across the Channel to South East England, with an arm reaching up through Birmingham to the Mersey (see Figure 5.5a).

In most developing countries, the movement of people into metropolises is not yet tempered by secondary tendencies to scatter. People go right into the metropolitan district of Calcutta, Bombay, Rio, Sao Paulo, Lima, Caracas, Mexico City, rather than just into their general neighbourhood.

Specialised Cities

Beside the main bulk of the world city, there are likely in the near future to be a number of experimental city developments which will be both technologically exciting, and stimulating places to live in or visit. Here are three types which seem probable.

Cities with Climate Control

Cities may be required on parts of the earth's surface which are not *a priori* very attractive for human settlements; for instance, parts of Canada and Siberia, where it is often cold, or in parts of Africa and Australia, where the climate is too hot. A solution which will certainly be attempted is to air-condition the whole city. Already around many American cities there are air-conditioned shopping centres as large as old-fashioned villages. In Montreal, there are about 7 miles of pedestrian underground streets lined with shops and cafes, all air-conditioned and lit so that it is very pleasant to stroll along (although I am not sure what happens if there is a power failure).

Super Beehive Cities

These are very high-density three-dimensional arrangements of living units, not in the conventional rectangular tower blocks. One very promising preliminary step in this direction is the housing unit Habitat, erected at the 1967 Montreal World Exposition by the Israeli architect Mosche Safdie. Prefabricated units of a few different varieties were piled on top of one another in a pleasantly irregular arrangement to provide a number of apartments, each with its own private roof garden.

Figure 5.11: Habitat, Montreal

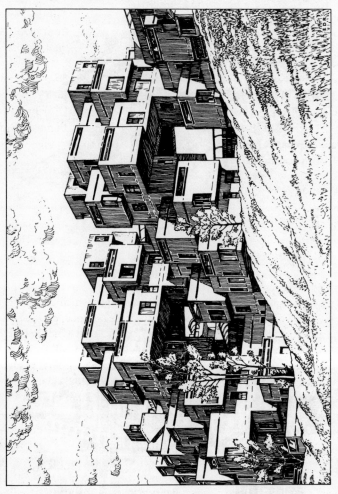

Figure 5.12: Part of Design for 'Babel 11C' by Paolo Soleri : a One-Building City for 350,000 People

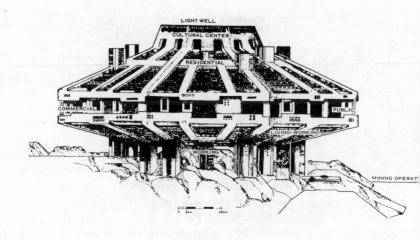

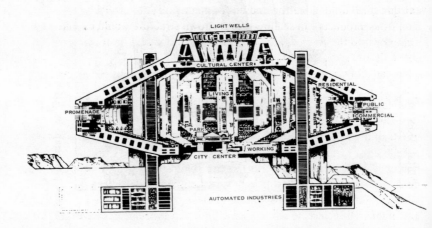

Source: Paolo Soleri, *Arcology : The City in the Image of Man* (MIT Press, 1969).

Buildings developed from this basic idea are already being erected in a number of places.

Much more fantastic, super-colossal three-dimensional structures, to provide living accommodation, work places and other facilities for populations of hundreds of thousands, have been proposed by a few architects, of whom the most fashionable is Paolo Soleri.[21] Such magnificent daydreams may fascinate sufficient people for some attempts to be made to realise one or other of them, but the circumstances in which this type of development can be of real importance are very special.

Ocean Cities

One development which seems not too unlikely is the building of cities for permanent habitation in the oceans. In theory there could be two forms of these; at the bottom, or extending down only to a moderate depth below the surface. It seems unlikely that there will be any urbanisation of the bed of the deep sea, because of the very formidable pressures, and it is difficult to envisage any reasons why anyone should wish to live down there. There may, of course, be small work stations, perhaps connected with mining, but that is not the same as a city.

Cities on the sea surface, extending down a few hundred feet, look much more attractive and may develop in the first place from the existing small drilling platforms used for mining oil (and probably later other products). In shallow seas the town structure would extend right down to the sea bed, although its upper part would be at and above the sea surface.

Ocean cities might also be built of nodes on transport routes. In the last two or three centuries, several coastal cities have been built to serve as nodes in sea transportation, located at previously unused areas of shore line — Singapore, Hong Kong, Aden and Bombay. These cities were conjured up out of mud flats and waste along the sea's edge, though some of them have quite large floating populations living in houseboats. If we needed any further communication nodes, we could now construct them as floating islands in the middle of the deep ocean, and it might well be attractive to do so. In a more leisured post-industrial society, in which many at present hidden costs have been brought out into the open, there may be many types of cargoes which it would be sensible to transport in a more leisurely way than by intercontinental jet or by super-colossal tanker. People may even prefer to cross the Atlantic or Pacific in several hops, stopping at a few interesting places on the way, and giving their biological clocks time to

Figure 5.13: Parts of City to Be Built in Tokyo Bay, by Kenzo Tange

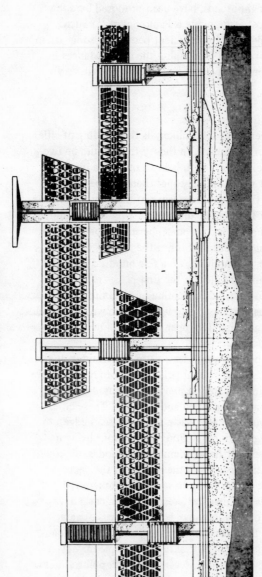

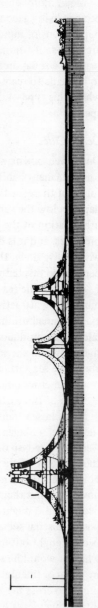

Source: Redrawn from Paoli Riani, *Kenzo Tange* (Hamlyn, 1969), Figures 27, 29.

catch up. One can imagine a few new Hong Kongs or Singapores floating in the middle of major oceans, servicing short-hop aircraft, possibly airships, normal cargo ships, and possibly cargo-carrying sub-mersibles; there might be some deep ocean fishing involved as well, and the city would probably extract large crops of energy from ocean waves. It is in cities of this kind that 'Soleri-like' structures seem most likely to find a practical use.

Less isolated types of floating city development have been proposed for the expansion of some densely built-up coastal areas. The famous Japanese architect Kenzo Tange has made plans for the development in Tokyo Bay of a number of floating suburbs, to relieve the pressure for space on the dry land. This would be following in the footsteps of Venice and could add an enjoyable variety to what may all too easily become a boringly uniform world city.

Further Reading

A. C.A. Doxiadis, *Ekistics* (Oxford University Press, New York; Hutchinson, London, 1968) is the definitive statement by Doxiadis, but is very long. *Architecture in Transition* (Oxford University Press, New York; Hutchinson, London, 1963) or *Between Dystopia and Utopia* (Trinity College Press, Hartford, Connecticut; Oxford University Press, NY, 1966) are shorter discussions of the same viewpoint.

B. Peter Cook, *Architecture; Action and Plan* (Studio Vista, 1967) is a short alternative view.

C. Buckminster Fuller, *Ideas and Integrities* (Macmillan, NY, 1969) gives the basic ideas of one of the influential though eccentric futurists.

D. Peter Cowan, *Developing Patterns of Urbanisation* (Oliver & Boyd, 1970) is mainly about British cities.

E. Kevin Lynch, *The Image of the City* (MIT Press, 1960) is an interesting description of what modern cities (mainly American) actually look like or are thought by their inhabitants to look like.

F. Gwen Bell and Jacqueline Tyrwhitt eds., *Human Identity in the Urban Environment* (Penguin, 1972) is a large collection of essays from *Ekistics*.

G. Lewis Mumford, *The City in History* (Secker & Warburg, Harcourt Brace & Wald, NY, 1961; Penguin, 1973) is a classic about cities up to the present.

Notes

1. Geoffrey Vickers, 'The End of Free Fall', in *Value Systems and Social Processes* (Pelican Books, 1970), p. 74.
2. 'Declaration of Delos Ten', *Ekistics*, October 1972, p. 230.
3. C.A. Doxiadis, *Ekistics* (Oxford Univ. Press, NY, 1968) is rather large. Smaller books by the same author are: *Between Dystopia and Utopia* (Trinity College Press, Hartford, Conn., 1966); *Architecture in Transition* (Oxford Univ. Press, paperback, 1968); and C.A. Doxiadis, 'A City for Human Development', in *Ekistics 25*, 151, June 1968, later developed into the book *Anthropopolis* (Athens Technological Centre, 1974).
4. Bill Hillier and Adrian Leaman, *Structure, System, Transformation*, Transactions of the Bartlett Soc. *9*, 36, 1972/73; Philip Tabor, 'Structures of Organisation', in *Architectural Design,* May 1971; see also 'Size and Shapes in the Growth of Human Communities', in *Ekistics*, October 1973.
5. Doxiadis, *Ekistics*.
6. A very attractive book on this phase of history is Jaquetta Hawkes, *The First Great Civilisation* (Hutchinson, London, 1973).
7. From *Ekistics*, February 1973, number on 'The City of the Future'. See also C.A. Doxiadis and J.G. Papaioannou, *Ecumenopolis* (Athens Centre for Ekistics, 1974).
8. See note 3.
9. Jane Jacobs, *The Economics of Cities* (Random House, NY, 1969).
10. See Report by the Royal Society Working Group on the *Biology of Urbanisation* to appear in 1975.
11. John Pappaioannou, in Waddington ed., *Biology and the History of the Future* (Edinburgh University Press, 1972), p. 9.
12. Ibid.
13. Rayner Banham, *Los Angeles; the Architecture of Four Ecologies* (Harper & Row, 1971).
14. See for instance Paul Andrews, Malcolm Christie and Richard Martin, 'Squatters and the Evolution of a Life Style', *Architectural Design,* January 1973; or Richard Martin, 'The Architecture of Underdevelopment', *Architectural Design,* October 1974 (both based on Zambia), and number on 'Housing the Poor in Developing Countries', *Ekistics*, July 1974.
15. See for instance, *The Conscience of the City*, Special Number of *Daedalus,* Fall 1968, especially Melvin Webber, 'The Post-City Age' and Martin Meyerson, 'Urban Policy; Reforming Reform'. For a British point of view on the American pr see Richard Llewellyn Davies, 'The American City through English Eyes', *Daedalus,* Fall 1972.
16. Jay Forrester, *Urban Dynamics* (Wright-Allen Press, Cambridge, Mass., 1969).
17. See note 15.
18. I. Papanek, *Design for the Real World* (Thames & Hudson, 1972).
19. Nan Fairbrother, *New Lives, New Landscapes* (Penguin, 1970).
20. See note 10.
21. Paolo Soleri, *Arcology: The City in the Image of Man* (MIT Press, 1969).

6   TRANSPORT AND COMMUNICATIONS

Transport

From Horse to Car

During the lives of people who are still with us changes in transportation have had more effect on the nature and quality of human living than those in any other field. My own early childhood, in a rural part of Worcestershire, was spent in a society based on the horse, supplemented for the movement of heavy goods by steam railways on land and steamships on the sea. The car was a rare spectacle, and all the children of the

Figure 6.1: Decrease in Road-space per Motor Vehicle: Great Britain, AD 1900–2000

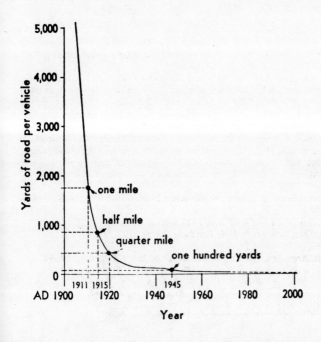

Source: J. Parsons, *Population versus Liberty* (Pemberton Books, 1971), p. 226.

village and many adults would turn out to watch if one were to go past. The normal way to get from the village to Evesham, the market town 5 miles away, was on a dray — a four-wheeled cart, whose super-structure was a flat wooden platform which could be stacked with wicker baskets of produce. After delivering their load to market, the young carters would show off their prowess, standing up loose-jointed on the jolting platform and whipping their horses into a canter down the steep High Street and over the humped bridge across the River Avon at the bottom — the horses' hooves and the iron-tyred wheels made as satisfying a racket as anyone's silencerless sports car, and their girls on the pavements were duly impressed.

The rapidity with which the petrol-driven motor car was adopted by society, and the desire which non-car-owners still show to get themselves one as soon as possible, are evidence of the great enrichment

Figure 6.2: Yards of Road per Vehicle, 1968 (Cars, Goods, Buses and Coaches only)

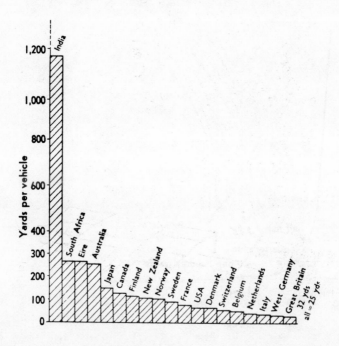

Source: J. Parsons, *Population versus Liberty* (Pemberton Books, 1971), p. 227.

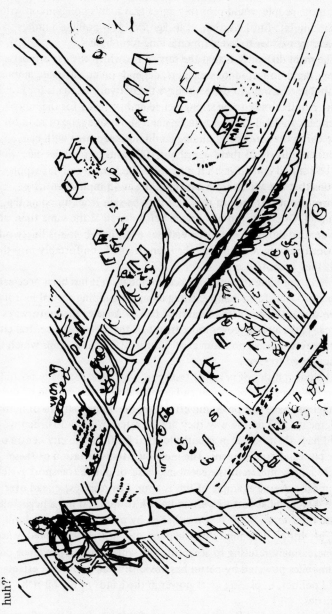

Figure 6.3: 'Welcome home, Luvah! Ah'm cookin yah favrit. Just slip down to the S Mart, buy li'l me pack spaghetti, huh?'

Source: Original

of human life which that piece of mechanism has produced. However, most people would probably agree that man's honeymoon with the automobile finished some years ago, and it is proving a rather demanding partner to live with on a long-term basis.

The main difficulty is that the service for which the car is most valued, rapid door-to-door transport, depends on an adequate amount of suitable roadway. In the early days the network of roads for horse traffic required only to be strengthened and surfaced for the much faster cars. In 1911 there was in England about one mile of road for every car in use, but road building could not keep pace with car production. By 1945 there was about 100 yards of road per car, while by 1968 it had fallen to about 32 yards. The Ministry of Transport reckons that a medium-sized car travelling at 45 mph essentially requires about 25 yards of road if it is to be safe from bumping the car ahead. Of course not all cars are being driven at the same time, also they are certainly not evenly spread out over the whole road network; but we already have more cars than can fit at all comfortably into the roads they want to use.

Even to provide this minimal accommodation it has been necessary brutally to transform many existing cities by building special motorways. There is also the problem of parking. In Los Angeles the motorways and car parks already cover more than half the area of the central city. Soon they will leave no room at all for the offices and shops which they are supposed to serve.

The possibilities of personal transport which the car made possible when the owners were a small and comparatively rich section of the population, have had profound effects on the whole pattern of human settlements, and on the way they are operated. Well-to-do urban workers could have their homes in suburbs located far from the city centre or their places of employment. The individual transportation of these people largely undercut the economic basis of public transport systems. The most extreme example of this is again Los Angeles, spread over some 40–50 miles east to west and north to south; it has a negligible public transport system – you either go by private car or you don't go. This inflicts a disability on the poor, old, infirm or disabled, who are increasingly refusing to accept it. The widespread dependence on automobiles powered by petrol has obviously had important effects on world politics, in placing great power in the hands of the oil-rich countries.

It also becomes difficult to stop pouring large quantities of noxious pollutants into the atmosphere. These results from burning petroleum

Figure 6.4: Commuting Fields of 11 American Cities in 1960

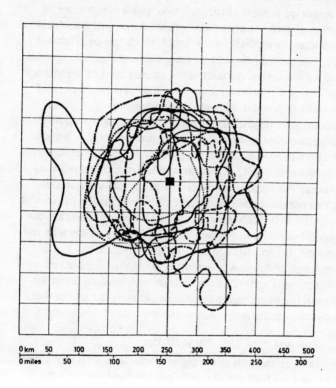

Source: C.A. Doxiadis, *Anthropopolis* (Athens Technological Centre, 1974).

without taking special precautions to prevent the formation of carbon monoxide and oxides of nitrogen, and also from very dangerous materials formed from some of the additives with which petrol is treated to increase the efficiency of conventional engines — for instance, volatile compounds of lead. They provide important additional arguments for reassessment of the internal combustion motor vehicle, and the ways in which it should be used in our civilisation in the future.[1]

It is not easy to find a satisfactory substitute for oil products as a fuel for cars (or aircraft). Active work is, of course, being done on the development of electric cars powered by batteries; but the known forms of batteries (lead-acid, zinc-air, etc.) make heavy use of somewhat more metals, and the supplies of these could scarcely support motor transport on the mass scale we have now, let alone what will be demanded by developing countries. In some ways hydrogen is an attractive fuel; it is easily transported and gives little pollution, but it is expensive, in energy terms — at present about twenty times the cost of petroleum. Other possibilities are methane or methanol, which can be produced biologically. This probably looks like being the long-term solution; but it will entail a good deal of restraint in the employment of the internal combustion engine, if the production of such fuels is not to demand the use of land which could otherwise grow food.

A final point to remember about the motor car is that at present it entails a casualty rate worthy of a sizeable war. In 1971 in Britain, somewhat over a third of a million people were injured in car accidents, and some 7,700 were killed.[2] The comparable figures for the 'Ulster Troubles' during the same period were 173 people killed on all sides. The average death rate from violence in Northern Ireland for 1969—74 was 12.4 per 100,000. The fatal accident rate, largely due to cars, for the same period was 35.3 in England and Wales, 74.3 in France and 54.1 in the USA (and, for another comparison, the homicide rate in US cities varied from 2.6 in cities of less than 10,000 to 17.5 in cities of over a quarter of a million). Car accidents have become the major source of disablement and death of citizens between the ages of 8 and 35 in this country (p. 210).

Transport Needs and How They Might Be Met

There is no agreed consensus at the present time as to what new forms of transport, or modifications of existing forms, hold out the most promise. Perhaps part of the difficulty is that we now rely on one basic form of vehicle — the car — for everything from running down to the nearest shopping centre to taking our family away for a continental holiday or transporting bulk goods. The most sensible way to approach the problem is to ask first what purposes are served by transportation, then to enquire what type of transportation looks like being most suitable for each purpose.

As a preliminary, note that means of transport always have important secondary roles in society. One is an expression of personal power and status and, in the male, of virility. This was as true of the highly decorated bullock wagons, used by Prince Genji and his friends in early medieval Japan, as it was of the Italian mercenary soldier sculptured by Colleoni in the well-known statue in Venice, the young bloods and huntsmen of Victorian England, or today's eminent personage in his Rolls or Cadillac. Probably society will always need some means of

Figure 6.5: Road Deaths per 100 Million Miles

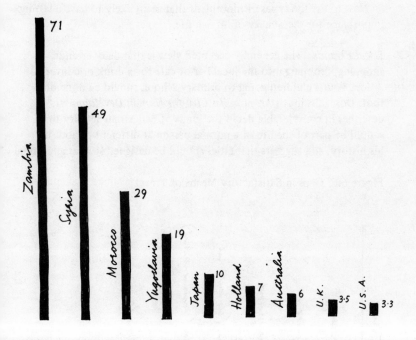

Source: Drawn from data in J.E. Baerwald, 'Traffic Safety: Problems and Solutions', *Int.J.Env. Studies, 3,* 209, 1973.

transport which offers the opportunity to show off as well as go places. Another important secondary role has been in providing privacy. Any young person who can get his hands on a car can easily escape the supervision of parents and neighbours; the effects on sexual morals and other aspects of personal life are too obvious to need exposition.

Now to list the types of movement that seem likely to have a lasting importance for the quality of human life.

Local Errands. The generally accepted view is that daily errands, shopping, dropping into the local bar or cafe for a drink or conversation, young children going to primary school, should be done on foot. Doxiadis, in *Anthropolis: City for Human Development*,[3] describes in considerable detail the kinds of pedestrian activity that should be part of the life of a normal person at different periods in his history, and suggests that cities should be designed so that all normal

Figure 6.6: Gaps in Satisfactory Means of Travel

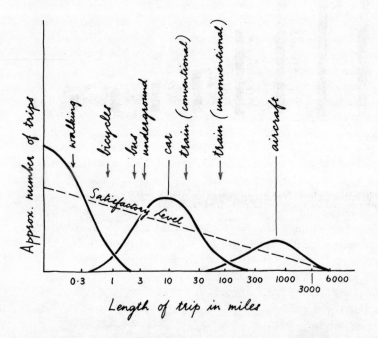

Source: 'Technological Forecasting Applied to Transport', *Futures*, April 1973.

domestic and minor leisure activities can be satisfied within a one mile
radius of the home. (It is possible that in some savagely cold climates
this cannot be satisfactorily achieved unless the cities are roofed-in and
air-conditioned.)

One to Five Miles. There is a range of activities which require movements
of about one to four or five miles. These might be leisure activities,
such as moving from home to swimming pool, tennis club, the theatre
or other cultural centre, or to a secondary or more advanced school; or
they might be movement associated with work and shopping in the
central areas of cities. The use of cars capable of carrying five people at
80 mph for satisfying these needs is wasteful of space and most productive of disturbance to other road users.

The use of the bicycle, or some more modern derivative of it, is
probably worth more consideration than has recently been given to it.[4]
The bicycle itself is a remarkably efficient and simple device for using
human muscular energy for transportation. In pure energy terms, it is
four to five times as efficient as walking, even though human walking
itself is twice as efficient as the movement of effective animals such as
dogs or gulls. It is still widely used, not only in some developing countries
where it and its relative the bicycle-rickshaw are major means of transport of people and goods, but in a few richer towns such as Amsterdam
in Holland and Cambridge in England.

It usually gives inadequate protection from the weather, is not very
suitable for carrying goods, and demands considerable muscular work
to make progress against the wind or uphill. It also offers its rider no
protection against collisions with other vehicles. All these difficulties
could, however, be greatly ameliorated, if not removed, with relatively
small changes in design. The whole machine could be enclosed in a
plastic bubble which would provide some protection in case of accidents.
It would be easy to add a small petrol or electric motor. A wide variety
of designs would be possible. As in rowing, we might employ the power
of the arms or the general body musculature, as well as those of the
legs; more muscular exercise would be good for the health of many
people in cities, and a wider use of bicycle-like muscle-powered
vehicles would be a useful way to ensure this. It could also provide
ample opportunities for 'showing off' by the young and vigorous.

It has been suggested that short-range transportation in central areas
of cities should be done by 'moving pavements' — horizontal versions
of the moving staircases common in underground systems. These could
be running at different speeds, so that you would first step on to a slow-

Table 6.1: Costs of Urban Transport 1970, Typical of South Asian Metropolitan Regions

Mode	Energy Cost	Capital Cost	Operating Costs	Time Cost	Total Cost
	passenger mile	passenger at peak	passenger mile	per mile	passenger mile
Walking[a]	100 Cal.	Rs. 100	Rs. 0.03	30 Min	Rs. 1.10
Bicycle[b]	25	250	0.05	8	0.35
Motor Scooter[c]	200	1,000	0.20	5	0.45
Bus[d]	100	1,000	0.10	10	0.30
Rapid Transit[e]	100	6,000	0.05	3	0.25
Automobile[f]	800	20,000	0.70	2.5	1.30

(Rs. = Indian Rupees).

a. Walks with drainage are assumed, as well as flat terrain, and frequent halts at intersections. Progress at 2 mph and average value of time is Rs. 2 per hour ($0.27–0.40).

b. A second-hand bicycle that will operate for several more years will need tyre repairs and drained paths or roads to average this speed.

c. A used light motorbike or scooter is assigned a 1.5 passenger capacity for the peak periods. Value of time is set at Rs. 3 per hour because they are used primarily by the young in the middle class.

d. Allows for delays equal to the riding time, but the value of time is the same as for pedestrians and bicyclists.

e. Waiting time is half the riding time but average value of time is equal to motor scooter users.

f. Whether taxi or private, an auto averages about two passengers at peak. Cost of extra roadway and parking space are included in estimate. Average value of passenger time is set at Rs. 5 per hour since autos are used for higher priority movement.

Source: R.L. Meier, 'Resource-conserving Urbanism: Progress and Potentials' in Proc.Int. Future Research Conference, Kyoto, 1970, p. 396.

Figure 6.7: A Bicycle Designed for Carrying Loads in Rough Country

Source: I. Papanek, *Design for the Real World* (Thames and Hudson, 1972), pp. 174–5.

moving one, and then pass from that on to one moving a few miles per hour faster, until you got up to quite fast speeds. However, the capital costs of installing the network arrangements to move backwards and forwards across a city, and the power costs of running them, would be formidable. They are adequate for straight runs of a few hundred yards in very large airport buildings, but it would be a very difficult matter to provide an adequate service covering the area from Marble Arch to Tottenham Court Road, down to Charing Cross and along again to Hyde Park Corner — all of which would be within easy bicycling distance.

Journey to Work. One of the greatest demands on transportation is the 'journey to work', and back home again. The travel lengths involved are from about 3 miles (overlapping the previous category) up to about 25 miles. One of the basic questions is whether to use the same vehicles for the commuter journeys as are used for other purposes. Then, supposing one settles for a special commuter-type of vehicle, the alternative is whether this should be for individual use, or be some form of public transport, or a mixture of both.

If commuting continues to be carried out in the same vehicle used for a longer journey, the main development that can be foreseen is computerised control of traffic flow. Data about the number of vehicles on various segments of the traffic network can be fed to a central computer, which can adjust traffic control lights and operate other systems for indicating to the motorists the most favourable route to take at any given time. The total traffic through-put of the network can be considerably increased.[5] Experiments along these lines have already worked fairly well. However, the hardware involved in such installations is quite expensive and success depends very much on the readiness of drivers to accept the discipline imposed on them.

It is unlikely that computerised control of traffic flow together with the building of new roads can cope with the rate at which the number of vehicles is increasing. In 1968 there were in Britain about 14½ million vehicles. If the country achieves a reasonable but modest increase in real wealth this number is expected to rise to about 26 million in the year 2000, even if the population remains constant.[6] If, however, the population goes on growing, even at the rather slow rate it has been doing recently, the number will be more like 35 million, that is to say 2½ times the number there are at present. This looks to be a losing race for society as a whole.

One suggestion is to use much smaller vehicles, but anyone who has driven through Rome or Naples, where most cars are quite small Fiats, is likely to be sceptical whether this in itself would produce a solution. However, studies by the British Ministry of Transport have shown that small cars produce little saving, either in travel time or in parking space, if they are used intermingled with larger ones, but that they could in theory perform about twice as well as normal-sized cars if segregated with special roads and special parks.[7] They might therefore make an important contribution, given the right organisation and the necessary capital outlay to provide their special tracks.

Small cars for one or two persons with very low horsepower engines could do even better if they were moved rapidly through the middle section of the commuting journey. There have been several suggestions for such 'dual mode' transport systems. The general principle is that the commuter drives his own car from his home to some terminal, where

Figure 6.8: A Fully Enclosed Motor Cycle

Source: *Cars for Cities*, Steering Group, Ministry of Transport (HMSO, 1967).

Figure 6.9: A Two-Passenger Network Cab for Trips within a Major
Activity Centre

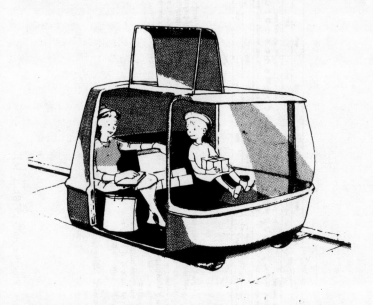

Source: *Tomorrow's Transportation*, US Department of Housing and Urban
Development, Washington, DC, p. 77.

it becomes connected to a general transport system which takes him
quite near his final destination, where he unhitches himself and completes the journey under his own control. During the central section
of the journey the individual cars might be physically linked together
to form trains, hauled by some form of engine; or they might be left
physically separate but come under the control of a power and
guidance system built into the track. With computerised control
of entry and exit of vehicles, the main stream of traffic could be
kept moving at high speed – 60 or more miles per hour – and there
would be no need for the continual stopping and starting at intermediate stations which so much slows up the present mass transportation systems in cities. Dual mode transport systems, which could also
be applied to larger vehicles such as buses, as well as the small individual
cars, seem among the most promising ways of solving the problem of
commuter traffic.

Another proposal, which depends on the ability of computers to

Figure 6.10: A Design for an Automated Highway

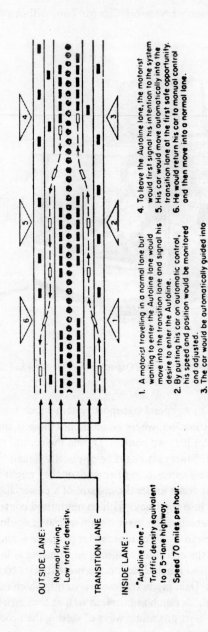

OUTSIDE LANE:
Normal driving.
Low traffic density.

TRANSITION LANE:

INSIDE LANE:
"Autoline lane."
Traffic density equivalent
to a 5-lane highway.
Speed 70 miles per hour.

1. A motorist travelling in a normal lane but wanting to enter the Autoline lane would move into the transition lane and signal his desire to enter the Autoline.

2. By putting his car on automatic control, his speed and position would be monitored and adjusted.

3. The car would be automatically guided into position at the end of the first available group on the Autoline lane.

4. To leave the Autoline lane, the motorist would first signal his intention to the system

5. His car would move automatically into the transition lane at the first safe opportunity.

6. He would return his car to manual control and then move into a normal lane.

An automated highway. *Courtesy General Motors.*

Source: Martin and Norman, *The Computerised Society* (Prentice Hall, 1970), p. 243.

react quickly and appropriately to highly complex inputs, is known as the 'Dial-a-Bus' system. This usually envisages relatively small buses holding 13–20 people. Anyone wishing to use a bus would telephone a central computerised office, which would be able to direct the most suitable bus to collect the passenger and to take him where he wanted to go. The problem of deciding an optimum route would be enormously complicated but this is just the kind of task which a computer is capable of carrying out. It is said that investment in the control side of the operation (though not in the buses themselves) would be only about 1 million dollars for an average-sized city.

A 'Dial-a-Taxi' system would be a more flexible system and could provide an even better service, but a difficulty is that there would have to be a large number of taxi drivers who would be available to meet the peak loads but would find little to do during the hours while the commuters were in their offices. This probably means that systems of this kind are more appropriate for general journeys about cities, but not for the specific needs of commuting.

50–250 Mile Journeys. These fulfil two different needs: there are business journeys between centres of population, usually both beginning and ending in areas of high-density traffic; and there are pleasure journeys, often beginning in a suburb and ending at some pleasure place which may not, but increasingly often does, have a high traffic density. These short pleasure trips, which can be completed in a day or a weekend, are the field in which the dominance of the car is most unassailable. It was because the car made possible such trips, too long for horse-drawn carriages, that society first took this new form of transport to its heart. But even if things very like our present cars continue in use for such purposes, they could be smaller, safer, more economical with fuel and less polluting, and be built for much longer effective lifetimes.

Short business journeys make much the same demands as longer-range commuting. They can be carried out wholly by private car, as occurs in many parts of the developed countries, but they make enormous demands on roadways and are responsible for a high proportion of the casualties and deaths in which a car is involved. In many other regions, and in some of the largest towns, such as London and Manhattan, a dual mode system would be safer, faster and less stressful for inter-city travel over short distances as much as for long-range commuting.

For distances of more than about 150 miles, changing from the approach vehicle into another in the rapid system, and at the other end from that again into another car, is not too much of a hardship. For the rapid part of the system, the main stand-by at present is still the conventional train moving on rails. This can undoubtedly be greatly improved even in its more or less conventional form, as is shown by the Japanese development of the Tokkaido Express and the plans for the San Francisco Bay area rapid transport system. More drastic improvements might come with new forms of track, such as monorails or trains running on an air cushion, perhaps powered by linear accelerators.

Journeys of Hundreds or Thousands of Miles. One of the greatest changes in the lives of ordinary people is that it has now become not

Figure 6.11: Journey Times, City Centre to City Centre

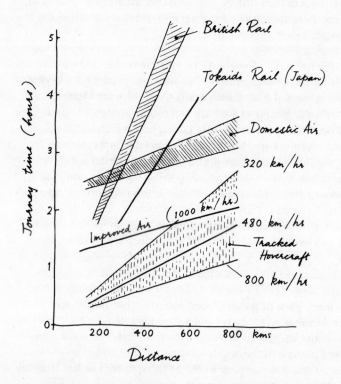

Source: W.T. Gunsten, 'Railways of the Future', *Ekistics*, 25, no. 146, January 1968, p. 36.

too outrageously expensive, or time-consuming, to travel between any two centres of population in Britain, or for British people to go to the coast of the Mediterranean, the Alps, or similar places for holidays or on business. In the United States, journeys from coast to coast, or from the Great Lakes to Texas, are only slightly longer.

For business or professional consultation the rapidity with which a journey of a few hundred miles can be completed may be critically important; for visits and holidays it is a convenience rather than a necessity. For air journeys in this category, e.g. from Edinburgh to London or London to the Mediterranean coast, the time actually spent in the air is rarely more than half the total door-to-door journey time, and may be considerably less. Slight increases in aircraft speed cannot bring any great gain in convenience. The only real improvement would be to reduce the time and trouble of travelling from starting-point to the take-off airport, and from the touch-down airport to the final address. There are difficulties in bringing the airports nearer to the centres of population. The cost of running an airport is reduced as its traffic volume becomes larger (up to a certain point at least) and so there is a tendency to develop very large airports handling an enormous amount of traffic, including intercontinental planes which require very long runways. Even if planes were built capable of a good speed in the air, but requiring only short runways suitable for confined airports within cities, these would be very noisy.

Indeed, improvements in land transport over these distances may offer more comfort and convenience than the air services. The journey time from terminal to terminal will almost certainly remain greater than from airport to airport, but the terminals themselves may be much nearer to one's point of departure and destination.

In journeys measured in thousands of miles the air has the field essentially to itself. The only possible competitor for crossing the oceans is the passenger ship. The unavoidable physical resistance of water limits ships to such slow speeds that their only possible attractions are the amenities, luxuries, social life they can offer to those who have plenty of time to spare. On the whole, at present, people who travel thousands of miles usually do so when there is some rather compelling reason to get to the other end as quickly as possible. In a more leisured and affluent post-industrial society, there may be enough custom to keep the luxury ocean-going vessel alive, but it is unlikely ever to regain its place as one of the main means of transportation.

Long-distance travel will be mainly air travel; but it is difficult to envisage any revolutionary advances in its technology beyond the stage

Figure 6.12: Size of the World in Travel Time

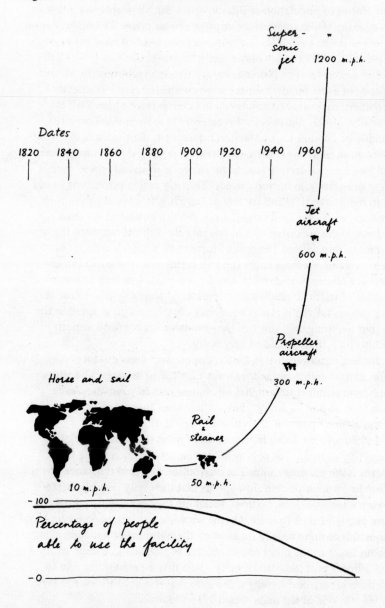

Source: Based in part on John McHale, 'World Facts and Trends', *Futures*, September 1971, p. 217.

we have already reached. Aircraft flying above the speed of sound *must* produce a shock-wave, which produces highly unpleasant 'noise pollution' affecting all people who live within a few tens of miles on each side of the flight path. Furthermore, they must fly in the upper reaches of the atmosphere and give out into this highly rarified region exhaust gases whose effects can scarcely be favourable and may be highly dangerous (see Chapter 2). Finally, there are physical limits to the maximum speed of air transport; if a vehicle goes too fast it goes 'out of orbit' and sets off away from the earth into outer space.

Figure 6.13: Increasing Speed of Travel

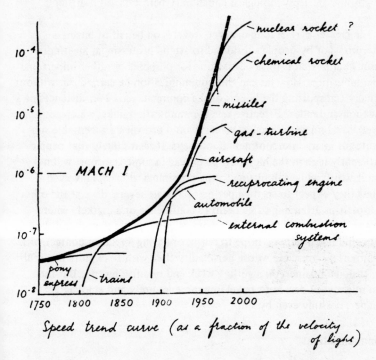

Speed trend curve (as a fraction of the velocity of light)

Source: John McHale, 'World Facts and Trends', *Futures*, September 1971, p. 271.

The speeds achieved by supersonic aircraft, such as Concorde, are now so near the natural ceiling set by the strength of the earth's gravitational field, that present speeds could not, in the next 30 years, be multiplied by anything like the same factor as they were in the previous 30 years.

There may also be another natural ceiling set by the biological nature of man. Like most biological organisms, we run on a set of 'biological clocks', which have deep-seated influences on our rhythms of sleeping, digesting, excreting, level of wakefulness and so on.[8] Already air transport from east to west, or west to east, is so fast that the crossing of time zones – leaving London at lunchtime and seven hours later coming down in New York with still four hours to wait before dinner – considerably upsets the traveller's mental awareness and fundamental physiology. Some national administrations and big business firms insist that any administrator or executive who has to fly across a number of time zones to his meeting, must allow 24 hours to recover his physiological/psychological equanimity before facing a difficult decision.

The greater part of long-distance travel is on behalf of business enterprises, or by people subsidised to attend professional meetings of various kinds; that is to say, it is done for purposes of rather impersonal communication. How far can this communication be carried out without actually transporting the bodies of the communicants over distances of a few thousand miles? Effective tele-communication links, which conveyed visual images as well as voices, would provide an acceptable substitute for many intercontinental journeys. It seems likely that people sufficiently high in the hierarchy to engage in sonic transport will not find it worth while submitting to the physiological insults involved unless they expect to spend a period of at least several days at the other end; perhaps attending some event (a conference or a market) where they anticipate making personal contacts with people they do not know and could not otherwise hope to reach; or having a relaxed contact with an important associate whose personality they wish to explore in a multi-dimensional manner, on a golfing week-end or a fishing trip. But then you might even decide to travel in a more leisurely and enjoyable manner, possibly even by ship.

Communications

In Rich Countries

For the richer parts of the population in the developed world the ease of communication with other members of society even over long distances has increased fantastically in the last half-century. Anyone who has become used to living among friends and associates all of whom have telephones, and then has to spend some time in a pre-telephone part of the world, will soon get a vivid impression of what this change has meant. Of course, there are still large sections of the population, even in the rich countries, who do not have easy access to telephones, and this is the case for the vast majority of people in the poorer countries. A large element of 'growth' is required to bring these poorer sections and nations up to a reasonable level of inter-personal communication. Similarly there are large sections of the world who do not enjoy the benefits of access to centralised radio and television networks – and these certainly are very real benefits, although one may often be tempted to respond more strongly to their inadequacies than to their advantages.

The significance for human life of these increased facilities for communication are not so easy to assess. Marshall McLuhan[9] has argued, with considerable wit and showmanship, that the available means of communication play a major part in shaping the way the human mind works. In *The Gutenberg Galaxy* he traced the effect on human thinking of the invention of books printed in enormous numbers by movable type; he believes that at the present time electronic modes of communication – radio, television, video-tape and so on – are not only supplanting the printed word as the accepted medium for transmitting information but, by doing so, are completely changing the character of thought. The title of one of the best known of his books is *The Medium IS the Message*. That will certainly seem an exaggeration to anyone who has to act on the factual content of messages, whether he is an engineer or a housewife laying out the week's spending money. But, even if exaggerated, McLuhan's thesis is a warning that profound changes will take place in the cultural life of the poor parts of the world which are only just entering the period of the universal availability of information.

In many fields there is now so much information so easily available that no one person can handle everything that might be of interest to him. Even if they accept the most drastic specialisation, most scientists have to give up hope of reading all the relevant publications. The means of communication which have been developed are designed to disseminate any items fed into them, but there has been little attempt to provide adequate filtering, sorting or digesting devices, which could select what is most important in some connection.

The dominant role which communication has come to play in the modern world has led to the development of a theory of information, which some people have considered one of the great modern intellectual triumphs. But this theory measures 'information' as the number of separate 'bits', each bit independent of, and equivalent to, every other bit. In real life we need to make distinctions between different kinds of things which may be communicated; perhaps along the lines of the World War II Air Force slang, in which 'info' meant all the true but boring information in the handbook of a new mark of fighter aircraft, while what it was really important to know – how it handled in a dog-fight, its stalling characteristics and so on – were referred to as the 'gen'. The overload of communication to which we are now being subjected will force us to improve our ways of sorting out the gen from the info in many fields of interest. As in so many of the subjects discussed in this book, we are finding ourselves faced with a situation in which it is no longer possible to accept the simple idea that *more* is sufficient by itself to mean *better*; we are going to have to be more selective, and decide that more of some things may be better, but that more of everything might lead to disaster.

In comparison with the spreading of modern communication facilities to the poorer parts of the world and with the provision of better systems of filtering and digesting information, changes in the apparatus used for communication seem likely to be relatively minor in the near future. The most important may be a change in what one can communicate with rather than in the mode of communication. The general provision in offices or homes of an apparatus (usually referred to as a 'console') which will enable people to get in immediate contact with a large-scale computer system seems to be a very real probability. This will mean that one can have immediate access to an almost un-limited memory; not only could one get hold of any particular piece of information, either a scientific fact or a detail about one's own bank account or the price of groceries, but one would be able to call up any of a very large range of books, pieces of music, theatrical performances, etc., to be displayed in some form on a screen. There would, in fact be so much available on call that some people might feel no need to do anything else but sit and absorb it, without the bother and messiness of actually living. However, it seems to be more likely that after a short time saturation would occur, so that people would not actually allow themselves to be dominated by the availability of stored memories.

A similar development might be the provision of more cable tele-vision, which enables the home listener to have a far greater choice of programmes than is available on present-day television sets. The first step in this direction would probably be the cheap provision of cassettes of magnetic tape which could be attached to a normal television set and played rather as a cassette of music can be played in a tape recorder. Cable television would give one access to an enormous library of cassettes, but it would involve the laying of the necessary types of cable, which are more complex than present telephone cable (and much more costly). These cables would also make possible the use of a 'picture phone', that is to say, a telephone in which you can also see on a television screen the person you are talking to. The cables necessary to carry a signal complicated enough to present a visual picture are so expensive that it seems very unlikely that they will soon come into use for ordinary person-to-person communications, unless they are linked with a large development of cable television. However, the picture telephone could, and probably will, find a use for types of communication which are inherently very expensive, e.g. transatlantic flights. Instead of travelling long distances by intercontinental jet to carry out face-to-face negotiations (when one side or the other has a disturbed biological clock), it seems probable that much of the discussion will be carried out by picture telephone.

Video-tape recording, which is already coming into use, is likely to become much more widespread. A moving scene can be recorded in real time with its accompanying sounds on video-tape, instead of on film. The advantage of video-tape is that it does not require lengthy processing, but can be exhibited as soon as it has been made. Moreover, one recording can be wiped out and another put in its place if necessary. Many people see a future for this in local community television, in which problems are discussed and situations exhibited to the comparatively small number of people who live in a locality and have a personal interest in them. Similarly, in a university, lectures or other events could quite easily be recorded and replayed at a slightly different time or place, with much less trouble than is necessary to do the same thing nowadays with film.

Another change in the conditions of communication which will cause problems in the next few decades is a considerable increase in the difficulty of preserving privacy. There are already many 'bugging' devices which can be used to listen in to, and perhaps record, telephone or other conversations which the participants think of as being private. There are said to be, for instance, microphones which can pick up a conversation by the vibrations of the window panes resulting from the sound waves inside a room. So far it is difficult for anyone but a specialist to know how efficient these devices are. If they live up to their advertised abilities, it seems strange that several groups of conspirators in an embattled city like Belfast can arrange their operations, which must involve a great deal of conferring and consultation and eventual giving of orders, without either their rival groups or the authorities being able to find out what is going on. However, even if the devices at present are not all they are claimed to be, it is more than likely that their efficiency will greatly increase in the near future. People who really want to make secret communications may have to go to considerably more trouble than at present to ensure their privacy.

In Poor Countries

In the poor, developing, countries the bringing of radio to the masses of the population could be the first step in conveying to them some of the basic information about the natural world, and technological ways of dealing with it, which they need if they are to improve their material conditions. The provision of the necessary equipment need not be as difficult as one might think at first sight. Radio transmissions over a large area can be achieved, particularly with the aid of space satellites. A satellite can be launched in an orbit arranged so that it rotates round the earth exactly in time with the earth's own rotation, and thus stays continually over one region. Then such a satellite can be used to reflect a radio signal, beamed to it from a suitable transmitter, over a very large area of territory indeed.

If in any region there is only one radio transmitter, or if one radio signal is very much more powerful than any others (and this would be the case if such a system were set up in a poor developing country, such as India or much of Africa), then the apparatus necessary to receive the signal can be very simple, since it will not have to distinguish between many different wavelengths. In fact, one socially-minded industrial designer, Papanek,[10] claims to have designed a receiver which can be made for about 9 cents. It is basically a used tin can in which some fuel is burnt — cow dung will do at a pinch; the heat is converted to electricity by a small thermocouple, and this is sufficient to amplify the radio signal picked up by the old-fashioned device of a 'whisker', so as to give recognisable speech in an ear-plug microphone. Admittedly only one man could listen to such a receiver at a time, and it would require considerably more electric power to produce a signal which could be broadcast to a whole village, but Papanek's device shows that one could, at a very small cost indeed, make it possible for every village in India or Africa to receive, through its radio receiver in the hands of somebody who would act as a teacher, a nationally broadcast programme of information on such basic matters as agriculture, hygiene, health, the weather and other factors important to the life of a subsistence farming community.

John Platt[11] has been particularly emphatic in arguing that this possibility of communicating with isolated illiterate peasants in poor countries offers an extraordinary opportunity of giving them the kind of basic education that could be really helpful; but he points out that the opportunity is likely to be completely lost unless somebody writes the necessary programmes in time, before the satellite broadcasting systems are set up and begin to be used for less carefully planned, and probably commercial, programmes. This is an area in which pressure from interested people among the well-educated populations of the fortunately-placed parts of the world could produce really important results if it were applied with vigour and determination in the next year or two.

Further Reading

Transport

A. *Tomorrow's Transportation*, US Department of Housing and Urban Development, 1968.
B. *Cars for Cities*, Steering Group appointed by Ministry of Transport, 1967 HMSO, Study of Long-Term Problems of Traffic in Urban Areas.
C. Colin Buchanan & Partners, *Traffic in Towns* (HMSO, 1963) is a classic text.
D. Jack Parsons, *Population versus Liberty*, Chapter 12, 'Freedom of the Road' (Pemberton Books, 1971), pp. 214–54.
E. James Martin and Adrian R.D. Norman, *The Computerised Society*, Chapter 11, 'Cities and Transportation' (Prentice Hall, 1970), pp. 228–66.
F. *Ekistics*, October 1970, is devoted to 'Networks' in general; the numbers for January 1972 and June 1974 deal with in-town and inter-town transport; there is a summary of the discussions of networks over the years of the Delos symposia in the number for April 1972, pp. 328–38.
G. *The International Journal of Environmental Studies*, vol. 3, no. 3, (July 1972) is a special number devoted to the Motor Vehicle.
H. Terence Bendixson, *Instead of Cars* (Temple Smith, 1974).

Communications

I. Martin and Norman, as E above.
J. Marshall McLuhan, *Understanding Media* (Routledge, 1964) (Sphere, 1973).

K. Gerald E. Stearn ed., *McLuhan Hot and Cool* (Penguin, 1968).
L. Brenda Maddox, *Beyond Babel; new directions in communications* (Andre Deutsch, 1972).

Notes

1. See Independent Commission on Transport,*Changing Directions* (Coronet Books, 1974); articles by Gerald Leach, *New Scientist*, 8 November 1973 and 6 December 1973, and by R.S. Berry, *Bulletin of the Atomic Scientists*, May 1972; Terence Bendixson, *Instead of Cars* (Temple Smith, 1974).
2. Figures from D.R. Bates, 'Practising Science in Northern Ireland', *Nature*, *250*, 754, 30 August 1974.
3. C.A. Doxiadis, *Anthropopolis: City for Human Development* (Athens Technological Centre, 1974).
4. S.S. Wilson, 'Bicycle Technology', *Scientific American*, March 1973, pp. 81–91.
5. Martin and Norman, *The Computerised Society* (Prentice Hall, 1970), Chapter 11.
6. Steering Group, Ministry of Transport,*Cars for Cities*,(HMSO, 1967), p. 19.
7. Ibid.
8. P.V. Siegel *et al.*,'Time Zone Effects', *Science, 164*, 1969, p. 1249.
9. Marshall McLuhan, *The Gutenberg Galaxy* (Toronto University Press, 1964).
10. I. Papanek, *Design for the Real World* (Thames & Hudson, 1972), p. 163.
11. J. Platt, in *Future as an Academic Discipline* (CIBA, 1975).

7 HEALTH, WORK AND WEALTH

Health

Medicine and the World's Diseases

Health and wealth are usually accepted as being good in themselves, so that one cannot have too much of them; people are more in two minds about work, tending to resent it when they have it but to wish ardently for it when they have none. But the ambiguity about work — is its absence leisure or unemployment? — has parallels in uncertainties about the other two concepts also. What is true wealth? Surely not just money in the bank. And what is health, staying alive for a long time, or keeping fit?

The two meanings of health usually run parallel; in a population with little sickness throughout life, people tend to live long lives. The length of life a new-born baby can expect ('the mean expectation of life at birth') is one of the best indices of the general health of a community. On the whole the richer the social group, the longer its members may expect to live, and the more recent the period in history, the greater the expectancy of life.

There is little variation in the maximum length of healthy life. There is rather slender anecdotal evidence that in a few local groups living in some kind of peasant economy considerable numbers conserve their vigour and energy above the age of 100. But for the majority of mankind the maximum period of a normal lifetime is still the biblical figure of three score years and ten. The important question is how many people come near to achieving it. Until a few generations ago there were few populations in which the average expectation of life was more than half of this. The human individual takes a considerable time to become reasonably mature. If the mean expectation of life is only 35 years almost half of these would be spent before becoming open to the full range of human experience. So the great increases in the average expectation of life, which occurred first in Europe and are now spreading throughout the world, are more worth while even than the crude figures suggest.

The greatest contribution to the increase in the expectation of life has been made by reducing mortality caused by bacterial diseases in early childhood. The main technical triumphs of Western medicine have, in fact, been the discovery of germ-killing agents, such as

203

Figure 7.1: Expectations of Life

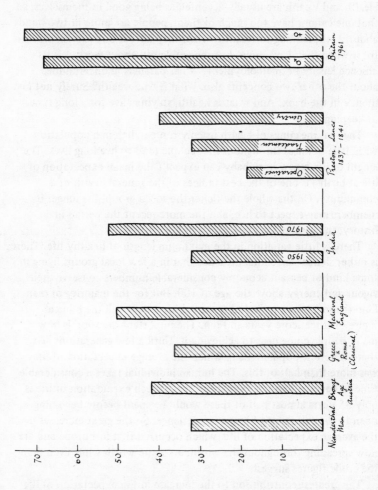

penicillin and other antibiotics, and the development of very effective surgery. We are still much less able to cure virus diseases, parasitic infections or mental disorders. But much of the reduction in the unpleasant effects of parasitic and bacterial diseases was actually achieved in Europe before the discovery of bacteria. This resulted from a general tidying up of the human ecosystem, by the provision of good water supplies, sewage and better food, following on the more efficient production of the early industrial revolution. Our increased knowledge of the basic causes of diseases should make it easier to reach similar levels of control in other regions of the world, but even the best science will not be able to get far unless more general economic and social advances are made.

Table 7.1[1] gives some idea of the incidence of diseases throughout the world:

Table 7.1: Major Communicable Diseases in the World

	Cases per year	Deaths per year (1963)
Common cold	3,500,000,000	Few thousand
Gastritis, duodenitis	750,000,000	3,094,000
Pneumonia, bronchitis	125–350,000,000	6,786,000
Measles	90,000,000	508,000
Whooping cough	70,000,000	112,000
Dysentry	50,000,000	202,000
Malaria	25,000,000	326,000
Respiratory tuberculosis	13,000,000	2,800,000
Tyhpoid	2,000,000	98,000
Diphtheria	1,270,000	127,000
Small Pox	430,000	172,000

Major long-lasting illnesses in the world

Respiratory tuberculosis	40,000,000	active cases
Leprosy	10,786,000	cases
Yaws	10–15,000,000	
Hookworm	715,600,000	
Schistosomiasis (= Bilharzia)	203,800,000	
Tapeworms	64,500,000	

Note: These figures date from a few years ago, and some progress has certainly been made in dealing with some, but not all, of the diseases. Moreover, the figures are certainly not as accurate as one could wish; but they give a not unduly misleading picture of the size of the problems.
Source: John Platt, *Medical Care and Society*, 9th CIOMS conference, Rio de Janeiro, 1974.

What kinds of resources has mankind organised to battle against these threats? John Platt[2] has recently distinguished four different levels of biomedical intervention in society:

(1) individualised medical and surgical care and treatment of illness with one doctor serving hundreds of patients per year;
(2) mass treatment, prevention and cure as with vaccines, contraceptives and generally available drugs, with one doctor and several paramedicals serving tens of thousands per year;
(3) public health and epidemiology (improved sewage disposal, chlorinated water, mosquito control or highway design) with each doctor, biologist, or engineer contributing to the health of millions;
(4) better diets, home sanitation, birth control, infant care, and family and self-help treatments, where the doctor or biologist using the mass media can bring about improved health for tens of millions.

In addition there is a research level, which does not usually treat patients, but attempts to discover the principles on which rational treatments can be based.

As Platt points out, the costs are roughly in inverse proportion to the number of people served by each doctor or biologist. Thus the per capita cost of level 1 intervention and associated services will be in the range of several hundred dollars per year, or several per cent of personal and national income. The cost of level 2 will be in the range of a few dollars per capita per year per person and levels 3 and 4 may produce great improvements in health for a few cents per capita per year.

Table 7:1 shows that still many of the greatest killers are bacterial diseases, for which adequate cures are known; they demand little activity from the research level and will probably be controlled best by activities at Platt's levels 4, 3 and 2, probably in that order of importance. Unfortunately the spirit of Western medicine has been in the opposite direction, towards the production of highly trained and specialised doctors. The countries with the worst health problems are mostly poor tropical lands, with very few doctors per head; and those mainly located in the town — the countryside usually gets much less than its fair share. The only region which, according to reports, is making really serious attempts to deal with this, for instance by encouraging the 'paramedicals' who are placed in Platt's level 2, is Mainland China.

Health care at Platt's level 2 should play a greater part in the

Figure 7.2: Number of People per Physician

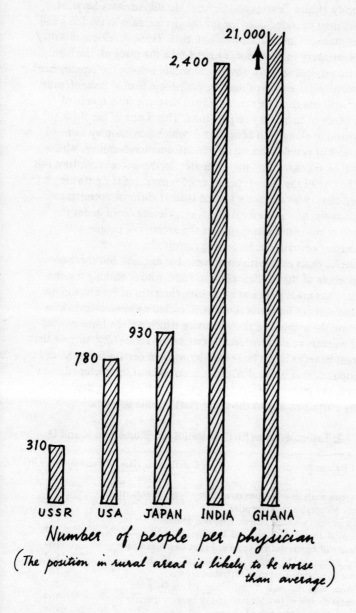

Number of people per physician

(The position in rural areas is likely to be worse
than average)

Source: *UN Statistical Year Book.*

ordinary lives of people in rich societies by such methods as
Community Health Centres and General Health Advisory Services,
which are now provided only for special groups, such as students and
in better managed industrial establishments. These developments may
be supplementary to, or to some extent take the place of, the highly
specialised services we have now. They would involve the employment
in the health service field of many more people than at present, most
of them with less thorough training than that of a fully qualified
doctor. Many of them may be part-time. This is one of the fields of
employment — along with education — which may mop up some of
the energies of people who are now in information-handling, whose
place will be taken over by the computer. In the poorer countries this
should be one of the main types of employment for the growing
educated class, who are likely to find their traditional openings as
office workers, minor administrators, etc. closing down under the
influence of computerisation, just as the number of people with
the necessary education is increasing rapidly.

Table 7.1 deals only with communicable diseases, but these are
not the whole of the medical picture. Platt, who is nothing if not a
bold man, has made a shot at estimating the ratio of benefit to cost
of various sorts of biomedical research, including research into how
to increase the amount of skilled service which a given force of
trained workers could provide. His estimates (Table 7.2)[3] suggest that
very great benefits might be reaped by work in certain fields. Since
most sophisticated medical research is carried out in developed
countries, the research effort at present is far from being deployed
in a way corresponding to the order Platt's Table suggests.

Table 7.2: Estimated Benefit/Cost Ratios for Biomedical R and D

Area of Research	$\dfrac{\text{Benefit/year after 20 years}}{\text{Cost/year today}} = \dfrac{B(T+20)}{C(T)}$
1. Systems analysis of problems, epidemiology, treatment	10^5
2. More acceptable contraceptive	10^4
3. New protein sources, genetic copying, protein from oil	10^4
4. Tropical disease, bilharzia and kwashiokor	10^3
5. Theory of biochemistry, sequence-structure-function	10^3
6. Fast automated biochemical and clinical analysis	10^3
7. Ageing research, enzyme controls or repairs	10^3
8. Cancer, viral studies and environmental carcinogens	10^3
9. Mental disorders, biochemical and behaviour therapy	10^3
10. Regeneration of limbs and organs	10^2

Source: Platt, *Medical Care in Society, op. cit.*

Health in the Rich Countries

The major killers in the rich countries now are the breakdown of blood vessels supplying the brain (a stroke), or the heart muscle (a coronary), cancer and automobile accidents. These conditions are being intensively studied to design ways of life which will reduce the likelihood of stroke or heart failure. Again, recent advances in molecular biology should give us some understanding of the origin of cancer, in the next ten or twenty years. This may not lead to a 'cure for cancer' which will prevent its occurrence, but will quite likely make it possible to diagnose incipient cancers early enough for them to be dealt with surgically or in other ways.

The death and maiming caused by automobile accidents should be dealt with in ways other than those conventionally classed as medicine, for instance by designing new systems of transport (see Chapter 6). However, certain animals, even as highly evolved as newts and salamanders, can regenerate (i.e. grow again) a whole new limb when one has been lost, whereas man is quite incapable of such a feat. When the human body is physically wounded, it can do little more to repair itself than closing together the cut surfaces. There is no reason why we should accept as a permanent limitation our present inability to replace the parts that have been lost. But the development of an effective capacity for regeneration in man would require a major research campaign and almost certainly a period measured in several decades.

When considering the future of medicine most people think first of new advances on the frontiers of medical research. We already know how to keep in a state of living a few types of patients in the terminal phases of illness who would a few years ago have died in short order. There have been spectacular successes in transplanting hearts, kidneys and other parts into people whose own organs have failed. Many more advances of this kind can confidently be foreseen. It is hardly fanciful to say that the time is approaching when, apart from drastic accident, a person could be kept alive indefinitely by supplying a new organ to replace whichever of his own wears out. Well before that stage of technological mastery is achieved, society will have to face the problem whether it wants to employ its medical resources in that way.

Traditionally in all parts of the world, medicine has concerned itself primarily with the interests of the individual rather than with those of society. The Hippocratic Oath, which has been the basis of medical ethics in Western Europe for the last 2½ millenia, specifically requires the doctor to look after the interest of his individual patient

Figure 7.3: Percentage of Deaths from Specified Causes – 1971

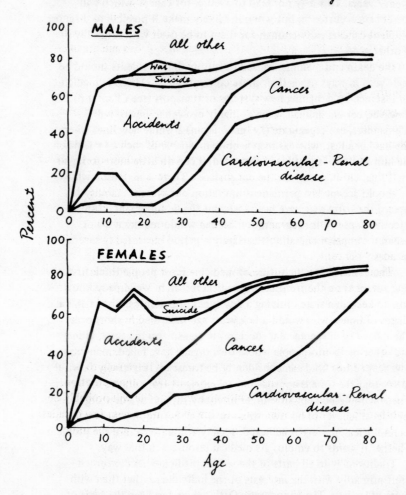

Source: *Statistical Bulletin*, April 1972.

above everything else. The individual nearly always wants to stay alive as long as possible, yet evolution of the whole human population depends on individuals dying and being replaced by new individuals with different hereditary potentials, which we may hope will be more useful ones. There is essentially no way to reconcile these two points of view, and fundamental questions are coming out into the open. Which people are to be the recipients of the grafts and which the donors? Can society afford the lengthy training of the surgeons and the skilled nurses involved in managing cases of this sort? From the point of view of mankind, organ transplantation and similar methods for preserving life in the essentially moribund are now rich men's toys and are likely to remain so.

Control of Ageing[4]

Advances in the control of stroke, heart failure and cancer, and the preservation of a few moribunds, would not bring about spectacular changes in the general system of society, but would lead to a slightly greater proportion of elderly people, and perhaps to some slowing down in the rate at which young people could take over the oldsters' jobs. Changes of this kind are already occurring; in the United States the proportion of people in the 45—60 year age group has increased in the last 10 years from 12 per cent of the population to about 20 per cent, while those aged 65 and upwards have increased from 3 per cent to almost 9 per cent.

There would be much more drastic changes if medicine learnt how to manage the underlying ageing processes, which cause people to grow old and eventually become senescent. If the average person did not begin to welcome the idea of retirement until they reached the age of 75 instead of about 65 as at present, what a difference this would make to the lives of everyone! Changes in the restructuring of the work functions of societies in rich countries are already beginning to be demanded by the development of automation and computerisation. An increase in the length of the effective working life will probably be another important factor in bringing this about in the next few decades.

Is the possibility of increased control of the ageing process more than a Utopian daydream?

The mechanisms of ageing are certainly not yet well understood, but rapid progress in understanding and probably in control is likely to start fairly soon. Three main types of theory are being considered.[5] One supposes that the physiological processes of living produce substances which tend to gum up some part of the works; for instance, it has been suggested that metabolic processes may immobilise proteins by linking together parts which should be free to move. Another type of theory appeals to the harmful effects of a gradual accumulation of accidental errors in the normal chemical processes. Sometimes there may be an error in the construction of an enzyme molecule or even of genes which should be reproduced exactly every time a cell divides but which do undergo occasional random changes or mutations. These theories can be regarded as variants on the theme of 'wearing out'. Theories of the third kind suggest that there may be errors in the construction of the proteins concerned with the steps by which the genetic DNA guides the manufacture of the proteins; then in every protein synthesis in which this altered molecule took part, something would go awry and a changed and presumably less efficient protein produced.

All these three types of process look as though they must occur to some extent. What is uncertain is which of them is most important. Possibly they all play some part; there is no reason to suppose that ageing is always a simple process with only a single cause. If it is not, control of any one of the factors contributing to it might lead to some lengthening of the normal life span. That is why the prospects for some increase in human lifetimes look rather favourable. However, the steps necessary to control the ageing process might not be pleasant, or even worth while. For instance, the length of life of rats has been considerably prolonged in experiments by keeping them on semi-starvation diets throughout their lives. A similar regime would be equally successful with human beings, but would anybody in their childhood and twenties be persuaded to the necessary self-control by the prospect of adding five or ten years on to their seventies?

Some Particular Problems of Poor Countries

In the poor countries the major killers are not cancer/stroke/heart attacks and car accidents, but are still mainly infectious diseases. Many people, particularly in the tropics, also suffer great losses in well-being from various parasites which do not directly kill. The magnitude of the problem is indicated by the figures for active cases of yaws, hookworm, schistosomiasis and tapeworms in Table 7.1 (p. 205). For several of these, no effective treatments are yet available, and a greatly increased research effort is needed. The US has in fact recently promised to devote much more effort to the attack on schistosomiasis, where an apparently promising line of attack using immunological methods has recently emerged from a team in Britain.

Some of the major infectious diseases have been mastered in some regions in the last few years. It is important for people whose whole lives have been spent in rich countries to appreciate just how much these successes, partial though they are, have meant to populations which have for generations lived with uncontrolled infections. Some inkling can be got by looking at the effect on infant mortality of using DDT to control the malaria mosquito in countries like Sri Lanka and Guatemala (Fig. 1.6 in Chapter 1).

A more graphic account, from Greece, a country one would not consider particularly poor or undeveloped, was given recently by Spyros Doxiadis, the physician brother of the ekistics Doxiadis.[6]

Please let me tell you a little story, the story of malaria in Greece.

Before the last war Greece had a total of 7 million inhabitants. Conditions were deplorable. Typhoid fever, gastric enteritis and malaria were rampant all over the country. We had a million cases of malaria every year and the people's resistance to infection was lowered. In various regions, like Thessaly, the people were thin and terribly pale, while the children roamed around pot-bellied and emaciated. Tuberculosis was raging. I recall that in 1925 or thereabouts the recruits in the Corfu regiment were found to have the highest percentage of grey TB in Europe! Then the war broke out and these weak men were the first to put up a victorious fight against fascism. In the end, however, our country was conquered, and one of the first things that the occupation forces did was to confiscate the Greek government's supply of quinine.

In 1942 we had over 2 million cases of malaria. So, when Greece was liberated, it was decided that we should serve as the first guinea pigs in the testing of DDT. It was first used in 1945/46 at a village called Souli near Marathon, where the population had 100 per cent malaria. The experiment was a success and the next year they sprinkled DDT all over Greece like salt and pepper. There was not a house, room or yard left without DDT. Then the miracle happened. Greece and her population have changed. Our country is no longer infested by insects, vermin, flies and mosquitoes, and we have not seen Rachel Carson's 'Silent Spring' either. On the contrary, malaria is gone and the emaciated children have given way to the wonderfully healthy youngsters we see around us today. We lack malaria cases even for demonstration purposes in our medical school. TB has almost disappeared and — something the medical experts say is unrelated — we no longer have typhoid fever. Today Greece has one of the lowest morbidity rates for tuberculosis etc.

Speaking as a clinician, I have seen nothing over the last 25 years that could be ascribed to the ill effects of DDT. I have no doubts that there must be valid reasons for banning it, but I cannot help smiling when I read 'Letters to the Editor' expressing the writers' concern for the fate of insect life as a result of that evil thing DDT!

Today, however, I feel this is the right spot and the proper moment for a respectful requiem for the greatest benefactor that has ever come to Greece.

Another example of success in dealing with malaria is Sri Lanka. The island had been plagued by the disease for centuries, but a vigorous campaign against mosquitos with DDT resulted in reducing the incidence to only 100 cases in 1963. Then there was a relaxation on the control measures — and by 1968, the number of new cases had shot up to over a million; so the battle had to be renewed.

In spite of such set-backs, the over-all effect of anti-malarial campaigns, primarily based on DDT, has been little short of miraculous. According to the World Health Organisation (WHO), in 1971 about half the world's population (1,814 million people) were living in regions which had originally been malarious; but by that date malaria was no longer a serious problem for nearly three-quarters of them (1,374 million).[7]

So far, so good. But things — particularly living things — do not always stay put. The evolution of pesticide-resistant strains of insects is one of the ways in which the ecosystem we inhabit shows its complexity and its ability to exhibit 'buffering reactions' which tend to keep things going on much as before. Nearly all the disease-carrying insects — mosquitoes, fleas, lice — which man started to control with DDT succeeded, usually within ten years, in producing strains which were more or less immune to the poison. It has been one of the most striking examples of an evolution occurring as an unwelcome and unforeseen response to human action. We have, therefore, had to go to other insect-killing poisons; so the man-insect battle sways to and fro.

Another reaction, which one might not expect unless one is in the habit of thinking about complex systems, involves the human population itself. Protected against the major killer like malaria, populations have usually responded by breeding so many offspring that they outrun the food supply and get themselves back into a situation very little less miserable than that from which the pesticide seemed to be rescuing them.

These difficulties do not mean that pesticides and such 'cures' are useless and should be given up; it does mean that they are specialised weapons, which give control only over parts of the total system, and that other measures must be found which can be combined with them to give adequate advance over the whole broad front with which anything as complex as an ecosystem confronts us.

Work

Pre-agricultural Leisure and Post-industrial Leisure[8]

Throughout the 10,000 years or so since the invention of agriculture, men and women have become habituated to spending most of their waking hours performing work — work being defined as tasks which the people concerned would not choose to do if they could avoid it. This was probably not so in man's hundreds of thousands of years in the hunting phase before agriculture was invented, and it is also not clear that it is going to be true after the end of this century.

Before young people of today become middle-aged they may run into the same problem of disposing of their time as their hunting forebears did. Pop sociologists argue that the instincts of the hunter have been built into the human constitution through the long period of pre-agricultural evolution, and hence that man is inherently aggressive, with instincts such as territorial possessiveness. Before swallowing these arguments, remember that hunting has nearly always been an exclusively male pursuit, and that the human individual inherits his potentialities from a mother as well as from a father. Perhaps there was some evolutional selection for males to be effective hunters; but what was evolution selecting females to be? The food eaten by hunting societies (for instance Australian aborigines) consists mainly of wild roots, fruits and seeds, collected by the women. While women collect the essential sustenance, the men, according to Margaret Mead[9] (with, dare one suggest, a slightly Women's Lib slant) go off on a hunting expedition; seeing nothing very obvious around, they spend the day sitting in the shade telling stories or playing games, and come home in the evening saying 'Sorry, no, we did not get a kangaroo today. What have you got in the pot?'

That is by way of a parenthesis. In the last few millennia the majority of the human population have lived by agriculture which has demanded long hours of continuous work, usually from dawn to dusk, by both men and women for most seasons of the year, with

Figure 7.4: Average Lifetimes and How They Were Spent

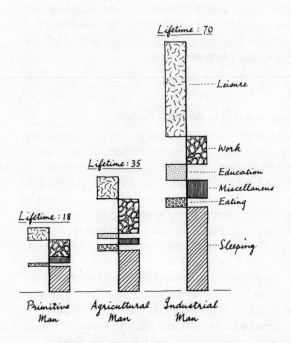

Source: J. McHale, *Futures*, September 1971, p. 260.

a few interludes of winter or dry season when nothing will grow.

The future will involve both changes in the hours devoted to work and the nature of the work. There has already been some reduction in working hours since the early days of the industrial revolution. In the rich countries, the age at which children can be sent out to work for wages has been raised, while old age pensions have shortened the working life at the other end. Furthermore, the number of hours per week that can be legally worked in one job has been reduced, although this reduction has not been proceeding very fast in the last few decades. However, even when the length of the official working week is reduced, a number of workers prefer to earn more by taking a second, part-time job, so that their actual hours of work are as much as, if not more than, before. They have preferred greater affluence to increased leisure.

It is doubtful whether this can continue much longer. Over the last

Figure 7.5: Daily Time Budget of German Worker

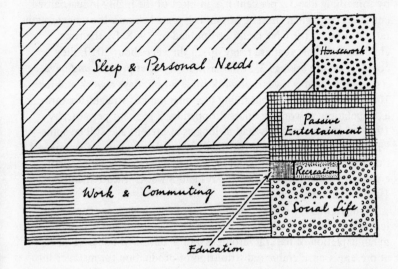

Figure 7.6: How an Average European Worker Says He Would Spend
an Extra Hour's Leisure

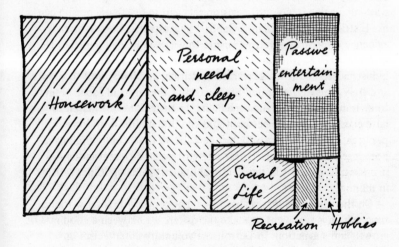

Source: Redrawn from E. Fontela, 'Communications in European Social, Economic
and Political Environments, 1970–1990', *Futures*, June 1972. The original data are
in a large study – Alexander Szalar ed., *The Using of Time* (Menton, The Hague, 1972).

ten years or so the Gross National Product (GNP) has been increasing
by something like 3½ per cent p.a. in most of the highly industrialised
countries (though at present Britain is lagging behind). If such a growth-
rate continued, the GNP could be doubled by 1988. By the time
children born this year are rising 40, in the year about 2010, they
could be on the average 3½ times as wealthy as at present, *and* have
six months holiday a year; or work three 8-hour days a week and take
10 weeks' vacation.[10] Continuing the same kind of straight-forward
extrapolation, if working hours dropped by 3 per cent per year, by
1990 we could work only half as long as at present and still be somewhat wealthier. Martin and Norman suggest that a plausible estimate is
that by 1990 there might be an increase of the GNP by 50 per cent,
a working week of five 7½-hour days and 3 weeks' vacation and
10 public holidays a year.

It might be very difficult indeed to cope with such an increase in
real wealth, if the products were of the present kind and caused as
much depletion of natural resources and pollution as our GNP does
at present. Considerable redistribution of production for instance into
building new cities and improving old ones, might make things easier
from this point of view. However, it will be difficult for families, of
the size possible at a time of population crisis, to find a use for much
more than 3 cars and 2 houses; and the number of refrigerators,
washing machines, colour television sets and so on, that a person can
use is strictly limited. Dennis Gabor[11] suggests that there is already
evidence of people preferring leisure to wages in many countries. He
refers in 1970 to 'the spreading of voluntary absenteeism' in most
industrialised countries. It started in Britain, and has spread to France
and Italy, and to the United States. Only Germany and Japan seem
to be immune to it for the time being. In Britain it is estimated to
have caused the loss of between 200 and 300 million working days
per year, which is at least 30, but perhaps 40 times, more than have
been lost by strikes. This varies widely between different industries;
it is about 2 per cent in the electrical industry, almost 20 per cent
in mining.

On the whole the loss is about 5—6 per cent of the total working
time, which is sufficient to make the difference between a good rate of
growth and stagnation. In Detroit the voluntary absenteeism on
Mondays is of the order of 5—10 per cent, caused mostly by young
workers. It is likely to increase steadily as the older workers are being
replaced by the younger, who have greater expectations of what they
are entitled to receive from life.

Monday morning absenteeism to recover from the weekend is a symptom of a tendency which is likely to become much more widespread. Most people would like to have more control than at present over the hours at which they put in their work. Some firms already experiment and many more will, with methods of organisation by which a person who is due to work, say, 40 hours in a week can do 20 of these at previously agreed times, and is free to contribute the other 20 more or less when he pleases. This involves more organisation by management, but appears to be feasible in many types of employment. But, of course, the simplest course, which involves the least reorganisation of production methods is to keep some people in full employment (and high wages) and let the others be unemployed, on the dole. In Britain, there are at present pressures which would result in this, both from employers and from trades unions. It is a real dilemma, and we will return to it after discussing likely changes in the character of work to be done.

Types of Work

It is worth while to consider, in this connection, some of the ideas about work and leisure which have been developed in other societies, which have been less influenced by the masochistic Puritan ethos than our own. I will quote two paragraphs from an article on Buddhist Economics by a Western but sympathetic writer, E.F. Schumacher.[12]

The Buddhist point of view takes the functions of work to be at least threefold: to give a man a chance to utilise and develop his faculties; to enable him to overcome his ego-centredness by joining with other people in a common task; and to bring forth the goods and services needed for a becoming existence. Again, the consequences that flow from this view are endless. To organise work in such a manner that it becomes meaningless, boring, stultifying, or nerve-racking for the worker would be little short of criminal; it would indicate a greater concern with goods than with people, an evil lack of compassion and a soul-destroying degree of attachment to the most primitive side of this worldly existence. Equally, to strive for leisure as an alternative to work would be considered a complete misunderstanding of one of the basic truths of human existence, namely that work and leisure are complementary parts of the same living process and cannot be separated without destroying the joy of work and the bliss of leisure.

From the Buddhist point of view, there are therefore two types of mechanisation which must be clearly distinguished: one that enhances a man's skill and power and one that turns the work of man over to a mechanical slave, leaving man in a position of having to serve the slave.

Perhaps we shall find ourselves driven towards this sensible point of view, if not by our own good sense, then by applying our Puritan efficiency so effectively that eventually there is not enough 'work' (in the unpleasant sense) left to occupy the whole of our time.

Up to the beginning of the Industrial Revolution, the great majority of workers were engaged in primary production, that is to say the production of food by agriculture and of raw materials by mining, forestry, etc. This phase was succeeded by one in which agriculture became more organised for producing saleable crops rather than for personal subsistence, and the majority of the labour force moved into factories engaged in industrial production. About the beginning of this century this phase was succeeded by one in which most people are being employed in organisation, information processing, communication, research and so on.

The great reduction in the proportion of the labour force employed in agriculture in modern industrial societies is rather misleading if taken at its face value. The figures usually quoted refer only to those working directly on farms. The real situation was discussed on pp. 87–9. Even with all the benefits of modern technology, man still does not get food for nothing. This raises the whole problem, which is basic for man's future and will probably quite soon be recognised as urgent, of the real value to society of different types of work. Clearly the mere reduction in the proportion of the population employed in primary industry does not justify the conclusion that it has become unimportant; the social muscle which can be exerted by the organised coal miners or power station workers, or potentially by the poorly organised food producers, or by certain groups in secondary industry, such as transport, is enough to show that. At the other end of the scale, a good deal of the tertiary (service) and quaternary (information processing) types of employment, into which people have been moving in increasing numbers, might be accused of being nothing more than parasitic paper pushing: questionnaires, reports by observers of what other people have done, have proliferated prodigiously since World War II.

An experienced United Nations diplomat, considering what efforts the UN might make to help developing countries, wrote:

Figure 7.7: Percentage Distribution of Economically Active Population

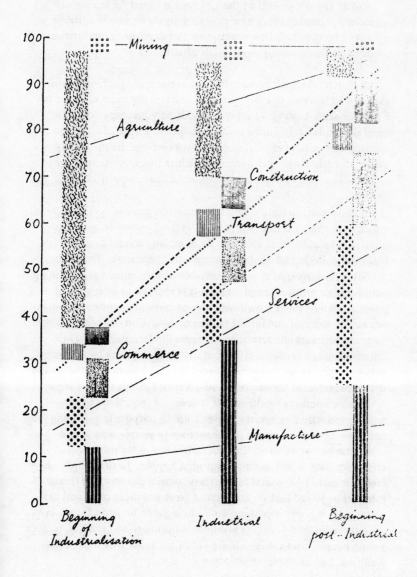

Source: Redrawn from J. McHale, *Futures*, September 1971.

A few years ago, I calculated that it would take seventy government officials working eight hours a day throughout the year, just to read all the documents of the UN system (apart from summary records, agendas, etc.); now probably eighty or ninety officials would be required. Few governments of developing countries can devote so much manpower to UN affairs. . .[13]

Of course, there are some information-processing activities which do yield an increase in efficiency. It is fractionally more efficient for a shop or store to keep a supply of goods only just big enough to meet demands likely during some appropriate length of time. A fraction of one per cent difference in working out the maximally efficient method can spell success or failure in a very competitive world — but will, or need, the world remain as competitive as all that?

Again, there is a third type of information processing, the value of which — in theory if not in practice — is hardly open to question, namely, education in all its forms from nursery school to university, technical colleges and all the forms of adult education. This is already probably the largest of all industries in developed countries, providing about 5 per cent of all employment. It is also the most rapidly growing, and its rapid growth will almost certainly continue for many years. The value of our formal system of education has been attacked by some believers in a return to a simpler life (see Illich).[14] Their criticisms may have some effect but, by their emphasis on intimate person-to-person interaction, will probably lead to an increase, rather than a decrease, in the hours the adults spend in this type of work.

Much quaternary work, even if it does not contribute to the actual production by society, serves a useful purpose in providing jobs and thus serving as a means of subsistence to people who would otherwise be out of work. The main increases in technological efficiency have been labour-saving; what happens to the people whose labour is saved? In general terms, the situation can be eased if new jobs can be found that do not require great resources of capital or materials — e.g. paper pushing, or again higher education for all, even if, in its traditional form, its main contribution to society is to remove young people from the labour market in a manner which seems less insulting than unemployment pay.

Computerisation and Personalisation[15]

The joker that is going to make itself felt in the next round of this game is computerisation. Computers can carry out most forms of clerical work, managerial organisation, operation of productive machines, and information processing, including much of education, faster and better than human workers. Increasingly, they are being able to carry it out more cheaply too. When a computer is first introduced into a new technical field, it is usually more expensive than traditional methods. The experience has been that it very rapidly becomes possible to cheapen it, until it becomes so much less expensive that it is almost bound to become adopted. Martin and Norman write:

> ... in business and industry one application after another falls within the province of the computer. Machines will eventually handle school room drill more cheaply than teachers; using a domestic terminal will be cheaper than driving to the bank, travel agent or super-market; data banks will be cheaper than repetitive form-filling. The rate of increase of the number of computer terminals in use in countries like the United States and in Europe is in the early phases of an exponential rise.
>
> By 1984 we think that the terminal industry will have matured to the position of the automobile in the late twenties — as an accepted part of life — one might foresee a terminal in every home, a terminal in every manager's office and one for every few students at school or college. The price and universality will approach that of television or telephone.

Increasing computerisation will do away with many of the clerical information-processing and quaternary jobs which are at present providing a living for those released from productive industry by increasingly efficient labour-saving processes. In looking at other possible effects of the computer revolution, it would be as well to consider a general picture of the 'employment mix' into which society seems to be moving in the next couple of decades. Dennis Gabor[16] has offered a map of the situation in the form of an 'intelligence occupation matrix'. Accepting that the population contains individuals of different abilities, he classifies them into a number of groups, ranked according to their IQ. Then he classifies types of work and for each category of work he gives an estimate of the contribution which each IQ group is now making. Then he gives a guess how the same ability might be distributed to a different mix of employment in 20 years' time.

Table 7.3: Gabor's Employment Mix for 2000 AD
(Bracketed figures are guesses for present situation.)

IQ brackets	133 +	126.5 133	120.7 126.5	113.6 120.7	104.1 113.6	91.5 104.1	75.1 91.5
% of Population	2	3	5	10	20	30	35
Science, Arts learned professions	1.6 (1.0)	2.0 (1.2)	2.4 (1.8)				
Higher Administration	0.4 (0.3)	0.8 (0.6)	1.0 (1.0)	1.8 (3.1)			
Pre-University Education	– (0.4)	0.2 (0.7)	1.6 (1.2)	7.0 (2.0)	7.0 (0.5)		
Clerical	– (0.1)	– (0.2)	– (0.6)	1.0 (3.0)	3.0 (10.0)	6.0 (6.0)	
Technicians	– (0.1)	– (0.2)	– (0.2)	0.2 (0.4)	2.0 (2.1)	3.8 (1.0)	
Production operatives including farming	–	– (0.1)	– (0.1)	– (1.2)	7.0 (6.4)	11.0 (17.0)	2.0 (15.0)
Service	–	–	– (0.1)	– (0.5)	1.0 (1.0)	9.2 (6.0)	23.0 (10.0)

Source: D. Gabor, *The Mature Society* (Secker & Warburg, 1972), p. 93.

In Gabor's mix the number of people employed in education is multiplied by about three, the number in clerical jobs and in production operations are halved, and the number of people employed in service jobs is almost doubled. Probably some of the more enthusiastic advocates of the computer revolution would suggest that the production operatives might be reduced even more. The clerical workers would also be further reduced, unless indeed one included some of the simpler types of computer programming in this category of employment.

Computerisation is likely to have a very strong influence on the nature of society in several ways. Working with a computer essentially involves a communication channel connecting the computer terminal with the computer itself — there is no need for a worker to be physically in central location. He can work at home obtaining any information he needs from the computer store on the wire and sending back his own contribution by the same channel. Whereas the telephone has not been able to counteract all the other influences which tend to bring work-places together into city centres, computerisation may succeed in doing so.

Computerisation is also likely to lead to increased ability to satisfy individual needs and desires. Paradoxically, the computer — a machine — provides more personalised service than do human administrators. The computer has unlimited memory and inexhaustible patience. When one books a long air journey through a computerised reservation service, one can put all sorts of special requests — window seat, forward on the starboard side, in the part reserved for smokers and not subjected to a film show; and one can keep changing one's mind about the exact places to be visited, times of departure and arrival, etc. — and these requests will be recorded and probably acted on, whereas a few years previously human clerks found it too complicated to take them all into account. And with computer-controlled tools and assembly lines it will be perfectly feasible to produce an enormously wider range of individually slightly different products than are practical for the mass production methods of today.

Much of the 'personalisation' could be carried over into transactions in which the computer is not involved. If people became used to obtaining a personalised service from machines, would they not expect it, and expect to supply it, in their dealings with each other? In the age of mass production, work consisted mainly in dealing with individual identical parts, according to a precise schedule; bank clerks, sales assistants, barbers and other service workers who meet people face to face tended to treat them also as a set of identical units, all to be given the same treatment. Computerisation may bring about an ethos in which the person providing the service takes a pride in giving exactly what the individual client wants, and also perhaps an equal pride in expressing his own personality in the work he performs.

The simplest way in which people are using their already increasing leisure for their own personal development is by participating in sport, not merely as spectators (live or TV) but as performers. There has been a spectacular increase in the membership of clubs for active sportsmen; some British figures are shown in Figure 7.8. But for most people, there is only a rather short period of life in which sport provides an adequate form of activity for anything more than a minimum of leisure.

The possibility of some creative expression of personality is one of the attractions of some of the tertiary or service activities available now; for instance, for dressmakers, people who run small restaurants, boutiques, or the like. There are many other types of service, excluded by our present economic set-up, which would greatly enrich living if carried out by people who enjoyed doing them; an example is the gardening and care of spaces in the improved and beautified cities which we must hope for.

Even the highly unfashionable field of domestic work may again come to seem attractive. It is one of the paradoxes of history that the trend of employment away from productive or secondary industry into tertiary service work has been accompanied by a reduction in the status of domestic service. Not long ago a trusted personal servant to an important family had considerable prestige. The trouble was that the servant became almost wholly dependent on the master, both for security of living standard and for orders about the details of the work to be done. With highly mechanised domestic appliances there might in the future be domestic professionals, such as house cleaners, cooks or people who might service ten or a dozen families, becoming acquainted with them on a personal level, without the unacceptable dependence. Pre-nursery schools, which relieve young mothers of the task of baby minding, are one of the first examples of such a development. Further such developments in a wider range of domestic services might have a profound effect on family life and child up-bringing. For instance, Alvin Toffler[17] has suggested that, in a more leisured society, people of the 'young grandparent' age group might develop some kinds of special services for families with young children.

Further automation and increased leisure, combined with respect for conservation of natural resources and prevention of pollution, is

Figure 7.8: Trends in Selected Sports

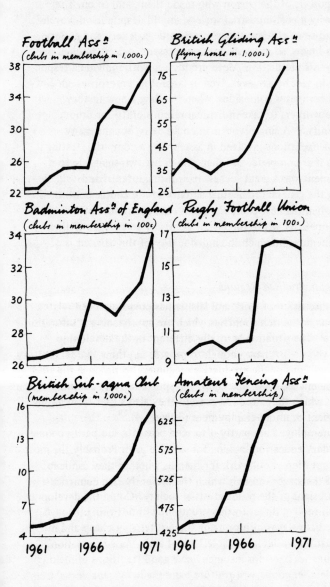

Source: Sports Council, *Sports for All*, 1973, p. 11.

likely to lead to a revival of craft production of many items of equipment, made to last, out of good quality materials, and expressing the individual powers of the person who made them, and so on. There is no reason why a post-industrial society should despise hand-woven fabrics, hand-sewn clothes, shoes, hand-made crockery and cutlery and pots and pans, so much as does our present society, hooked on profit and mass production. More production with individual responsibility can in fact be achieved even in large-scale enterprises. One of the French computer companies, when building a new factory, allowed the workers to take individual responsibility for producing complete units.[18] A single workman could carry out the many hundreds of operations involved in assembling a computer, testing it and passing it as complete, and then attach his own signature to it. The experiment was a great success in arousing interest and stimulating the general intellectual activity of the people concerned. However, when the new plant was ready, the economics of the present competitive world forced the company to go back to their normal procedures in which the individuality of the workers is submerged.

In the Pre-industrialised Regions

The above discussion of work and leisure has obviously been related to conditions in the rich countries which are approaching a 'saturation of affluence'. The situation is totally different in the developing countries, who do not have enough to provide anything like satisfactory material conditions or the productive machinery to produce the steel, fertiliser, chemicals, food, machines, transportation and communication equipment, which they need. At present they also suffer from intense unemployment or under-employment (Table 7.4).[19]

These unemployed are partly displaced peasants and partly people with secondary education looking for suitable jobs. Probably the most important question about work for them is whether they can leap over any of the stages through which the presently rich countries have come within sight of the post-industrial society? Could the developing countries aim to get direct to this situation, without going through the intermediate stages of producing the not terribly cheap and not very long-lasting products characteristic of early mass production?

Poor countries may, for instance, have good traditions of making pottery or leather goods, or furniture hand-made by capable carpenters from sound hard wood. Their needs may be quantitatively so large (remember the 2 billion chairs needed for the developing

Table 7.4: Unemployment and Under-employment in Developing
Asian Countries

India:

    Unemployed rose from 5 M in 1961 to 15–20 M in 1971.

    Under-employed, 30–45 M in 1971.

    Total population around 550 M.

Pakistan: (undivided)

    Un- and Under-employed about 17.7 per cent of work force in 1970.

Indonesia:

    Unemployed about 10–11 per cent of work force in 1970.

    Under-employed about 3 times as many.

Sri-Lanka (Ceylon):

    Unemployed about 12 per cent of work force.

These unemployed are partly displaced peasants and partly people with secondary
education looking for suitable jobs.
Source: *Ceres*, September–October 1972, p. 31.

world, p. 165[20]) that the native handicraft productions may in the first
place have to be luxury goods for the better-off citizens, while the
mass needs are met by some sort of mass production. But would this
not be better than for the leading citizens in the poor countries to
acquire a taste for the type of articles that are smart and fashionable
in the rich countries at present, but which are likely to be out of
date in the next decade or two? The aim of these countries should be
to jump into the twenty-first century without having to go through
the worst of the twentieth.

Wealth

I am not intending here to provide a potted survey of Economic
Theory. It would be impossible to do so in the space available, nor am
I competent to attempt it. I only want to draw attention to a few
points about real wealth which are often overlooked but which
seem likely to become more important in the future.

    Real wealth is something broader and more inclusive than monetary
values. Figure 7.9 may serve to suggest the complexity of the network
of social and economic relations which underlie its creation. This
diagram has been translated from a German discussion, which takes
as its key value 'self-realisation', which one can provisionally accept as
at any rate closely connected with the kind of 'real wealth' we wish
to discuss. The diagram indicates that almost every activity of society
has some influence on it, directly or indirectly, and either positive
(solid lines and arrows) or negative (dotted).

Figure 7.9: The Causal Network Which Converges on One Aspect of Real Wealth, namely Self-realisation

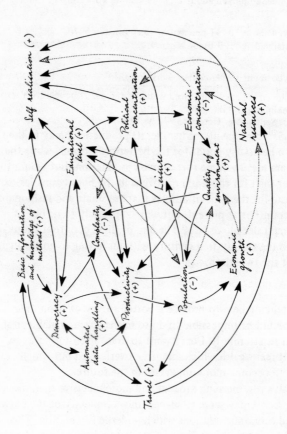

Source: Translated from H.H. Koell, 'Über die Aufgaben und Hilfsmittel der Zukünftsplannung', *Analysen und Prognosen*, September 1974, p. 16.

Total Wealth and How it is Divided Up

The total wealth of a nation is more usually discussed in simple
monetary terms, as its Gross National Product (GNP). This, divided by
the number of people in the population, gives the average GNP per
head, or per capita. The percentage by which the GNP of a country
increases from one year to the next is spoken of as 'the growth-rate'.
Countries are often arranged in a sort of league table, either by their
GNP per capita, or by their growth-rates. It is important to realise
what extremely rough and inadequate measures these indices provide
of the real situation.

In the first place, the GNP is based on monetary transactions,
and there are a great many aspects of life which are not at present
measured in money terms, and are therefore not included in the GNP;
as, for instance, various aspects of pollution. Again, some monetary
transactions can scarcely be considered as benefits. For instance, if
somebody falls ill and pays his doctor, that adds to the GNP; but if
he stays well and does not pay his doctor, that does not increase the
GNP. As coal seams get worked out and it costs more in wages to
mine a ton of coal, so the GNP goes up. Of course, the GNP does not
include many of the important factors in the well-being of a nation,
such as the amount of food, the roads, water, education, manufactured
products and so on. Gross differences of the GNP per capita between
countries (e.g. the United States and Brazil, or Europe and India)
undoubtedly do reflect, even if crudely, the real differences in
standard of living. One of the most important facts about the world
is that large differences in material wealth not only exist between
various regions, but are actually increasing. The 'developing nations'
are in fact developing less fast in material terms than the richer
nations. Even though material terms are not everything, the increasing
disparity in available goods is certainly one of the major factors
bringing about instability in the world system.

A figure like GNP per capita conceals the disparities in wealth
between different citizens. In the United States, with the highest per
capita GNP in the world (bar some of the small oil kingdoms), there
are at least 26 million people, about 12 per cent of the population,
living below the officially recognised poverty line. It has been claimed
that, in the US, the total income of the richest 2 per cent of the
population is equal to that of the bottom 40 per cent. Enormous
inequalities often arise within even the poorest nations when they
begin to raise their standard of living. In Kenya, an African business
man in Nairobi may spend on lunch in a posh hotel as much as six

months' wages for a rural labourer.[21] This is in part an indication of the unreality of present money values; the rural labourer can live for six months on the food he buys, while the business man can certainly not live for that long on the food he bought for the same money.

Growth in Wealth

All national governments and most of the people within all nations seem always anxious to increase the GNP per capita of their society. The problem is obviously most pressing for those countries lower down on the development scale. What does GNP depend on, and how can a country set about increasing its material wealth?

Natural Resources. One factor which is often of crucial importance is the availability of easily exploited natural resources. This is perhaps most obvious in situations like that in the Middle East where many small and previously very impoverished Arab nations along the Persian Gulf found themselves sitting on one of the world's major oil fields, and rapidly became exceedingly wealthy, whereas nearby the large, populous and ancient country of Egypt, with an intelligentsia with many centuries of sophistication and education behind it, has no such easily exploited resources and remains extremely poor.

Table 7.5:[22] Material Sources
Value of natural resources in less developed countries (dollars per capita, current prices).

Country	Population 1967 est. (millions)	Agric. forest & fisheries	Coal reserves	Iron ore	Petroleum	Non-fuel, non-ferrous reserves	Hydro-electric power	Totals (rounded)
China	750	10	655	80	30	14	10	800
India	500	13	410	120	3	14	6	570
Pakistan	106	16	5	–	1	–	5	30
Indonesia	105	–	11	12	150	24	1	200
Nigeria	60	70	33	–	75	6	–	200
Philippines	34	121	5	300	–	32	13	500
Turkey	32	110	37	7	–	12	6	170
Thailand	31	116	–	1	–	40	1	160
Egypt	30	37	–	5	21	2	15	80
S. Korea	29	19	590	25	–	38	–	700
Burma	26	81	–	–	4	47	60	200
Iran	24	13	–	–	3000	4	3	3000

Source: Meier in R. Jungk and J. Galtung (eds.), *Mankind 2000*. (Allen & Unwin, 1969)

The availability of resources has also had a great influence even in those countries which we now think of as highly developed. The lead taken by Britain in the Industrial Revolution, which for a time made it the richest country in the world, was quite largely dependent on easily worked supplies of primary fuel (coal) and ores of some crucial metals, such as iron. The great wealth which the United States has developed in the last couple of centuries arose as much from the fact that the immigrants into that continent found that they were sitting on a gold mine — or rather an Aladdin's cave, full of resources much more diversified than mere gold — as from the much-flaunted merits of the capitalist economic system.

Technological and Social Factors. Most countries have some natural resources, but the exploitation of almost every kind of natural resource requires that capital be invested in mines, refineries, factories, improving the land and so on. Until a few years ago it was generally believed that, if the rich countries would only make available to the poor ones enough capital and technical skill to start exploiting their own resources, these countries would soon reach the 'take-off point' at which they would enter into a phase of rapid growth under their own steam. These ideas seemed to receive support from the success of the Marshall plan in Europe, by which the United States, shortly after the end of World War II, pumped large quantities of money into the shattered European economies, with the result that they very rapidly rebuilt new factories and facilities which enabled them to make use of their own resources. It turned out, however, that it is by no means so easy to do this when the receiving countries have not an already existing tradition of generating material wealth within their own boundaries.

The kind of difficulties that arise differ in different places. In some countries the most important factors may be medical, such as substandard health, or it may be a lack of literacy, or the system of land tenure. As an example of an analysis of the situation by a competent group within one of the developing regions, Figure 7.10 summarises a study by a group of Brazilian economists and developers. The system does not consist only of interacting economic factors, such as a lack of capital and low productivity of labour. They suggest that one has to consider at least four interacting cycles: an economic one, an agricultural, a social, and one concerned with education and health. It is impossible to improve one, such as the economic cycle, unless there are improvements in the other cycles to back it up. Thus, even if one is content to measure the well-being of the country in monetary terms,

Figure 7.10: Social Cycles Affecting Output in Brazil

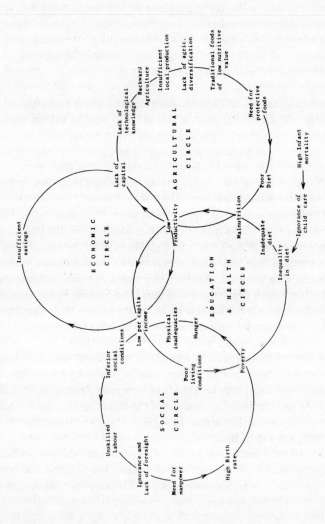

ECONOMIC CIRCLE

AGRICULTURAL CIRCLE

EDUCATION & HEALTH CIRCLE

SOCIAL CIRCLE

Insufficient savings

Lack of capital

Low Productivity

Low per capita income

Inferior social conditions

Unskilled Labour

Ignorance and Lack of foresight

Need for manpower

High Birth rate

Poor living conditions

Physical inadequacies

Hunger

Poverty

Inequality in diet

Inadequate diet

Malnutrition

Ignorance of child care

High Infant mortality

Poor Diet

Need for protective foods

Traditional foods of low nutritive value

Lack of agric. diversification

Insufficient local production

Backward Agriculture

Lack of technological knowledge

Source: Based on work of the Fundacao Geulio Vargas. See O. Ballarin, 'The Brazilian Food Riddle', *Ceres*, May–June 1972.

such as those in the GNP, those terms are not sufficient for planning
how to improve the situation; for that one has to take into account
many non-monetary factors as well.

Social Indicators

It would be useful to have indices more comprehensive than GNP,
which include factors, other than purely monetary ones, contributing
to real wealth and happiness. These are often known as 'social indicators'.
Many efforts to devise them are being made in various parts of the
world, particularly in America and Japan. The Japanese have been
extraordinarily successful in raising their national GNP, but at the cost
of extremely bad pollution, overcrowding, noise and general disamenity
in their cities;[23] they are, therefore, attempting to develop an index of
Net National Welfare (NNW) which will take account of these factors
and give a better measure of the real state of affairs than does the
GNP.

Most of the social indicators proposed are based on already
ascertained statistics of material fact. One which illustrates their
general character was published by the weekly paper *The Economist*
at the beginning of 1972.[24] This was based on available statistics about
15 features in 14 well-developed countries, concerning factors like
population density, the number of people per doctor, the murder-rate,
infant mortality, the number of television sets per head and so on. For
each item, the percentage by which each country differed from the
average of all 14 countries was worked out. For example, the average
number of deaths from road accidents in all 14 was, in 1967, 22 per
hundred thousand people; in West Germany the figure was 29, or 31
per cent above the average. So West Germany scored 31 for this item.
The score was marked either positive or negative according to whether
it was a Good Thing or a Bad Thing. Obviously road deaths are a Bad
Thing, so Germany's score for this item was minus 31. On the other
hand it was reckoned that population density is a Bad Thing, so
Australia, with a low population density, gets a high positive score on
that account. All scores, positive or negative, which a country made
on all 15 items were then simply added up. *The Economist* could not
make up its mind whether a high rate of divorce should be counted
as a Good Thing, or a Bad Thing, so it is omitted from the final scores.

When this more broadly-based index is used, the countries come
out in quite a different rank order than they would on the basis of
GNP alone. However, the weaknesses of the scheme are very obvious.

Table 7.6a: Social Indicators

	Population density	Early marriage	Population per doctor	Suicide	Murder	Deaths from Road accidents	Infant mortality
	−	+	−	−	−	−	−
Australia	+ 99	+29	−18	−10	− 1	−27	+11
Belgium	−121	+11	+11	−11	+ 42	−16	− 9
Canada	+ 99	+29	− 3	+35	− 15	−22	− 4
Czechoslovakia	+ 21	+51	+33	−77	+ 21	+22	−15
France	+ 36	− 4	− 7	−15	+ 35	−24	+17
Germany (Fed.Rep.)	− 66	− 7	+18	−60	+ 6	−31	−17
Holland	−120	−26	+17	+55	+ 63	− 1	+33
Italy	− 24	−22	+22	+56	+ 28	+ 2	−51
Japan	− 94	−77	−27	− 3	− 1	+21	+23
Spain	+ 55	−55	− 6	+69	+ 86	+47	−49
Sweden	+ 87	−33	−11	−60	+ 35	+34	+34
Switzerland	− 6	−11	+ 9	−27	+ 42	−11	+22
UK	− 59	+29	−14	+31	+ 49	+32	+ 6
USA	+ 85	+88	+ 9	+21	−395	−21	− 4

Source: 'Social Indicators', *The Economist*, 22 January 1972, p. 18.

Table 7.6b: Social Indicators

	Students in higher education	Proportion of dwellings with baths	Ratio of TVs to people	Ratio of telephones to people	Circulation of daily newspapers	Car ownership	Economic growth	Divorce
	+	+	+	+	+	+	+	+|
Australia	+ 5	+85	− 9	+ 5	+11	+ 45	− 27	± 6
Belgium	− 48	−56	−12	−32	−20	− 4	− 4	± 28
Canada	+ 78	+51	+23	+53	−37	+ 48	− 34	± 37
Czechoslovakia	− 21	−38	−12	−56	−13	− 77	+ 45	∓ 59
France	0	−47	−15	−44	−23	+ 15	+ 16	± 14
Germany (Fed. Rep)	− 42	− 3	+10	−26	+ 1	+ 1	− 13	∓ 14
Holland	+ 18	−51	− 6	−13	− 8	− 14	− 7	± 33
Italy	− 41	−47	−28	−43	−26	− 18	+ 23	±100
Japan	+ 13	+11	−10	−17	+46	− 67	+150	± 4
Spain	− 58	−56	−29	−57	−52	− 70	+ 25	±100
Sweden	+ 1	+14	+27	+89	+58	+ 33	− 27	∓ 55
Switzerland	− 50	+29	−22	+54	+13	0	− 38	± 2
UK	− 38	+45	+19	−11	+47	0	− 62	± 5
USA	+179	+66	+67	+98	+ 3	+107	− 47	∓201

Source: 'Social Indicators', *The Economist*.

Table 7.7: Final Scores

Canada	+ 301
Sweden	+ 281
USA	+ 256
Australia	+ 198
UK	+ 74
Switzerland	+ 4
Japan	− 32
France	− 60
Holland	− 94
Czechoslovakia	−116
Spain	−150
Italy	−169
Germany (Fed. Rep.)	−229
Belgium	−269

Getting a high score for television sets is counted as having exactly the same value as a high score for having many doctors, or a high rate of growth of GNP. It would be more satisfactory if one could find some way of weighting each score according to the real importance of the item under consideration, but it would be very difficult to find how to do this. Moreover, *The Economist*, which obviously did not itself take this exercise very seriously, points out that there may be other factors involved in the pleasantness of life which are not included in these figures, broad though they may be. For instance, its last paragraph points out:

> Canada's easy triumph suggests that one should perhaps add a column on mean temperatures. They have not been included because of internal variations in, for example, the United States; because averages hide unpleasant extremes; and because too hot is as nasty as too cold. But it is possible to imagine that on these indicators the South Pole might, when sometime in the future it is scooped into the statisticians' net, emerge as the pleasantest place to live — no road accidents, low population density, good economic growth and a fair level of amenities, because otherwise no one would be so daft as to go there at all.

Probably it is misguided to try to summarise the whole well-being of a country, or the national wealth, in a single figure at all, but we should use clusters of indices or what might be called 'welfare profiles'. One scheme of this kind has been suggested by the French Canadian ecologist Pierre Dansereau.[25] He does not rely on the figures already available, but tries to lay down theoretically in very general terms what he considers to be the major factors of the quality of life. He enumerates 23 factors which are concerned with individual and social life in physiological, psychological, social, economic, political and religious, ecological and evolutionary aspects. He then made a survey, in which people were asked whether the conditions of their life were good, average, bad or very bad, in relation to each of these factors. He exhibits the results as a sort of rosette for each person, the boundary of the rosette sticking out further from the centre when the answer was that that condition was good, but being pulled back towards the centre when the answer was that the condition was very bad. One could, of course, find ways of superimposing a great number of these rosettes to average out conditions over the whole population, and there are many more refined statistical methods which could be used ('multivariate analyses').

Dansereau's scheme at least tries to take into account the whole range of factors which contribute to real wealth or well-being. His use of the method has so far depended on the subjective evaluation by people of the satisfactoriness of their own conditions. One would like a more objective judgement as to the adequacy of life in all its aspects, but it is not easy to see how to arrive at it.

Dansereau's scheme is attractive not only because of its comprehensiveness, but also because it could be developed so that it could be used to describe different sorts of well-being. There is no reason why everybody, or all societies, should adopt the same criteria of value in their estimations of the quality of life. That is another reason for the inadequacy of a single figure index.

Or would even an attempt to summarise a desired life-style as a rather complex profile or cluster of indices be going too far towards quantifying something which may be inherently non-quantifiable? An attempt to express something as a figure, or a set of figures, or, even more vaguely, as a set of orders of rank, may not always be the wisest or most rewarding way of treating some subjects. We cannot meaningfully treat music or art or literature like that. It is possible that real wealth, the actual fulfilment of all one's human potentials in balance with one another, may always remain essentially a matter for discussion between human beings, rather than for measurement. It is already clear that we should not allow ourselves to be intimidated by an index like GNP, which is precise about something which is obviously inadequate.

Figure 7.11: A Few Specimens of How People Rate the Satisfaction of the Way they Live.

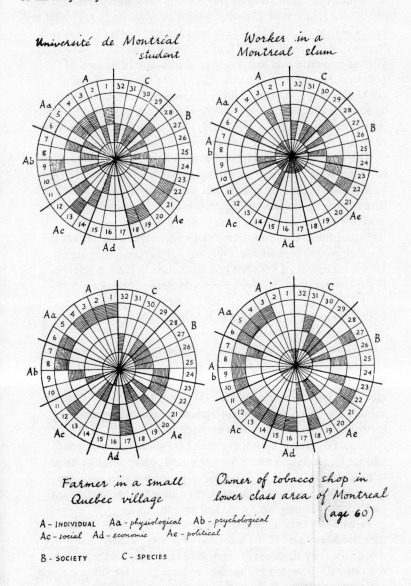

Université de Montréal student

Worker in a Montreal slum

Farmer in a small Quebec village

Owner of tobacco shop in lower class area of Montreal (age 60)

A - INDIVIDUAL Aa - *physiological* Ab - *psychological*
Ac - *social* Ad - *economic* Ae - *political*

B - SOCIETY   C - SPECIES

Source: Pierre Dansereau, 'The Dimensions of Environmental Quality', Commonwealth Human Ecology Council Conference, Malta, 1970.

No Growth, Restricted Growth or Directed Growth

Admitting that there are more things in life than money does not
abolish the fact that most people want their situation to get better and
better as time passes, and this has been brought about by economic
'growth'. But growth in GNP is by no means an unmixed blessing; the
GNP of a country is in fact a very good indicator of its level of
pollution. Some people have therefore called for a no-growth or
stable economy.[26] Others point out, however, that there are still
an enormous number of poor people even in rich countries, let alone
in the developing parts of the world, and that growth is undeniably
necessary if they are to be provided with proper conditions of life.

This question could be treated in a much more rational way if we
had some better means of measuring growth than GNP. We certainly
need growth in some directions, but not in others. But until we
have something like the welfare profiles considered above, we will
have to carry on the discussion in ordinary language.

Conventional economists are usually reluctant to discuss systems
in which growth is restricted. Professor John Pringle, who has since
1969 been running a full-scale honours course in Human Sciences
at the University of Oxford, has contributions to his course from
many fields,[27] but he has confessed, 'there should probably be
some economics, if there were an economist willing to compromise
on the desirability of unlimited growth.'

In view of professional economists' reluctance to comment I can
offer no more than an amateur opinion. It is fairly clear that in the
western capitalist countries, the main motive force which has been
used to propel the economic machine is profit, and that is after all
another way of saying growth in monetary value. To repudiate
growth is to tamper with the main force in the running of the economic
machine. But even in countries which have given up a complete
reliance on profit and which operate mixed economies, like Britain,
or have reduced profit to a very minor personal matter, as in the
Soviet Union, economists do not seem willing to contemplate any
basis for an economy except over-all growth.

Perhaps this is an inevitable result of what was originally one of
the great advantages of the invention of money; namely that it was a
way of reducing all values of every kind to a single measure. Money
was originally invented as a method of barter; but we now use money
not only for current exchanges, but for every kind of investment and
enterprises which are intended to bring in benefits of many different
kinds. Probably we need to invent some drastically new mechanisms

which could function as several different sorts of money, appropriate either to exchanges of goods or to investments in certain particular kinds of growth, rather than in growth in general.

At the Delos Symposia on Ekistics, or the Science of Human Settlements, I once argued that the existence of large areas of slums, which ought to be knocked down and rebuilt — inhabited by healthy people who were well capable of knocking them down and rebuilding them, but had to stay out of work supported by welfare payments — simply meant that money was not doing the job which we relied upon it to do; namely, to enable society to use its resources to produce improvements in its conditions. If money cannot do this task then we need to invent something else which can.[28]

The suggestion was at first greeted with polite silence, but the next day Charles Haar, a senior administrator in the US government department concerned with housing, said that something of the kind had already been done in America, by the introduction of a system of government-guaranteed mortgages on newly built houses, which in effect pumped a quantity of newly invented money into this area.

But although government-backed housing mortgages are new money, they are still interchangeable with the old money. What is really needed is an invention of much more novel character. To facilitate growth in areas which contribute to long-term social well-being requires a medium with some money-like properties (e.g. leaving a good deal of freedom of choice to the possessor as to how it should be used in detail) but which cannot be used quite outside the field it is supposed to help. Two scientists in Australia have recently suggested[29] that national governments should issue each citizen, each year, with a certain number of 'Natural Resource Units (NRU)'. In a democracy, there would be the same number for everyone, though there might be fewer for babies and children. Any object or activity would have not only its financial price, fixed as at present, but also a price in NRUs fixed by the government in accordance with its impact on existing and future resources. In their scheme, child-bearing would be an activity with a definite, probably fairly high, NRU price; if a man and wife wanted to have many children, they could do so, but only at the cost of having little NRU-resources left to pay for other resources, like using things (such as a car). How such a scheme might work out in practice has not yet been thought out (in detail), but here is a scheme for an alternative or supplementary exchange medium like money, which is not obviously absurd or impossible.

Recent developments in using computers may also have drastic effects on the workings of our present monetary system.[30] Computers could do one of the main things for which the western industrialised world has so far relied on 'the free market', that is, balance out the factors in situations which we find too complex to analyse rationally. The classical theory of economics takes it that, if the market is left 'free', the forces of supply and demand will, in not too short a time, see to it that prices, wages and investment become adjusted to one another in a manner which is near the best possible. At least since Karl Marx, we have been forced to doubt if this really works out so well. The market has produced the glaring inequalities referred to at the beginning of this chapter, and also other, lesser, but still in the long run unacceptable maladjustments of earnings to the social value of work done. Many societies, both officially socialist ones, such as the Soviet Union, and officially 'mixed-capitalist' ones, such as Britain, have tried to improve on the brutality of the free market, but so far none of their 'Planning Boards', 'Wages Boards', or 'Relativities Boards' seem able to provide a convincing answer. The problems are probably just too complex to be thought through to a finish, and have to be settled by the old rough and not very ready method of arguing round a table. Now the most important character of a computer is that it can take an enormous number of factors into consideration; it is not bowled over by complexity as such, but it can only give these factors that 'consideration' which has been built into it, as its 'logic'. If its programme is based on a faulty theory, its results will be of little use, even if it has not left any factors out. At present, I doubt if we have an adequate theory to programme a computer to work out satisfactorily the tasks we now leave to the market. But perhaps to start with we should not ask for too much; even a computer whose theory was not quite right would find it difficult to do much worse than the market at the present time. Within the lifetimes of young people of today many of the functions of the market in fixing prices and wages, and levels and types of investment will probably be done on computers. That will also amount to 'an alternative to the money system'.

Appendix: Dansereau's 'Rights'

A. *Basic Ecological Rights of the Individual*

a. *Physiological Rights*

1. The right to daylight normal for the latitude.

2.   The right to breath air containing normal proportion of oxygen and free from toxic or otherwise noxious substances.
3.   The periodic right to a minimal quantity of water or equivalent liquids for drinking and washing.
4.   The periodic right to a minimal amount of edible, digestible, and innocuous plant and/or animal products.
5.   The right to shelter from excessive cold, heat, wind, and other environmental adversities.
6.   The right to procreation.

b.   *Psychological Rights*

7.   The right to minimum space in which to move and exercise.
8.   The right of freedom from sensorial shocks that might cause blindness, deafness, loss of sense of touch or taste, or lameness.
9.   The right to fulfil the sexual urge.
10. The right to engage in a wide range of attachments involving exchanges at several levels.

c.   *Social Rights*

11. The right of choice of abode.
12. The right to manage a household, involving minimal space, privacy and association.
13. The right to devote gainful energy by working on chosen resources by applying techniques that have been duly mastered.
14. The right to association for personal, professional, and other purposes.

d.   *Economic Rights*

15. The right to a minimum income that lifts barriers to the satisfaction of other rights by adequate participation in regional or national wealth.
16. The right to influence the channelling of resources and to determine priorities of exploitation.
17. The right to conserve and dispose of property.

e.   *Political Rights*

18. The right to an education that insures minimal access to the accumulated treasury of mankind's information and knowledge.
19. The right to accurate and timely information in all matters concerning the exploitation and management of all resources.
20. The right to minimal participation in decision-making.

f. *Religious Rights*

21. The right to adhere to a creed, whether personal or historically defined.
22. The right to join with others of similar persuasion in occasional or periodic worship or exercises and to acquire and conserve adequate facilities therefor.
23. The right to manage and employ resources in a way that is compatible with an accepted ethic prescription.

Further Reading

Health

A. G. Wolstenhome, M. O'Connor eds., *The Health of Mankind* (Churchill Livingstone, 1967).

B. Alex Comfort, *Biology of Senescence* (Routledge & Kegan Paul, 1956).

C. R.R. Kohn, *Principles of Mammalian Ageing* (Prentice Hall, 1971).

Work

D. Dennis Gabor, *The Mature Society* (Secker & Warburg, 1970).

E. James Martin and Adrian R.D. Norman, *The Computerised Society* (Prentice Hall, 1970) Chapters 2, 3, 4, 21, 23 and 29.

F. For leisure, see Jack Parsons, *Population versus Liberty* (Pemberton Books, 1971), Chapter 13; Ralph Glasser, *Leisure: Penalty or Prize* (Macmillan, London, 1970); or Fred Best ed., *The Future of Work* (Prentice Hall, 1972).

Wealth

G. J. Galbraith, *The Affluent Society* (Penguin, 1970).

H. Kenneth E. Boulding, *Beyond Economics* (Univ. Michigan Press, 1968).

I. E.J. Mishlan, *The Costs of Economic Growth* (Penguin, 1967).

J. Gunnar Mydral, *The World Poverty Problem*. 1972 Book of the Year, *Encyclopedia Britannica.*

K. For poor nations, see *Development & Environment* ('The Fauna Report'), UN Document GE 71–1378, and the 'Cocoyoc Declaration' from the UNEP/UNCTAD Symposium 'Patterns of Resource Use, Environment and Development Strategies', Cocoyoc, Mexico, October 1974, published in *Development*

Dialogue, September 1974, p. 88.

L.   For UK statistics relevant to social welfare, see the annual *Social Trends*, HMSO. Recent American discussions are: *Towards a Social Report* (Moncur Mason Report), US Dept. HEW, 1972. *The Quality of Life Concept*, US Environmental Protection Agency, Washington, DC, 1973. William Watts and Lloyd A. Free, *State of the Nation* (Universe Books, NY, 1973).

M.   There is now a quarterly journal *Social Indicators Research* (Reidel Publ. Co., Dordrecht, Holland), vol. 1, no. 1, May 1974.

References

1.   W.H. Le Riche, *Health of Mankind*, CIBA Foundation Symposium, 1967, p. 42.
2.   John Platt, *Medical Care and Society*, 9th CIOMS Conference, Rio de Janeiro, 1974.
3.   John Platt, 'The Urgency and the Pay Offs for Biomedical R and D', IUBS – Battelle Symposium on 'Biology Relevant to Human Welfare', Seattle, 1971.
4.   Alex Comfort, *Ageing, the Biology of Senescence* (Routledge & Kegan Paul, 1956).
5.   A.R. Kohn, *Principles of Mammalian Ageing* (Prentice Hall, 1971).
6.   C.A. Doxiadis, *Anthropopolis: A City for Human Development* (Athens Technological Centre, 1974), p. 278.
7.   From *World Health Chronicle*, 1973, *25*, 498, quoted in *Endeavour*, September 1972.
8.   Good general discussions are Fred Best ed., *The Future of Work* (Prentice Hall, 1972) and Stanley Packer, *The Future of Work and Leisure* (Paladin, 1972).
9.   Margaret Mead (in conversation).
10. Figures from J. Martin and A. Norman, *The Computerised Society* (Prentice Hall, 1970), Chapter 21.
11. Dennis Gabor, *The Mature Society* (Secker & Warburg, 1972).
12. E.F. Schumacher, 'Buddhist Economics', *Resurgence*, January–February 1968 and Chapter 4 of *Small Is Beautiful* (Blond & Briggs, 1973).
13. Source unknown.
14. Ivan Illich, *Deschooling Society* and *The Tools for Conviviality* (Calder & Boyars, 1973).
15. James Martin and Adrian Norman, *The Computerised Society* (Prentice Hall, 1970).
16. D. Gabor, *The Mature Society* (Secker & Warburg, 1972), p. 93.
17. Alvin Toffler, *Future Shock* (Bodley Head, 1970).
18. For a more thorough and sustained effort in this direction see Lars E. Bjork, 'An Experiment in Work Satisfaction', *Scientific American*, March 1975.
19. *Ceres*, September–October 1972, p. 31.
20. I. Papanek, *Design for the Real World* (Thames & Hudson, 1972).
21. Quoted from Supplement on Kenya in *The Times*, 21 September 1973.
22. Richard L. Meier, 'Material Resources' in R. Jungk and J. Galtung eds., *Mankind 2000* (Allen & Unwin, 1969).
23. *Japanese National Welfare*, Tokyo, Club of Rome; see *New Scientist 53*, 1972, p. 282.

24. 'Social Indicators', *The Economist*, 22 January 1972, p. 18.
25. Pierre Dansereau, 'The Dimensions of Environmental Quality', Commonwealth Human Ecology Council Conference, Malta, 1970. For other attempts to formulate the factors in 'wealth' in the broad sense, see the journal *Social Indicators Research*, and in particular David E. Christian, 'International Social Indicators: The OECD Experience' in September 1974 issue.
26. One general discussion of 'no-growth' economics is in *Daedalus*, Fall 1973.
27. J.W. Pringle, 'Biology as a Human Science', *Biologist*, November 1970, p.204.
28. Papers of the 9th Delos Symposium, 1971.
29. W.E. Westran and R.M. Gifford, 'Environmental Impact: Controlling the Overall View', *Science 181*, 819, 31 August 1973.
30. J. Martin and A. Norman, *The Computerised Society* (Prentice Hall, 1970), Chapter 4.

8 CONTROLLING THE NATURE OF MAN

Advanced biology is opening up the possibility of interventions in the operation of the human body which go beyond anything previously possible in medicine. Quite new problems are raised of ethics as well as of social arrangements. The problems raised by techniques for organ transplantation or various forms of very intense care for moribund patients mentioned in the last chapter are already well recognised by the medical profession, and there have been several good symposia on them, at which non-medical thinkers – biologists, philosophers, theologians – have participated.[1] They will not be further dealt with here.

Improving Conventional Medicine

Procedures for dealing with many diseases are already so effective that, in order to verify that a new method is an improvement, it may be necessary to test it on quite large numbers of subjects. Moreover, if the groups of subjects are to remain comparable, they may have to be shielded from the psychological effects that would be produced if the rationale of the procedure under test were fully explained to them. This obviously raises difficult ethical problems, of which the medical profession is already well aware.[2]

There is often another very real dilemma; a procedure aimed at relieving a recognised injury may have some harmful consequences which are spread thinly throughout a large population in such a way that they are hard to identify. As long ago as 1941[3] in a book called *The Scientific Attitude*, I pointed out that:

> adoption of methods of thought which are commonplaces in science would bring before the bar of ethical judgement whole groups of phenomena which do not appear there now... If a man hits a baby on the head with a hammer, we prosecute him for cruelty or murder; but if he sells dirty milk and the infant sickness or death-rate goes up, we merely fine him for contravening the health laws.

Some years later, Warren Weaver coined the phrase 'statistical morality', but the point is slow in gaining acceptance. Kaplan[4] points out that even today

> Because as a Society we do not intend specific accidental deaths and
> have no knowledge of them in their specificity, we feel that no moral
> issue is involved; yet we adopt social patterns whose inexorable
> consequence is death to tens of thousands.

Henry K. Beecher, in the same book, shows that adopting these social
patterns is not always mere insensitivity or ignorance: a real dilemma
may be involved:

> For example, in discussing new and uncertain risk against probable
> benefit, Lord Adrian spoke of the rise of mass radiography of the
> chest in Britain. Four-and-a-half-million examinations were made in
> 1957. It has been calculated that bone-marrow effects of the
> radiation might possibly have added as many as twenty cases of
> leukaemia in that year; yet the examinations revealed eighteen
> thousand cases of pulmonary tuberculosis needing supervision, as
> well as thousands of other abnormalities. The twenty deaths from
> leukaemia were only a remote possibility, but, Lord Adrian asks, if
> they were a certainty would they have been too tough a price to
> pay for the early detection of tuberculosis in eighteen thousand
> people?

As Medawar says, in his essay in the same volume: 'The contribution
of science is to have enlarged beyond all former bounds the evidence we
must take account of before forming our opinions.' He does not, however, offer us any clear advice about how to form our opinions after
we have taken all the necessary factors into consideration. Perhaps,
indeed, there is no very clear advice to be given. Kaplan argues that

> We can solve some problems in human life, but they are usually the
> less significant ones. Those that are more significant we do not solve,
> but at best we only *cope* with them. This is to say that we have no
> way of disposing of them: at best we learn to live with them, and
> go on to the next.

Certainly mankind is unlikely to find a clear-cut solution to these
conundrums in the near future. However, there has as yet been no
attempt to focus a really international discussion on these subjects, to
which it might be expected that thinkers from the many different

religions and philosophies of the world — Buddhist, Mohammedan, Jewish, Pagan as well as Christian — would each have characteristic contributions to make.

Genetic Engineering

We have recently learnt in considerable detail the chemical constitution of the molecules which carry hereditary potentials from one generation to the next and have discovered an adequate, though not yet exhaustive, working knowledge of how these molecules are synthesised and reproduced, and how they control the machinery by which the living proteins of the body are produced. This 'cracking of the genetic code' allows us at least to contemplate the prospects of creating new heredity potentials, or being able to repair or compensate for deficient ones, or determining which potentials shall be realised in a developing creature, and which denied expression.

The expression 'genetic engineering' is commonly used to refer to all human interventions in the natural processes by which hereditary potentialities become realised during the processes of development. Man has been engaged in such activities since the earliest times in which he cared for domestic livestock, but the recent discoveries have opened the way to actions with so much more far-reaching effects that there is a pressing need to think deeply about possible consequences before developing some of the technologically feasible procedures. In fact some manipulations on the genes of bacteria have already raised very genuine fears amongst the few specialists who know what has been happening. The risks seemed to some biologists already so great and so little understood that they have called for a voluntary moratorium on certain experiments until the situation has been clarified by high-level international dicussions between those technically experienced enough for a judgement at least at that level.[5] This must be taken as an impressive event. It is the first time in history in which scientists have themselves suggested a limitation on their freedom to explore any aspect of nature which seems interesting. (They might well have done the same about the development of atomic explosions if they had not been in the middle of a war which most of them believed justified; even so some senior physicists, such as Oppenheimer, argued against the development of the more terrible fusion explosives.)

However, the term 'genetic engineering' is commonly used also in a wider sense, to cover not only actions directly aimed at the genes, but also the planned alteration of the first substances produced by the genes and, even more widely, various procedures for controlling the early stages of development of the egg as a whole. Actually many of the same procedures are undertaken not so much for immediately useful results, but rather as parts of fundamental science. It seems sensible to discuss some of the less direct actions first; although perhaps slightly more mundane, some of them might have consequences which most people will think far-reaching enough.

Eugenics

People have always been concerned about the preservation and, more optimistically, the improvement of the genetic potentialities of the human race. 'Eugenics', as Galton named this subject about a century ago, has usually been considered under two headings: positive eugenics, which attempts to increase the proportion of 'good' genes, and negative which tries to decrease that of 'bad' genes. This section will be confined to a short summary of the present 'state of play' on some of the new possibilities.

The main available technique for increasing the frequency of 'good' genes would be to encourage widespread use, by artificial insemination, of male gametes derived from donors who are held to contain valuable genetic qualities. The techniques for using sperm derived from a living man in this way are well known and reasonably satisfactory. Bull sperm can already be stored in a functional condition for long periods and it should not be difficult to do the same with human material. Moreover, the rapidly advancing techniques for cell and organ culture make it reasonable to suppose that in the fairly near future it will be possible to keep spermatogonial cells in healthy and growing condition more or less indefinitely. By one or other method sperm from a given individual may be made available long after his death.

Methods for handling eggs in similar ways are more difficult but not at all impossible.[6] Mature human eggs have already been collected from excised ovaries and more recently from living women. Further cultivation of ovarial tissue for longer periods should not prove too difficult, though it has not yet been done. Recently we have found adequate *in vitro* techniques for fertilising the eggs of most species of mammals, including man. Methods for implanting fertilised eggs into the uteri of hormonally prepared females, who then act as foster mothers, are easy and well understood.

There are, however, very considerable difficulties in the way of widespread use of such methods. These are partly social, concerned with the readiness of people to accept a vicarious paternity of this kind. Possibly even more serious are the problems of deciding who is a desirable donor. There are three categories of difficult questions. First, it would have to be decided that certain people are particularly valuable members of society. Although it might be possible to arrive at a consensus about the value of certain types of individual, it is very doubtful if one could get general agreement about the value of all the different kinds of people who contribute in different but necessary ways to a complex modern society. Moreover, there are very few, if any, individuals who possess nothing but valuable qualities, and how are we to arrive at a balanced judgement which takes into account a person's worst qualities as well as his or her better ones.

Secondly, gametes derived from a parent of one sex may give rise to an offspring of the other sex. Even if we could decide that a given donor carried qualities which would be valuable in offspring of the same sex, it would be much more difficult to determine whether those qualities would be valuable in the other. This is the type of problem which faces the dairy-cattle breeder. He deals with it by methods of testing the breeding qualities of his bulls by measuring the milk yield of their daughters. This is a time-consuming procedure, which involves much closer control over biological pedigrees than is likely ever to be acceptable amongst men.

Finally, the fact that sperm participate in the production of both males and females is only one example of the basic hereditary process of segregation. Genes which may be together in the diploid cells of an organism, and whose interaction endows that organism with desirable qualities, may very well become separated from one another in the gametes. It is by no means safe to predict an individual's breeding value from his actual appearance and performance during his lifetime. Positive eugenic measures of this kind therefore seem likely to come into use only very slowly in spite of the technical possibilities.

The problems of positive eugenics should most probably be considered in connection with the wider question of the control of the total number of births. This of course already raises many problems for members of certain religious communities. It was argued in Chapter 1 that the pressure of circumstances, and reflection on the implications of effective birth control, may lead to the transfer of religious significance from 'marriage as a license for sexual activity' to 'reproduction as a licence to add a new individual to society'. If any such shift occurred, it is likely that an increased awareness of the values attaching to reproduction might lead to a greater readiness to consider ways of ensuring that the new individual who is being conceived will have the best genetic constitution possible.

Negative eugenics also runs into great difficulties. The majority of obviously harmful hereditary conditions are determined by genes which are more or less completely recessive. The deleterious condition appears in a small fraction of the population, and even if these do not breed or are restrained from breeding, this will have little effect on the frequency of the gene, since most examples of it occur in apparently normal heterozygous carriers. The most likely developments in this field in the near future are improvements in methods for detecting the heterozygotes for certain harmful genes. An individual who carries one dose of a gene determining a biochemical deficiency may often appear normal enough under ordinary conditions, but the heterozygous state may produce an enhanced sensitivity to a degree of biochemical deprivation which the normal homozygote can deal with adequately enough. One can, for instance, distinguish heterozygotes for all the genes determining abnormal types of haemoglobin, and for quite a large number of metabolic disorders, such as phenylketonuria, cystinuria, galactosemia and several others.

It is likely that more methods of this kind will be developed in the next few years. In particular in recent years there has been a very rapid and continuing development of techniques for detecting defective embryos at an early stage in their development, when it may be possible either to treat them more effectively than later on, or even bring about their abortion at such an early stage that the objections to this procedure would be minimised. In the main these techniques depend on taking small samples of cells from an early developing embryo and checking these for the presence of hereditary defects.[7] This method is technically known as 'amniocentesis'. It can save a great deal of unhappiness due to the birth of defective children, and makes it possible for a couple who know they have a certain likelihood of producing a hereditarily crippled child nevertheless to proceed to conceive an infant in the confidence that if it is defective it could be aborted at an early stage so that they could try again.

However, even if we become able to detect heterozygous carriers of many deleterious genes, it is by no means clear what will be the right thing to do about them. It is a rather general, though by no means universal, observation that heterozygotes for 'bad' genes tend to do better in many respects than homozygotes even for supposedly 'good' genes. This probably applies more often when the 'bad' genes are not very harmful when homozygous. Where the homozygote is very seriously defective, the heterozygote is usually somewhat disadvantaged also; for instance, heterozygotes for phenylketonuria have a rather

higher than average incidence of mental disorder, those for
cystinuria some degree of renal disfunction. As examples on the other
side, heterozygotes for sickle-cell haemoglobin are more resistant than
normal to malaria (but poor at withstanding the low oxygen tension
at high altitude) and it has been claimed that artistic ability is higher
in schizophrenic pedigrees. But when the harmful effects are relatively
slight it is not unusual, in animals in general, to find that heterozygotes
enjoy some advantages over both types of homozygote. Human
individuals are heterozygous for such an enormous number of genes
that it seems more than probable that many of the most valuable
individuals in society are carriers of one or more genes which might be
considered unfavourable in the homozygous condition. The situation
is almost certainly too complex for it to seem sensible to formulate a
general over-all policy about the breeding of the carriers or harmful
recessives.

There is, however, a good case for a much greater development of
informed 'genetic counselling' which attempts to ascertain the facts
and expound their probable outcome in particular cases to potential
parents, allowing them then to make up their own minds.[8]

Molecular Biological Engineering[9]

The recent advances of genetics and molecular and cellular biology
suggest some methods by which we might be able to go well beyond
the types of interference with natural genetic processes that have
been considered above and to carry out genetic engineering in the
primary sense mentioned earlier.

By now almost everyone has learnt that the hereditary potentialities
of the genes are encoded in sequences of nucleotide bases which are
strung together to form the long thread-like double helical molecules
of DNA. People know too that this DNA is first transcribed into a
corresponding RNA and that the RNA is translated with the aid of
small bodies called ribosomes and other enzymes into sequences of
amino-acids which constitute proteins. It is the interactions of these
proteins with each other and with the pre-existing materials in the
egg cell which brings about the development of the egg into an adult
organism. Molecular biological engineering aims to control these
processes at some stage or other.

Before discussing some of the ideas which have been put forward,
there are two points which need emphasising. One is that many of the
notions advanced by the more euphoric biologists are still well over
the horizon of the possible. They are things which *might* be achievable,

not from what we know or can do already, but on the basis of advances we might hope, with more or less reasonable expectation, to achieve in the not too distant future. That is to say, they are not to be dismissed as mere 'science fiction' which assumes quite arbitrary advances; but they, or many of them, are still pretty far-out.

The second point is that it would cost a great deal to make the fundamental discoveries in knowledge and technique, and then much more again, probably ten or a hundred times more, to develop the methods to the standard of reliability and lack of undesirable side effects that are demanded of methods which are to be used on man. So, even if some of these suggestions do after all turn out to be practical, their use will be dependent on the expenditure of large amounts of time and money on development work — so much money that it is almost certain to be taxpayers' money. The taxpayer will therefore be able to have some say in whether the development is undertaken or not.

These methods are very unlikely to be used unless the majority of people in a society call for their use. Man has known for centuries of a somewhat slow, but eventually very effective, method of genetic engineering, namely selective breeding. This was the means by which he has produced such drastically modified individuals as those of different races of dogs, for instance. There is no biological reason why similar procedures should not prove equally effective with human beings. In practice social forces have prevented this being done. Many of the far-fetched types of genetic engineering discussed in the public press will meet similar repudiation. Moreover, it is difficult to see how any enterprising private firm could anticipate a sufficient margin of profit from socially undesirable developments in this field to justify the expenditure that would be necessary. There is, therefore, little need to fear that we shall be suddenly confronted with some new nightmarish genetic engineering technology without having had notice in advance, and even having been asked to foot the bill, which we can well refuse to do. There are, however, some of these possibilities which hold out considerable hopes and which society may think worth while encouraging and paying for.

The most radical type of genetic engineering would be to produce copies of the desirable forms of genes, or to manufacture new hereditary material designed to produce a given effect, and then to insert these into the hereditary constitution of an animal or plant.

In some instances we already know precisely the change in a gene-controlled protein which renders it ineffective in carrying out its normal biological role. For instance in sickle-cell haemoglobin the amino-acid valine has been substituted for glutamic acid at position 6 in the β polypeptide chain. The genetic code has been worked out well enough for one to have considerable confidence as to the nature of the change in nucleotides in the DNA controlling this haemoglobin. If we can specify, in as precise terms as this, the chemical nature of a deleterious hereditary factor, surely it might be possible for us to control it and to restore the mutated gene to a more usefully functioning form.

The manufacture of new DNA molecules with a preselected sequence of nucleotide bases would be a major step to understanding the biochemistry of this substance, and work is going on rapidly in this direction. However, the second two parts of the whole project are very probably much more difficult to achieve — we have, as yet, almost no understanding of the precise relationship between a certain sequence of nucleotide bases in DNA and the functional effect of the protein produced by this gene. We shall probably slowly approach an understanding of this problem, but it looks as though it will be a very, very long time before we get near to it. This means that we cannot expect, for a long time to come, to be able to design and build a gene which will produce a protein capable of doing a specific job. The best we could hope for is to rely on finding a suitable gene in some healthy organism and transfer it to the place where we want it. An even greater difficulty is that it seems certain that most of the really important features of the human character have, as their hereditary base, not a single gene but quite a large number. Everything we know suggests that we cannot ever hope to recognise a gene for intelligence, or honesty, or even cleverness in a single special ability such as mathematics, or efficiency at a particular task such as long-distance running or high-jumping. Excellence at such activities always depends on the combined actions of many genes (together with reinforcing effects of environmental factors). And, of course, if there is no one gene for such a character, we cannot synthesise it and put it into place.

When we are dealing with one of the simpler components of the human developmental repertoire, which does depend on the presence of a single enzyme controlled by a single gene, the final stage of incorporating the gene into the hereditary material is perhaps not quite so far away. We know that under some circumstances certain viruses can carry genes from one species of bacteria into another. It was, in fact, a rather unexpectedly rapid success in achieving this that has led to the suggestion that there should be a halt to this type of work until there has been time to digest its implications. Molecular biologists have normally used for their experiments a type of bacteria which is resident in the human gut, and a very harmless creature as bacteria go. They have therefore tended to be rather slack in their techniques of handling it, not taking the trouble to carry out all the rigorous checks and precautions which would be enforced in laboratories which have to deal with disease-carrying bacteria, let alone those which are developed for biological warfare laboratories. But no one can tell off-hand just what unpleasant and dangerous new strains of bacteria might be produced if new hereditary material becomes incorporated into a previously harmless type. For instance, the new material might render it resistant to some of the antibiotics on which we so much rely to suppress bacterial diseases; equally, if we could fully control the process, we might use it to render bacteria more sensitive to them. At the present time it looks as though the biologists in this field of work will have to learn to accept the much more rigorous, time-consuming and vexatious methods of always playing absolutely safe when handling bacteria which their colleagues in the medical field have already become resigned to; and there seems to be a good case for helping the leaders who called for the moratorium to enforce it until that time comes.

In higher organisms, such as man, the DNA of the genes is combined with protein, whereas in bacteria the gene-DNA is not protected in this way. This makes the transfer of genes into such a system much more difficult than into the pure DNA genetic system of bacteria. If any way is discovered for making the process work, then one might tackle the next stage of the difficulty, that of seeing that the virus picked up the right gene and transferred it into the right place in the recipient cell. It is just possible to contemplate the possibility of using some method such as this to exchange a defective gene for one selected from those already existing in healthy animals. To make the process work reliably enough to be useful even in such crude enterprises as animal or plant breeding would probably need at least one or two decades after the first demonstration of the mere possibility. To refine it so that it worked reliably enough for human use would probable take the same amount of time again.

The real drive to achieve transfer of genes into the genetic system of higher organisms seems to me likely to come, not from any ambition to alter the human genes, but in an agricultural context. All human food has been derived ultimately from the growth of plants, which get their energy from the solar radiation but require some mineral salts from the soil and some materials from the atmosphere. Almost all plants must take up their supplies of nitrogen, essential for the formation of proteins, from soluble salts in the soil; but in nature nitrogen gets into the soil in a form usable by plants, almost entirely by the action of a few types of bacteria, which can 'fix' atmospheric nitrogen, that is to say, convert it into a soluble compound. At present, man supplements this natural supply by an almost equal quantity of atmospheric nitrogen which he fixes by chemical reactions; but these demand very large quantities of energy, both for the fixation and for the transport and spreading of the product. As the world population grows and food resources need to be increased, the pressure to find other ways of providing nitrogen-containing fertilisers will become enormous. The nitrogen-fixing ability of those bacteria which possess it probably depends only on one or at most a few genes; could one transfer them to higher plants, endow our main crops, wheat, maize, potatoes and so on, with the capacity to manufacture their own nitrogen fertilisers?[10] It would be a gift to mankind almost as valuable as fire. Already the technical possibilities look sufficiently promising, for several groups of biologists — though probably not yet as many as might be — are working on it. This is where the problem of transfer of new genetic abilities into higher organisms is likely to be solved, rather than in the context of trying to breed 'improved' human beings.

There are much greater possibilities of altering hereditary constitutions by transferring not single genes but, rather, whole chromosomes which contain a few hundred or thousand genes. This is a trick that has been used for many years in the breeding of plants. It is relatively easy to make plant hybrids, and one can afford to produce vast numbers of infertile seeds or worthless plants for the sake of getting one with a good combination of hereditary characters. An important method of transferring disease resistance from a wild plant species into a more productive cultivated one has been to transfer single chromosomes from the wild species in the hope that one of them will carry the factors for disease resistance. In animal breeding, it has until recently not been possible to do this, but now techniques for achieving the result are in sight, though not yet developed.

Possible techniques for transferring, say, an antelope chromosome into the genetic apparatus of a cow were discussed in Chapter 3, in connection with developing new sources of animal protein.

It is perhaps worth noting that there is another technique for making rather a different kind of hybrid between strains of mammals. Several embryologists studying mammalian development have recently found it possible to fuse together very young embryos of different strains of mice, at a time when the eggs have divided into only four or eight cells. From these fused eggs they have been able to rear normal healthy adults, which are built up of cells coming from the two different strains.[11] Such an animal is known as a 'mosaic-hybrid', because its body is a mosaic of one type of cell mixed in with the other type. They have appeared quite healthy and surprisingly, perhaps to the biologist disappointingly, normal. Perhaps this is because in the experiments made so far the fusion was between strains which differed only in genes controlling easily recognisable but superficial characters, such as coat colour, type of hair and so on. One is bound to ask what would happen if one fused together strains which differed markedly in some aspect of their behaviour and brain functioning. This is a new type of genetic engineering which will bear watching.

There are a number of less basic manipulations of the genetic material which seem much more likely to become practical in the fairly near future. Many of these raise ethical and social problems of the gravest kind. One rather immediate prospect is that of being able to exert some influence on the character of those very few sperm, amongst the millions that are shed, which actually effect fertilisation. The sperm carry one representative of each type of gene, and there is no *a priori* reason why one should not find methods of eliminating from effective action those sperm which carry genes of a kind against which one wishes to discriminate.

Probably the most immediate prospect is to discriminate against sperm determining one or other of the two sexes.[12] Here one only has to distinguish between sperm which differ by as much as a whole chromosome, the female-determining type carrying an X and the male-determining a Y chromosome. Work is quite actively in progress in several centres on this problem. If, or perhaps one should rather say when, it is solved man will be faced with the possibility of determining whether his next offspring will be a son or a daughter. One wonders whether we are intellectually, emotionally, or morally prepared to face such choices. As mentioned in Chapter 1, it might be very important for attempts to control population growth. A recent study of opinions in America[13] came to the conclusion that 'there would be a temporary surplus of male births in the first couple of years. This would be followed by a wave of female births to achieve balance, and the oscillations would eventually damp out.' Ultimately, under conditions of sex pre-selection, the sex ratio would be similar to the existing natural sex ratio at birth of 105 males to 100 females. So the US population, at least, might not behave so irrationally as some people fear.

In Chapter 3 we also discussed the possibilities for producing multiple 'identical twins' of high-grade hybrid animals. The reader may well ask; but could we not use the same processes to make multiple copies of humans, or the most sinister hybrids between man and his anthropoid ape cousins? It is certainly not looking very far ahead to envisage the technical possibility of producing a human zygote by controlled fertilisation between an egg and a sperm from designated individuals, allowing this to cleave into a number of cells which would be transplanted individually into a number of foster-mothers, and in this way producing a clone of genetically identical human individuals. These would be like identical twins, except that there might be many more than two of them and, although genetically identical, they would have been nurtured in the uteri of different mothers. The consequences, for the people concerned, or even for the whole concept of human individuality, are impossible to foresee. But there would have to be much more experience of such processes in domestic animals before society would be in a position to decide whether anything of this kind can be allowed to occur among human beings. The inherent costliness, and the implied control by the state, provides assurance that society will have an opportunity to take the decisions. Summing up then, it seems that the main immediate dangers from genetic engineering lie in the field of tampering with the genetic systems of bacteria. If factors conferring resistance to antibiotics became incorporated into disease bacteria, and these modified strains escaped from the laboratories into the general public, our present medical resources would be severely strained. It was probably wise of the biologists concerned to call a moratorium on this type of research until they had discussed plans for dealing with this threat — plans which will probably involve insistence on expensive and time-consuming protective measures, such as those already in use in laboratories which cannot avoid handling dangerous micro-organisms, such as public health laboratories or the former Biological Warfare Establishments. An additional safeguard is to use for such experiments only strains of bacteria which die unless they are provided with special substances available in a laboratory, but not in the world outside. The other genetical engineering projects seem all to demand such large-scale funding, and such considerable periods of research and development before they could be made to work, that it seems that society could keep control of them, provided, of course, that suitable organisations were set up to keep watch on their progress. But most of these projects look as though the main interests likely to urge their development will be agricultural rather than medical; and agricultural research is rather well organised, mostly under government auspices. The genetical engineering which man has freely engaged in in the past, such as selective breeding of improved strains of plants and animals, has provided the agricultural world with considerable experience in such matters, and I see no reason to doubt that it can deal with the new more radical, but more speculative, prospects also.

Personality Control by Chemicals[14]

The development of drugs capable of affecting mental sensations, such as pain, and mental states and emotions, including those involved in many types of illness, has long been one of the central tasks of pharmacology. With the increasing importance of mental illness among all causes of ill health, these efforts are bound to increase in the future. It seems certain that we shall reach a much greater understanding of the biochemical mechanisms involved in brain function, and a very much greater ability to affect these processes in subtle and sophisticated ways. Along with the many benefits that such advances will bring there are obviously many dangers.

One of these major problems is already with us in many parts of the world; namely the conscious use of mind-affecting drugs. It is, of course, true that for many centuries men have accepted as normal the use of different substances; for instance, alcohol and nicotine in some regions, marijuana, opium and various fungi in others. The circumstances in which the substances are used have often been codified or ritualised in various societies, but even so there have been deleterious effects on certain individuals. Even after many centuries of the socially acceptable employment of alcohol in western societies, pathological alcoholism is still an important problem.

The difficulties that can be foreseen in the future arise from the availability of a much greater variety of agents, some of them more potent than almost anything man has used before, and most of them probably producing long-term or delayed effects about which extremely little is known. Many, but not all, of the substances, are likely to be habit-forming. There is already, of course, international recognition of the dangers of this situation, and a considerable body of international action is taken in connection with it. It may be doubted, however, whether this machinery is adequate to deal with the vastly greater range of synthetic drugs which are beginning to be available now and will certainly increase in the future.

Nowadays there is widespread questioning of the validity of the conventional accepted definition of the 'harm' that drugs may produce. To many people, particularly younger ones, it is by no means self-evident that all abnormal mental states are necessarily harmful or to be condemned, or at any rate that they are more reprehensible and deleterious than the abnormal states induced by socially accepted substances such as alcohol. Already carefully reasoned arguments are being put forward in many countries for the legalisation of some mind-affecting substances which have previously been banned by law, e.g. marijuana in Europe and North America. Since these substances are relatively easily transported from one country to another, it is clear that some international agreement about such matters is greatly to be desired.

Socially powerful agencies of one kind or another might use mind-affecting drugs which are difficult to detect in an attempt to control the reactions of great masses of the population. This is a conceivable mode of warfare and, in the context of peace, the threat would amount to a more subtle and powerful form of the old policy of keeping the plebs in passive contentment by bread and circuses. It might be argued that much of the highly publicised sport and television and other public entertainment, which are such obtrusive features of civilised societies today, already to some extent limit the freedom in practice of many individuals to develop as fully adult responsible human beings by seducing their attention on to trivialities. Such 'dangers' to man's right to a full development are at present generally accepted by society. The question arises, at what point do practices aimed at diverting attention from important issues become unacceptable?

The conscience of mankind would surely be outraged if a ruling autocracy put a tranquillising drug into the water supplies or the bread, but what if they lifted all taxation or control of alcohol, marijuana and other such substances? Has mankind the right to be protected from the exercise of such powers against it? And if so, at what point in the spectrum does this right begin to be important? Furthermore, can mankind in practice be defended in this respect? In a pluralistic democratic society any widespread attempt to influence political or other opinions by means of drugs would be detected and countered by opponents of the agencies that tried to put it into effect. It is only in societies with a clearly defined ruling class, sharply differentiated from the large body of the populace, that the danger could arise; and in such societies it is difficult to see how an outside authority could materially affect the situation, except by expressing moral disapproval.

Other Techniques of Controlling Human Behaviour

A rapidly advancing area of biology is concerned with the study of learning in animals and the methods by which this can be accelerated, so that the behaviour of the animals becomes adapted to the will of the experimenter or the person setting the task to be accomplished. Some of these techniques might be effective in controlling the behaviour of man, at least in certain respects. The limitations of their use in man are not well understood, and it seems likely that more and more powerful techniques will be discovered for controlling human behaviour over a wide range of activities. Moreover, besides these methods derived from the experiments on animals (such as Skinner's method of 'shaping behaviour' by instant reinforcement),[15] there are other methods applicable primarily to human beings (such as subliminal suggestion) and, although many of these are of doubtful effectiveness, others of greater power may well be developed in the future. Again there is an important question; which of such methods can be judged offensive to natural human rights and dignity, and under what circumstances?

B.F. Skinner, who developed many of the most powerful methods pertaining to animals, pointed out that man in his natural social relations already uses many of the processes for reinforcing tendencies of behaviour which he wishes to encourage and which provide the basis for the systematic practices of animal training. Although few human beings have a formulated understanding of their methods of influencing other people's behaviour, many individuals (politicians, salesmen and the like) are exceedingly skilful in employing their semi-conscious skills. We can perhaps rely on native shrewdness to guard against the orator or persuasive arguer, but can we legislate against similar influences on the ground that they are being carried out according to consciously thought-out rules and theories?

Even if we had good reason to believe that the science of psychology had developed methods of influencing behaviour more powerful than those of Hitler and Stalin, it is not obvious at first sight what actions could be taken to prevent abuse of such methods. It may well be that this is an area in which the individual man has to take responsibility for his own actions and his own response to the various forms of social pressure and persuasion to which he will be subjected. Possibly his greatest safeguard will be to ensure the continuation of political systems which allow the existence of conflicting and competing pressures and persuasions. But the possibility of control of the actual nature of the methods used for persuasion does require further debate before it is rejected as impractical.

Most people have seen these new techniques of 'shaping behaviour' as a threat to human self-integrity and responsibility, but Skinner himself, and also such a perceptive writer as John Platt, argue that they have a great potentiality for good if rightly used. Even they would, I think, be unlikely to approve the imposition of such 'behaviour shaping' on criminal prisoners as methods of rehabilitation; this has been tried in some American prisons, but seems to have been discontinued after a fairly short trial.

There are other new methods of influencing behaviour for which their sponsors express great hopes. They fall nearer to the norm of educational practices. It is clear that, if we realise the increase in leisure, in knowledge and understanding, and the greater flexibility in life-styles which we may anticipate, mankind will experience a pressing need for more effective education, lasting through a longer period of his life. We have already come a long way from the days of learning purely by rote, when the children repeated the orthodox texts over and over until they knew them by heart, but we still know very little about the best methods of training young minds to be receptive, critically flexible and with a reasonable store of useful data in their memory. Some scientists, such as Seymour Papert, argue strongly that allowing quite young children to play with simple computer programmes, which they can write themselves, then feed into machines and watch the result, opens quite new doors of mental development. The children may, for instance, play specially devised games, or follow out the results of applying a set of logical rules to some simple axioms. They are then likely to acquire some skill in reasoning or some understanding, not always clearly formulated, about what axioms are necessary and what logical rules allow if anything sensible, or even anything at all, is to emerge. It is perhaps too early to say whether the promised results of such new educational techniques will actually be realised in practice. But here, at least, is a very up-to-date technique of modifying man's character which seems to hold out more promise than threat.

Further Reading

A. Alun Jones and Walter E. Bodmer, *Our Future Inheritance: Choice or Chance* (Oxford University Press, 1974).

B. Gerald Leach, *The Biocrats* (Penguin, 1972).
Some earlier general discussions, still very worth while, are:
C. Joshua Lederberg, 'Experimental Genetics and Human Evolution',
    Amer. Nat. 1966 and *Bulletin of the Atomic Scientists,* October
    1966. Th. Dobzhansky, *Mankind Evolving* (Yale University Press,
    1962) and *The Biology of Ultimate Concern* (New American
    Library, 1967). C.H. Waddington, *The Ethical Animal* (George
    Allen & Unwin, 1960; Chicago University Press – paperback, 1971)
    and *Biology, Purpose and Ethics* (Barre Westover, 1971). ·

Notes

1. *Ethics in Medical Progress*, CIBA Foundation (Churchill, 1966); F.J. Ebling
    ed., *Biology and Ethics*, Institute of Biology Symposium (Academic Press,
    1969).
2. For instance, 'Ethical Aspects of Experimentation on Human Subjects',
    Daedalus, Spring 1969; Sissela Bok, 'The Ethics of Giving Placebos', *Scientific
    American*, November 1974.
3. C.H. Waddington, *The Scientific Attitude* (Penguin Books, 1941; revised
    1948, 1968).
4. Edward Shils and others, *Life or Death: Ethics and Options* (University
    Washington Press, 1968).
5. This may be said to have been begun by a letter to *Science 185*, 26 July 1974,
    p. 303, by Paul Berg and others ('Potential Biohazards of Recombinant
    DNA Molecules'). This led to an international conference of biologists
    ('Asilomar Conference on Recombinant DNA Molecules', Paul Berg and
    others, *Science 188*, 6 June 1975, p. 991). There were also official enquiries:
    in Britain, the 'Ashby Report', submitted to Parliament, January 1975 (Cmd.
    5880 HMSO); and in the USA a Program Advisory Committee on the subject
    was set up in the National Institute of Health.. Legislation is being prepared
    at the present time in both countries; and some action by the UN seems
    likely.
6. Alun Jones and Walter F. Bodmer, *Our Future Inheritance; Choice or Chance*,
    for Brit. Assoc. Adv.Sci. Working Party (Oxford University Press, 1974); C.R.
    Austin and R.V. Short, *The Artificial Control of Reproduction* (Cambridge
    University Press, 1972); Robert G. Edwards and David J. Sharpe, 'Social
    Values and Research in Human Embryology', *Nature*, 14 May 1971.
7. Arno G. Motulsky, 'Brave New World?', *Science 185*, 23 August 1974, p. 653.
    Amitai Etzioni ed., *Symposium on Ethical and Public Policy Issues in
    Amniocentesis and Biomedical Innovation*, Amer.Assoc.Adv.Sci. San
    Francisco meeting, 1974; Maureen Harris ed., *Early Diagnosis of Human
    Genetic Defects*, US Dept. of Health, Education and Welfare, Public no.
    NIH 72–25, 1972. *Genetics and the Quality of Life*, World Council of
    Churches, June 1973.
8. Alun Jones and Walter P. Bodmer, *Our Future Inheritance; Choice or Change*,
    for Brit.Assoc.Adv.Sci.Working Party (Oxford University Press, 1974).
9. See refs. 5 and 6.
10. W.D.P. Stewart ed., *Nitrogen Fixation by Free-living Micro-organisms* and
    P.S. Nutman ed., *Symbiotic Nitrogen Fixation in Plants,* will appear soon
    as vols. 6 and 7 in the series of IBP Monographs, published by Cambridge

University Press.
11. See for instance, M.S. Stern, 'Chimaeras obtained by aggregation of mouse eggs with rat eggs', *Nature*, 22 June 1973, 243: 472.
12. C.H. Kiddy and H.D. Hafs eds., *Sex ratio at Birth – Prospects for Control*, Symp.Amer.Soc.Animal Sci., 1971.
13. Charles F. Westoff and R. Rindfuss, 'Sex Pre-selection in the US: Some Implications', *Science*, 10 May 1974, *184*: 633.
14. Charles T. Tart ed., *Altered States of Consciousness* (Wiley, New York, 1969); Charles T. Tart, 'States of Consciousness and State-Specific Sciences', *Science*, 16 June 1972, *176*, p. 1203; Roland Fischer, 'A Cartography of the Ecstatic and Meditative States', *Science*, 26 November 1971, p. 897.
15. See B.F. Skinner, *Beyond Freedom and Dignity* (Cape, 1972) and, for criticism of it, the review by Noam Chomsky in *NY Review of Books*, 30 December 1971, and discussion in Harvey Wheeler ed., *Beyond the Primitive Society* (W.H. Freeman, 1973).

9 POLLUTION

The pollution of the environment has been perhaps the most widely publicised of the difficulties man faces in the next few decades. It made its first major impact on the public imagination with the publication of Rachel Carson's book *The Silent Spring* in 1962. She argued that residues of insecticides, such as DDT, were accumulating in the environment at such a rate that they would soon kill off nearly all the birds and animals that we are used to finding in our surroundings. Since then various other forms of pollution have been at the top of the list of subjects for arousing public indignation. So much so that there has been a considerable backlash. It has been easy to show that some of the dire prophecies of gloom were grossly exaggerated. For instance, 'doomsters' claimed that the escape of mercury and its salts from industrial processes and from anti-fungal seed dressings used in agriculture was in danger of causing a complete poisoning of the seas. But, the growth-promoters countered, the sea already contains mercury that has been slowly washed into it off the land throughout geological ages and a calculation shows that if the whole mercury production of the world's industry went straight into the sea, it would take between 2,500 and 10,000 years to double the quantity that is there already. That sounds very comforting, but actually it does not change the fact that quite a large number of people, some thousands at least, have died or become gravely ill from eating seafood taken from waters in which industrial effluent has raised the local mercury content to quite unacceptable levels.[1] Thus problems of pollution need looking into with some care.

There is certainly not time and space here to examine each of the pollution problems in detail. I will only deal with some general principles and one or two instances where it is arguable that pollution might become of global importance.

There is pollution of air, of land and of waters. Probably the last is in the long run most dangerous, but we will deal with them in this order. Before discussing modern types of pollution, it is as well to remember that pre-industrial environments were, and in many parts of the world still are, highly polluted with agents very dangerous to man. These are basically biological agents, such as viruses, bacteria and eggs of intestinal and other parasites. Modern industry is putting some nasty things into our environment now, but at least it has removed these even nastier ones from the regions where it is at all well developed. The mean expectation of life is almost always increased in a region when industry begins to be developed there, and this shows that modern industrial pollution on balance is less harmful to health than the biological pollution of low-technology societies. This is no reason to be complacent about industrial pollution, but it does put it into some perspective.

It is in fact often very difficult to decide about the real importance of pollution. For instance, one of the most quoted examples of the insidious effects of slightly elevated concentrations of an industrial pollutant concerns lead. No one doubts that this is a poison at high concentrations. The main evidence that fairly small increases in the level of lead in the blood have harmful effects comes from studies on children living in rather derelict old tenements in the centre of American cities. The paints used many years ago contained much more lead than would be permitted nowadays and, now that they are dry and flaking, young children have been seen picking off and eating flakes of dried paint for the sake of their slightly sweet taste; and, of course, there is a good deal of lead from automobile fumes in the streets. The children have somewhat elevated levels of lead in their blood and show a some-what lower scholastic performance and mental alertness than is typical for their age group and the country as a whole. Where the problem arises is that they are on the whole members of very poor families. How far is their low performance due to the lead pollution and how far to general poverty? Only a very elaborate, expensive and time-consuming series of experiments could sort out precisely the relative importance of the two. Of course, the practical thing to do is not to fuss about the academic problem of assigning so much of the harm to poverty and so much to lead, but to get busy trying to alleviate both these pernicious influences by any means that are available and efficacious. But this is a situation that should put one on one's guard against being tempted to attribute some social evil wholly to a fashionable external material cause like lead pollution and to take this as an excuse to forget a much more general and powerful source of evil such as simple poverty.

Air Pollution

The modern pollution of the air in industrial societies comes from two main sources which it is useful to distinguish. The first are the materials — either gases or small particles of soot or ash — emitted into the air through the chimneys of industrial factories, power-generating or refuse-incinerating plants and the like; and the second is the automobile with its internal combustion engine.

Contamination of the air by industry is not at all a new phenomenon. It is doubtful whether the polluted air of present industrial cities is any more malodorous or obnoxious to health than the stinking smoky atmosphere of pre-technological cities, inadequately drained and warmed by fires of wood, soft coal or dung, from ancient Rome to modern Calcutta. Even the smogs of Los Angeles are probably little worse than the infamous pea soup fogs of Dickensian London. Industrial pollution of cities may have reached its peak of intensity in the early years of this century. The typical conditions about 40 years ago in a city (Leeds, England), dominated by industry in an early technological stage of development, have recently been described by a very responsible English scientist (Dr Kathleen Lonsdale, FRS):[2]

When as a young scientist 42 years ago, I married and went to live where my husband worked in Leeds, I found that life, although delightful in many ways, was rather grim in others. The countryside was easy of access but looking back from the higher land a few miles from the centre, Leeds could never be seen. It was covered by a pall of smoke. This was not ordinary smoke. It consisted of large sticky particles of soot. In order to be able to open the windows, we made special frames covered in net that could be place in the openings. Otherwise the carpets and furniture would have been covered within an hour with a film of smuts. Leeds housewives were remarkably houseproud. They cleaned and washed and cleaned and washed endlessly. They had to, if they wanted to keep reasonably clean. I was not so houseproud, because I wanted to continue my scientific research at the University. But even I washed my curtains every week. Now, in rural surroundings, I only wash them once a year, and they hardly look as if they needed even that. When we had our first baby and wanted to put her outside in her pram, we covered the whole pram with a net, a fresh one every time; I brought it in spotted like a leopard after two or three hours; big black spots of soot, that would otherwise have fallen on her, as they did on all the Leeds buildings. This was my first real experience of technological pollution. It made a lasting impression on me.

Such conditions scarcely exist any longer in the most advanced industrial countries. They have been overcome by legislative measures such as Clean Air Acts, or regulations establishing smokeless zones. They may well recur in countries which are rapidly developing their industrial potential, but the conditions that give rise to them are well understood and the hazards to health which they offer fully appreciated. The difficulties which may lead to their recurrence are primarily economic; all it takes is legislation, and money, to deal with this relatively primitive type of industrial pollution.

There is a simple mistake about the economics of pollution-control, into which people often fall. All control costs something; they argue that the best policy would be to go on paying until the total benefit obtained is equalled by the total cost involved. (The benefit is not necessarily proportional to the reduction in concentration of the pollutants; there may be very little benefit from a slight reduction, advantage coming only when the pollutant is considerably reduced; reduction beyond a certain level may again bring little real gain. It is important to measure the real, effective benefits.) But the optimum policy is not to go on until benefits equal costs; one should go on until the 'marginal' benefit is equal to the 'marginal' cost. That is economists' jargon for the situation when, for every extra pound or dollar spent, you will reap one pound or dollar's worth of benefit. In many situations, the graph of benefits against cost looks something

Figure 9.1: Costs and Benefits in Pollution Control

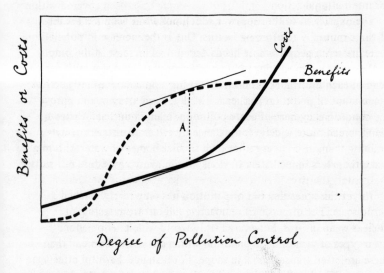

Source: S. Fred Singer, 'Emission Standards; Costs and Benefits', *Science 186*: 689, 22 November 1974.

like Figure 9.1.[3] The first improvements may be quite expensive, then there may be a phase in which extra costs bring rather bigger benefits, but eventually there will be a phase of diminishing returns, and further improvements will be more and more expensive. Very often, this last phase occurs long before costs and benefits become equal. Then is the time to stop, when the two curves are parallel, so that costs and benefits are increasing at the same rate; an extra unit of cost purchases just its own value of benefit (at A in the diagram).

The real dangers in the decades immediately ahead are more insidious. They arise partly from the quantitative increase in the area, and the increasing proportion of the total population, which is affected by technologically produced pollution; and partly from the fact that, although this pollution is not so gross as that described above, it does contain, in doses which might under certain circumstances be actually encountered in the environment, substances which are of much higher immediate toxicity than anything in more primitive types of pollution and which may also have very insidious but eventually far-reaching effects, in low doses spread over long periods. It is these two factors — pervasiveness over enormous areas and the inclusion of the substances with very powerful and inadequately understood long-term effects — that add new dimensions to the modern problem of pollution and call for international action.

The expansion of the area over which pollution occurs is the result of three mutually reinforcing factors. One is the increase in population; there are more people whose needs demand an increase in the output of the pollution-producing industries. Secondly, the real wealth per head of each individual has been increasing, and concomitantly so has the amount of pollution per head. Thirdly, in an attempt to improve the conditions in areas of acute pollution, many industrial wastes are being spread more widely, for instance by tall smoke-stacks or by draining them into larger rather than smaller bodies of water; this may make them less immediately obvious, but in many cases does not reduce their total quantity.

As yet this spreading out of pollution has only rarely reached a world scale. The dispersal of radioactive fall-out from testing of nuclear weapons was, however, a truly world-wide phenomenon. Even types of atmospheric pollution which are less widespread than these are often transnational in scope. For instance, harmful effects are being produced in the forests and freshwater lakes of Sweden by industrial effluents (acids, heavy metals, etc.) the origins of which are the smoke-stacks of the Ruhr in Germany.

Methods are already known for removing most, if not all, of the toxic substances that these industrial processes send up the smoke-stack into the air. All these methods cost money, which means that they cannot be adopted by any manufacturer unless his competitors are made to adopt them also; and since pollution is no respecter of frontiers, this requires international action. This is a sphere in which an effective world organisation with real powers is obviously required.[4] Possibly the formation of the EEC will turn out to be a step in the right direction, in that highly industrialised region.

Pollution of the air by the automobile is of a rather different character from its pollution by industry. The car produces a fairly small range of harmful pollutants, mainly carbon monoxide, incompletely burnt hydrocarbons, some oxides of nitrogen, and volatile compounds of lead, derived from dope put into the petrol to give it anti-knock properties. These substances already produce extremely unpleasant effects in a few parts of the world. This is so particularly in regions like Los Angeles, where the meteorological conditions cause the exhaust gases to be trapped in a fairly low layer above the city, without being able to escape into the upper atmosphere, and they are then subjected to strong sunlight which causes the incompletely burnt petrol fumes to combine with the nitrogen oxide to make some very nasty choking and eye-watering gases.

Technical methods for greatly reducing the output of the pollutants from cars are known, but again they are costly, in two ways; extra pieces of equipment have to be built into the car, and the reduction of pollution reduces the efficiency of engines of given size and petrol consumption. The American public and the American automobile industry are at present wrestling with this problem, with a good deal of hysteria on the public side and a good deal of what looks like irresponsible exploitation on the side of the industry. Public pressure has resulted in legislation which sets very severe limits on the amount of pollution legally allowable in car exhausts. These limits are so stringent that, early in 1973, William Ruckelshaus, then Director of the US Environmental Protection Agency, stated in Los Angeles that the only way he could see to meet the legal requirement was for the volume of automobile traffic in the city to be reduced by 1977 by 82 per cent. Since Los Angeles is a city measuring about 40 x 30 miles, with no other way of getting about it except by automobile, this proposal was clearly fantastic. It may indeed have been intended only to show that the proposed legal standards are unattainable. Meanwhile, on the other side of the picture, the automobile manufacturers compensated for the reduction of power in the low-pollution engines by increasing the size of the engines. This brought the power up to what it had been before at the price of using more fuel — which can hardly be regarded as acceptable in the present oil situation.

Carbon Dioxide in the Atmosphere[5]

The size of the atmosphere is enormous and the quantities of energy involved in its circulation are colossal. In a highly industrialised country such as Britain, the amount of man-made heat is less than one per cent of the energy received from the sun over the same area, while for the world as a whole, the total output of heat from industry is less than one per cent of the kinetic energy involved in the circulation of the atmosphere. Nevertheless, there may be some critical points in the heat and energy balance of the atmosphere at which human interference is large enough to have noticeable effects. A possibility that has been widely discussed is that the man-made output of carbon dioxide, arising from the burning of fossil fuels, might begin to be large enough to interfere with the transference of the solar heat through the atmosphere down to the earth's surface and its reradiation back up again into space. Clearly, unless the earth's reception and output of heat are kept in balance, the earth must gradually get warmer or colder. The processes of heat transfer depend on a number of factors, of which the most obvious is the extent of cloudiness, which may shield the earth from incoming solar energy and can also slow up the rate at which energy leaves the earth and escapes into space. Carbon dioxide also tends to prevent the reradiation of heat and the possibility arises that an increase in the atmospheric carbon dioxide, particularly at high levels, might have a 'greenhouse effect', which would raise the average temperature of the earth's surface.

Quite a small rise in the average temperature of the earth's surface may have profound effects on the climate. The last major Ice Age, which brought permanent glaciers and Arctic conditions to the south of England and large parts of northern Europe and North America, ended only 10,000 years ago. Since then the average annual temperature has probably varied by only about $2°C$, but even this was enough to cause a considerably warmer climate throughout England in the Middle Ages, followed by a much colder period — a mini-Ice Age — about the seventeenth century. The causes of these natural fluctuations are very little understood and almost certainly depend on very complex inter-relations of processes, involving both positive and negative types of feedback. Any reduction of temperature which leads to an extension of the Polar ice sheets tends to cause the earth to reflect, instead of absorb, more of the sun's energy, and this will be a factor of positive feedback tending to lower the temperatures still further. On the other hand, a slight rise in temperature will lead to more evaporation of water and this will have two opposite effects: on the one hand, it tends to prevent heat being radiated away from the earth and thus produces a hothouse effect, like carbon dioxide, tending to increase the earth's temperature still further; on the other, increased water vapour may lead to more cloudiness which reflects the sun's heat before it arrives at the earth, and thus tends to reduce temperature. The relative magnitudes of these two effects are not fully understood. Moreover, the formation of clouds depends greatly on wind velocities, and these again are affected by the distribution over the earth's surface of land masses, oceans and areas of special reflecting abilities such as snow fields or deserts. Man has always depended for the climate in which he lives on the interplay of this highly complex meteorological situation, the workings of which still remain to be unravelled in detail.

Against this background, one has to consider the possible effects of recent changes such as the greatly increased production of carbon dioxide by burning fossil fuels. It is fairly easy to calculate how much carbon dioxide is being added to the atmosphere in this way. We have very good measurements of the actual carbon dioxide content of the atmosphere over the last 10 or 15 years, made at places (the South Pole and Hawaii) far away from local sources of carbon dioxide and therefore probably good samples of the atmosphere as a whole. It turns out that the carbon dioxide in the atmosphere definitely has been rising. It was 312 parts per million in 1958 and had reached 319 parts per million by 1969 (near enough to a 2 per cent increase over a 10 year period).

However, this increase is only about half that which would have been expected if all the CO_2 produced by man's industrial activity had actually remained in the atmosphere. The other half must have been removed from the atmosphere in some way. The two obvious places where it can have gone are into vegetation and into solution in the sea. Both these great natural storages tend to act as buffers preventing the rise in the atmosphere's CO_2 content (see also p. 56). Presumably they could absorb a still higher proportion of the excess CO_2 if the concentration in the atmosphere increased further. This makes it difficult to foretell exactly how much the CO_2 content in the atmosphere will be raised in the future if fossil fuels continue to be used at the rates which now seem probable.

There are many other uncertainties about calculating the likely effects of the increased production of CO_2 on the earth's temperature. The most recent authoritative estimates arrive at a figure of an increase in temperature of about 0.6°C by the end of this century. This is considerably less than the approximately 2° fluctuation which seems to have occurred through natural causes since the end of the last Ice Age. It is, however, rather larger than any fluctuations which have lasted for several years during the last century or two, although occasional years have varied from the average by more than that. These results suggest that we need not expect any catastrophic climatic alterations as a consequence of the production of increased CO_2, but there might well be some appreciable changes in climate, particularly in certain localities, if the use of fossil fuels continues at the presently foreseen rate.

Water Pollution

Industrial man puts much more of his unpleasant wastes into water than into the air. The devastating effects on rivers which receive the effluent from some types of industrial activity are well known to everyone by this time. The argument in the past was that whatever poisons were dumped into a stream would only have a relatively local effect and would eventually be carried out to sea — and the sea is a big place in which they would be diluted enough to be harmless. It has, however, become clear over the last few decades that the quantities of toxic substances being put into some rivers are so massive that they produce unacceptable damage all the way downstream to the river mouth, and sometimes there are dangerously high concentrations in local regions of the sea. Moreover, the substances which have been disposed of in this way are becoming more and more toxic. One single sack of an insect poison which fell off a barge in a tributary of the Rhine was enough to kill practically all the fish from there to the river mouth — some 50,000 tons of fish.

People are already aware of this situation; in fact an international network of stations is being set up to keep watch and report on new dangerous pollution. Techniques to neutralise the toxic substances are known and legislation to control their disposal is being introduced and put into practice fairly rapidly — although certainly not rapidly enough, and public pressure to tighten up the regulations is still called for. The legislation is much easier to introduce and enforce when only one national sovereignty is involved, as in the clearing up of the Thames. The political problems are more difficult when a river passes through several national territories, as does the Rhine, and this is another good reason for pressure to form effective supra-national legislative bodies furnished with real power.

There is another matter of general principle which demands international action. Little is yet known about the long-term effects of low doses of deleterious substances, such as pesticides and herbicides, on more highly evolved animals, such as fish, birds and mammals, and our knowledge about such effects on man is completely inadequate.[6] For instance, although a powerful campaign has already been launched in the United States and a few other countries to ban or restrict the use of such pesticides as DDT and dieldrin, this is not on the basis of firm evidence of actual harm but on the grounds that these persistent substances have already, in a few restricted localities, reached concentrations producing ascertainable harmful effects on certain species, and have more widely reached levels which might *a priori* be expected to be deleterious. The 'Wilson Report'[7] on the situation in Great Britain points out that the evidence associating pesticide residues with pathological changes noticed recently in wild fauna, such as thinning of the egg shells of certain predatory falcons and hawks, is circumstantial rather than conclusive; and states that, although it can be shown that dieldrin, and DDT or its derivative DDE, occur in human body fat, there is 'no evidence that this results in any adverse effects on man'. It concludes, however, that laboratory experiments on the effects of relatively small doses of these substances suggests conclusions 'the implications of which could be so important that we believe that these data must be discussed, and agreement on their interpretation reached, on an international basis'.

Investigation of the effects of low doses of agents applied over long periods of time must necessarily be a time-consuming and relatively large-scale operation. As the conclusions reached will have a bearing for mankind as a whole, it seems eminently suitable that international organisations (e.g. the UN Group) should undertake the work. Some studies of this kind are already carried out by the World Health Organisation. Some years ago WHO discussed a plan for a large international laboratory, one of the tasks of which would have been the investigation of the problem of long-term effects of low-dose toxicity. Unfortunately this aim became involved with several other possible functions of such an international laboratory, and the plan finally did not reach fruition. There is a good case that such a scheme should be resuscitated, with the investigation of the eventual effects of environmental 'pollutants' as its central aim. It may be remarked that such a laboratory need perhaps not be centralised in one place. It has been suggested that it would require a 'mega-mouse facility', which could breed a million mice a year. But there would probably be an advantage in using several different experimental species, since extrapolation from any one species to man is always unreliable. It might be preferable to have a series of laboratories located in different parts of the world, organised as a co-operative network. Many of these laboratories might be very helpful to countries which are engaged in building up their scientific talent and which can offer access to experimental animals more closely related to man than the mouse (monkeys in India or Brazil, for instance).

Heat Pollution

Warm-blooded animals, such as man, must radiate away some heat from the surface of their bodies, however non-technologically they run their lives. Some writers who take a science-fiction attitude to the future[8] have pointed to this unavoidable 'heat pollution' of the planet as the inescapable limit on the growth of the human population. So it would be, if we ever came within sight of it. But even in the industrialised regions of the world today, the heat produced by man's activities is only about 1 per cent of what that region receives from the sun, and over the world as a whole the sun appears still more powerful. Heat pollution will not be a planetary matter for ages to come, if ever. The problems, which are real enough, are local.

There are already a very few places (e.g. Los Angeles, see p. 138) where local heating of the atmosphere is a nuisance. There are many more in which 'waste heat' carried off by water, from industrial installations such as electricity-generating plants, is producing un-desirable effects on the capacity of rivers, or even small lakes, to support a healthy biological ecosystem. These are problems for which there are many technological solutions; in a world which is short of energy, it is a confession of failure to label large quantities of it as 'waste heat', even if it is at rather low temperatures. There are many things it could be used for, such as heating houses, or greenhouses, or encouraging growth of algae on fish farms, or under-soil heating on crop land, and so on. As usual, the difficulties are financial. Most of these uses demand substantial capital outlay, for instance, to instal insulated pipes to carry the warm water to the places where it can be used. This is the reason why so few cities have so far followed the example of those (largely in Sweden) which have used 'waste heat' for central heating.

Solid Wastes

Man has always found it difficult to get rid of the solid wastes produced by his activities. Many Stone Age villages are now represented mainly by the mounds of oyster and mussel shells that their inhabitants left behind, and much of archaeology is based on more or less indestructible remnants of domestic pottery. With the development of richer industrialised societies and higher population densities there is more waste to be disposed of, and it is spread much more widely. Thor Heyerdahl, floating across the Atlantic slowly on a raft, had time to notice that there was floating debris, including globules of oil, even in the loneliest stretches of the ocean. Recently some marine scientists, operating in a remote region of the central North Pacific, 600 miles away from Hawaii and well off any normal steamer routes, kept an eye out for floating objects, large enough to be seen from the deck.[9] They looked at about 12½ sq. km of ocean surface, and in that saw 53 objects. Twelve of these were glass fishing floats which one might say had some sort of right to be on the sea, but two-thirds of all the objects were recently manufactured plastic objects. They estimated that there was one plastic bottle every 2 sq. km, which would work out at about 35 million plastic bottles in the Pacific as a whole. This can scarcely be regarded as a threat to mankind's existence, but it is certainly an unpleasant reduction in the amenities of the planet, and it is an indication of a problem that is getting worse.

In energy terms the waste is trifling. Most plastics are at present made from oil and account, in Britain, for only 5 per cent of the energy from that source; plastic packaging materials use only about ½ per cent of the total energy consumed. It is not in energy terms that the undoubted nuisance arises.

The increasing use of plastics for packaging is not without some good reason. They are not permeable to water, and thus protect food better than paper wrappings against moisture and the bacteria which can enter or grow faster when water gets in. The oil from which most plastics are made is an increasingly expensive and rapidly depleting resource, but it would be not much more difficult to use coal, which will soon become the cheaper raw material. Eventually one could make most types of plastics out of waste carbohydrate — wood, sawdust or the very large quantities of waste materials from food-processing plants — a good sized potato-chip factory may throw out 400 tons of peelings a day. So it would not be difficult to find substitutes for oil as a basis for plastics.

But can we prevent the discarded plastics being so offensive to the eye? There seems little chance of recycling them to form new plastics at reasonable cost — it costs more in energy to collect them, except from industrial users, than one can get back from either recycling or burning them as fuel. A possible method would be to ensure that they are 'biodegradable', that is disintegrate after a specified length of exposure to normal outdoor weather. Probably the most hopeful is to incorporate into them an agent which, under the influence of sunlight, turns into something which oxidises the plastic into a form which tends to disintegrate into small pieces, and also changes it chemically so that it is subject to bacterial attack, under which it effectually disappears from the scene. It is very useful to carry on with campaigns to persuade people not to discard plastic litter all over the landscape — farmers using plastic sacks for foodstuffs and fertilisers are some of the worst offenders. But the crucial steps in dealing with the problem will probably be the chemical ones just mentioned.

The problem of solid waste disposal is seen at its most intense in a city like New York. In 1970 each New Yorker threw away 5.3 lb of solid waste every day, and the quantity is increasing. It is expected to be 7.5 lb by 1980, and unless something is done about it, up to 10 lb by the end of the century.[10] A great deal of this is packaging material, most of it completely unnecessary to protect the goods involved. It takes 14,000 men to collect this waste in the city; and how to dispose of it is quite a question. A certain amount is burnt in incinerators. This reduces the volume of solid material, but the incinerators in use are old-fashioned and produce smoke and air pollution. Another solution has been to dump the waste as land-fill into swampy areas along the coast fairly near New York City, but they are now rapidly becoming used up, and soon there will be no more convenient rubbish dumps available. New York is proposing to build vast new modern incinerators. It will need three or four of them, costing around 80 million dollars each, and even then the present plans still leave a 'disposal gap' of about 4,000 tons a day with nowhere to put it or get rid of it.

This sort of problem is, of course, not confined to New York. There is plenty of solid waste to dispose of in Europe. The problem is in fact so acute that there has been a scheme, proposed by a Dutch group, to build an island of about 125 acres in a shallow region of the North Sea, perhaps near a gas field, to which solid wastes could be shipped for processing.[11]

Such a scheme should make it easier to introduce more sensible ways of handling waste than simply burning or dumping it. There is a

Figure 9.2: New York's Solid Waste Problem

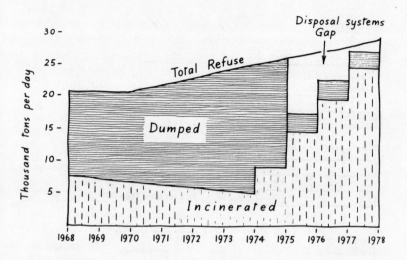

Source: Article in the *New York Times*, 24 March 1970, quoting the Regional Director of the Federal Bureau of Solid Waste Management.

certain amount of useful material which can be recovered, though not as much useful material as optimists sometimes suggest. Paper is one of the most useful things in most waste, and this can be recovered in much better condition if it is separated at the place where it has been used and is not mixed in with the other rubbish. A table of costs and benefits of waste-recycling in 1972 is diagrammed (Figure 9.3).[12] At that time, no technologies could recover enough useful material to have more than a bare chance of paying for themselves, but there were foreseeable technical advances which might make several of them, including composting and various systems of sorting, actually show a profit as well as disposing of the material. Once again, therefore, the main question is whether enough effort will be made to develop such techniques and to put them into operation soon enough, and on a large enough scale, to prevent still further destruction of environmental decencies.

How Important Is Pollution?

Should one really rate pollution as one of the major world problems of today? It was among the variables selected as crucially important by

Figure 9.3: Economics of Recycling Solid Wastes

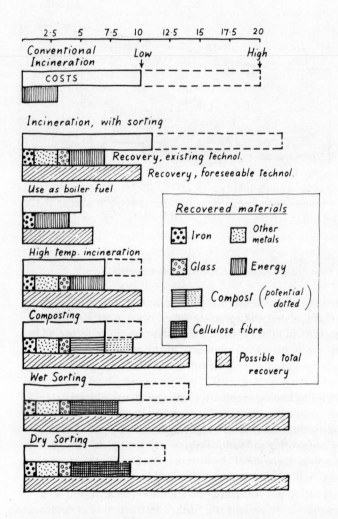

Note: The upper white bar in each group indicates costs, the bars with variable shading the recoveries possible with existing methods, the lowest bar with diagonal shading the total recovery possible with foreseeable technical advances.

Source: Robert R. Grinstead, 'Machinery for Trash Mining', *Environment*, 14 May 1972, p. 34.

the MIT team (Meadows and others) who first used the computer
simulation method to study the 'World Problematique'.[13] Probably
the most forceful and influential person who argues that it should go
near the top of the list of critical problems is Barry Commoner.

In a book *Science and Survival*,[14] published some ten years ago,
Commoner appeared as one of the earliest and most eloquent of the
scientific Jeremiahs who emphasised the potentially disastrous consequences of thoughtless applications of modern technology. That
book was largely concerned with the hazards to mankind of the
designing and testing of nuclear weapons. It played a worthy part in
the movement which has achieved a considerable control over the
danger of radioactive fall-out, and brought about a still hazardous
stalemate in the deployment of atomic weapons themselves. In his
later book *The Closing Circle*[15] Commoner focuses on the inter-
related problems of population growth and environmental pollution.

He begins by arguing that the dangers to the natural environment
are much more obvious and imminent in the developed than in the
developing countries. They do not arise primarily from pressure of
population or a rise in affluence, but rather from changes in
technology, most of which have been introduced since the end of
World War II. During this period the output of basic goods has done
little more than keep pace with the increase in population, except in
the field of personal transportation. There has been a considerable
increase in the vehicle-miles travelled per capita per year — much of it
due to the shift of urban populations into the suburbs, further away
from their places of work. Commoner provides figures to show
that the increase in pollution of various kinds has been much greater,
often by at least an order of magnitude. For instance, the total number
of vehicles on the United States roads increased 166 per cent between
1947 and 1968, but 'studies of the amounts of lead deposited yearly in
glaciers show that the annual entry of lead into the environment, almost
entirely from gasolene, has increased by about 400 per cent in the last
25 years', while 'a reasonable estimate of the increase in the smog
levels in the United States' cities since World War II would be tenfold
or so'.

The increase in pollution has usually been much faster than in
production. Commoner argues that this is a consequence of a number
of changes that have taken place in production technology, both in
industry and in agriculture. One tendency has been to substitute
artificial materials for natural ones; for instance, synthetic fibres and
plastics for cotton, wool and cellulose products. The synthetic materials

often involve types of chemical bonds which do not occur in the
natural environment and which cannot be degraded by the normal
decomposing organisms. Moreover, drastic chemical means may be
needed to synthesise these bonds, which lead to such results as an
increase since 1946 of 21,000 per cent in the use of mercury for
chlorine production in the United States. There has also been a
tendency to move from materials such as steel and timber, which
require rather little energy for their production, to materials such
as aluminium, which requires very much more. Then new systems
of agricultural production, such as reliance on heavy applications of
fertilisers and pesticides and on intensive management of livestock,
increase the pollution effects of production much more than its
over-all efficiency.

Commoner's conclusion is that

the increased output of pollutants per unit of production, resulting
from the introduction of new productive technologies since 1946,
accounts for about 95 per cent of the total output of pollutants,
except in the case of passenger travel, where it accounts for about
40 per cent of the total.

Commoner proceeds to examine the reasons for these changes in
production and technology, and argues that they are a consequence of
the fact that economic systems, both in capitalist and in communist
countries, do not at present take account of the full social costs of the
goods which they produce. An adequate cost-benefit analysis should
include the impact of the production processes on the natural environment; but since the costs of that impact are borne by society at large
and not by the customer for the particular goods produced, they get
left out of the equation which determines the profitability, or
assessed efficiency, of the production process. Moreover, when profit
is the recognised goal of the exercise, as in capitalist countries, there
is an inevitable tendency to cash in on the high profits which are
characteristically earned in the first few years after a new product has
been discovered and produced.

Commoner pays little attention to the political implications of his
analysis of the causes of the pollution of the environment. He finds
that the basic fault is an inadequate philosophical outlook; 'this fault
is reductionism, the view that effective understanding of a complex
system can be achieved by investigating the properties of its isolated
parts.' It is this outlook, he believes, that has led to the one-sided

emphasis on the single factor of immediate profit or productive efficiency, and the neglect of the 'inevitable side effects that arise because, in nature, no part is isolated from the whole ecological fabric'. Reductionism is certainly an inadequate philosophy (see Chapter 12); whether, in this connection, it merits all the blame Commoner lays on it is for the reader to decide; personally I would transfer some from the philosophy to the politics.

Commoner accepts that it would be exceedingly difficult to design and operate an economic system which does adequately allow for all the side-effects of industry, but he does not find the task impossible. He argues that 'the world is now no longer willing to tolerate even the present level of environmental degradation, much less its intensification.' However, 'ecological survival does not mean the abandonment of technology. Rather it requires that technology be derived from a scientific analysis that is appropriate to the natural world on which technology intrudes ... Since the environmental crisis is the result of the social mismanagement of the world's resources, then it can be resolved, and man can survive in a humane condition when the social organisation of man is brought into harmony with the ecosphere.'

Commoner's book is primarily concerned with the situation in the highly industrialised countries, but he does devote a chapter to the problems of the developing countries, in particular their populations. He points out that there are almost certainly tendencies towards the regulation of human populations, acting by a reduction of birth-rate when a high enough standard of living has reduced both the over-all death-rate and in particular the infant mortality rates (the 'demographic transition', p. 25). He seems to be more optimistic than many authors in feeling that these factors come into operation early enough to forestall major problems of over-population in most of the developing countries. He is probably too single-minded in refusing to allow the population problem to divert him from his main thesis — the valuable partial truth that several major recent technologies do greater harm to the environment than is warranted by their increased efficiency. It is a good point, but very far from being the whole problem mankind faces in trying to work its way into the twenty-first century.

Barry Commoner's emphasis on special polluting forms of technology and his low opinion of the relevance of population growth, provoked a bitter controversy between him and another of the great Old Testament prophets of the wrath to come, Paul Ehrlich.[16] Ehrlich claimed that Commoner was unduly simplifying the situation, and that population increase was, or could be, more important than pollution. Commoner replied that in the present situation of the western world population pressure was not of major importance, and that in any case the situation could not be looked at in purely scientific terms, as Ehrlich seemed to wish, but that it involved political issues which were critically important.

In my opinion, Commoner is right in arguing that population pressure is not a major factor in producing pollution in America or Western Europe, but Ehrlich is also right in emphasising the crucial threat it offers to man's future in the world as a whole. Dennis Gabor[17] was probably correct when he wrote 'Pollution is a major scandal, but a minor problem.' The only proviso is that some particular pollutant might turn out to have a trigger effect, producing much more damaging results than expected. The climate *might* be more sensitive than we think to small changes in concentration of CO_2 in the atmosphere; it is just conceivable that some chemical, such as DDT, might get into the oceans and prove to be particularly poisonous to the phytoplankton. If something of that kind happened we should be in bad trouble, but the chances of it happening seem considerably less than those of many other dangers that threaten mankind. The types of local pollution which are dangerous to the health of man, or to the planetary ecosystem of the biosphere, will certainly have to be controlled, even at considerable cost. The many types which are a nuisance or an eyesore, harmful but not lethal, have to be regarded as negative items on a budget sheet which includes many other items on which society could spend its money — schools, transport, pensions and so on. It will be a question of priorities; how much to reduce sulphur dioxide in the atmosphere, or to get fish to come back into a stream, as against how much to spend on other things which society wants. The priorities of these 'nuisance pollutions' will be, and probably should be, assessed differently in the rich and poor countries. It is important that even the poorest countries do not, in pursuit of immediate improvements for their peoples, do things which might bring long-term dangers to the planet as a whole; but there are not too many things within their reach which could be as dangerous as that. Yet no one should take it amiss if they decide, like early Victorian Britain, that what they need is the steel, coal and heavy chemicals, even at the cost of the sort of local pollution which Kathleen Lonsdale described for Leeds.

Further Reading

A. Nigel Calder ed., *Nature in the Round* (Weidenfeld & Nicolson, 1973).

B. Barry Commoner, *The Closing Circle* (Cape, 1972).

C. Paul R. Ehrlich, Anne H. Ehrlich and John P. Holdren, *Human Ecology* (Freeman, 1973), particularly Chapters 5, 6 and 7.

D. An early 'classic' (though not very reliable) is Rachel Carson's *Silent Spring* (1962, Penguin 1970).

E. The most balanced account of the world-wide situation is probably C.L. Wilson and W.W. Matthews eds., *Man's Impact on the Global Environment*, Report of the Study of Critical Environmental Problems (SCEP) (MIT Press, 1970).

F. Official assessments of the British situation are in the Reports of the Royal Commission on Environmental Pollution, annually from 1971–74 (HMSO); and for the USA, the Annual Reports of the Council for Environmental Quality (Government Printing Office, Washington). Lord Ashby (Chairman of the Royal Commission) summarised his views in a paper 'Prospect for Pollution', *Roy.Soc. Arts.J.*, June 1973.

Notes

1. Leonard J. Goldwater, 'Mercury in the Environment', *Scientific American*, May 1971.
2. Foreword by Kathleen Lonsdale to J. Rose ed., *Technological Injury* (Gordon & Breach, 1969).
3. S. Fred Singer, 'Emission Standards; costs and benefits', *Science, 186*: 689, 22 November 1974, 689, and for a good discussion of the difficulties of putting this admirable theory into practice, see M.S. Common, G.A. Norton and D.W. Pearce, 'The Economics of Pollution and its Control', *The Biologist*, February 1975, *22*, p. 5.
4. The main international organisations concerned with pollution now in being are the inter-governmental UNEP and MAB programmes, and the non-governmental SCOPE (see Further Reading note at end of Chapter 2).
5. J.S. Sawyer, 'Man made carbon dioxide and the "greenhouse" effect', *Nature*, September 1972, *239*, 23; also P.V. Hobbs, H. Harrison and E. Robinson, 'Atmospheric Effects by Pollutants', *Science*, 8 March 1974, *183*, 909; and *Inadvertent Climate Modification* (MIT Press, 1971). For another view of climatic changes towards a possible Ice Age for which pollution may, or may not, bear much responsibility, see Nigel Calder, *The Weather Machine and the Threat of Ice* (BBC, 1974).
6. Kenneth Mellanby, *Pesticides and Pollution* (2nd edn., Collins, 1970), and *Further review of certain persistent organo-chloride pesticides used in Great Britain* ('Wilson Report') (HMSO, 1969).
7. See note 6.
8. See note 5.

9. *Nature 241*, 26 January 1973, p. 271.

10. From an article in the *New York Times*, 24 March 1970, quoting the Regional Director of Federal Bureau of Solid Waste Management.

11. *New Scientist*, 13 July 1972, p. 150.

12. Robert R. Grinstead, 'Machinery for trash mining', *Environment*, 14 May 1972, p. 34. See also James G. Abert, Harvey Alter and J. Frank Bernheisel, 'Economics of Resource Recovery from Municipal Solid Waste', *Science*, 15 March 1974, *183*, 1052; 'The Useful Conversion of Waste', *Roy.Soc.Arts.J.*, June 1973.

13. D.H. Meadows *et al., Limits to Growth* (Potomac Associates, 1972).

14. Barry Commoner, *Science and Survival* (Cape, 1966).

15. Barry Commoner, *The Closing Circle* (Cape, 1972).

16. The extended battle between these two giants, involving a good deal of name calling, was published in *Bulletin of the Atomic Scientists*, May 1972, and also in Commoner's own Journal, *Environment, 14,* April 1972. A chatty account of the squabble is in *Science*, 31 July 1972, *177*, 245.

17. Dennis Gabor, *The Mature Society* (Secker & Warburg, 1972).

10 WAR

A few years ago most people would have said that the most immediate problem threatening the future of mankind was the possibility of an all-out war. If this were to happen the whole of civilisation as we know it, even possibly the entire human species, and conceivably every form of life on earth, might be wiped out, either by the direct effect of atomic explosions or by the longer-term effects of the radiation produced. At present these apocalyptic fears are not so vividly present in the public consciousness, but they are not far under the surface. Although mankind has achieved some degree of control over the potentialities of destruction, this control is still very precarious. It has been calculated that, since 1946, the sums spent by the US Department of Defence ('The Pentagon') amount to $1,100 billion, which is the value of all the structures existing in that country at the present time. Unless further mechanisms can be found for preventing the power struggles from escalating, global nuclear war seems inevitable; though, if one is optimistic enough, one might believe that it might be stopped before absolutely irreparable damage has been done and there is an increase in the use of these terrible weapons in more limited wars or even by terrorists.

The Nuclear Set-up

As social activities go, waging war is relatively simple; simple in its objectives, which are to destroy the enemy's capacity for carrying on, while retaining that capacity oneself; and fairly simple in the types of factor involved — although, of course, each factor, such as a weapon or a delivery system, will nowadays be extremely complicated in detail. In nuclear war there are only seven major components: the bombs themselves; the vehicles which carry them; the bases from which these vehicles operate; the systems which detect vehicles or bombs; devices used to intercept the vehicles; equipment used to deceive the enemy in various ways; finally the targets on which the bombs are being dropped. We will consider each of these in turn.

The Bombs

There are basically two kinds. The first to be developed was the atomic bomb, or A-bomb, which derives its energy from the splitting of the

Figure 10.1: Comparisons of World Expenditures in 1972 and 1973

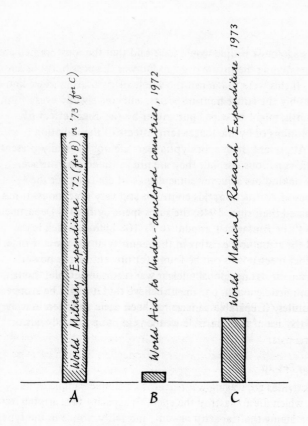

Source: Based on covers of SIPRI Yearbook Summaries, 1972 and 1973.

atoms of a few special types of very heavy radioactive elements (uranium, plutonium, etc.). This is the only type of bomb which has as yet been used in war. The two that were dropped on Hiroshima and Nagasaki, and completely destroyed each of those cities, produced an explosive blast equivalent to about 20,000 tons of the most powerful chemical explosive, TNT, and also released enormous quantities of radioactive material, which can injure people and other things, by radiation damage, long after the explosion is over. The second type of nuclear bomb is the 'thermo-nuclear' or 'H-bomb'. This operates by forcing atoms of a light element, hydrogen, to fuse together to form atoms of the slightly heavier element, helium. This process only occurs at an exceedingly high temperature, which is not easily attainable by the use of an A-bomb, so the thermo-nuclear bomb usually has a small atom bomb as a trigger to get it started and to produce an even more devastating effect. Whereas the effect of the A-bomb is measured in thousands of tons of TNT (called kilotons), the effect of thermo-nuclear bombs is measured in millions of tons of TNT (i.e. megatons). One megaton bomb can completely eliminate a moderate-sized city.

Because of the way they work, A-bombs are sometimes referred to as fission bombs, while thermo-nuclear or hydrogen bombs are referred to as fusion bombs.

The Vehicles

In a global strategic war the bombs would, of course, have to be sent across oceans, over distances of several thousand miles. Vehicles to carry them may be long-range aircraft. They have the great disadvantage that they must operate from large bases, which are difficult to protect. Moreover, the aircraft are relatively easy to detect and intercept. The vehicles which are most likely to be used are, therefore, unmanned rockets. These are usually referred to as ballistic missiles, and those capable of travelling across the oceans are known as intercontinental ballistic missiles (ICBMs). Until recently, their main snag was that they were relatively inaccurate. In the last few years, the accuracy with which a bomb can be landed on its target has been greatly improved. A further, enormously important, recent advance has been to increase the number of bombs which any given vehicle can carry. We shall come back to this later when discussing the way nuclear strategy has been evolving, and the major problems at the present time in stabilising the stalemate between the superpowers.

The Bases

For aircraft these must be aerodromes with long runways, which therefore present large targets. Rockets can be launched from much smaller sites, and these can be given a considerable degree of protection in two different ways. One way is to sink the actual tube, out of which the rocket is launched, quite deep in the earth and surround it with heavy masses of rock or concrete. This so-called 'silo' is safe from anything short of a hit by an atomic missile in its near neighbourhood. The other method is to make the rocket-launcher mobile and unfindable. The main way of doing this has been to build rocket-launching submarines.

Figure 10.2: The Components of an Air Strike

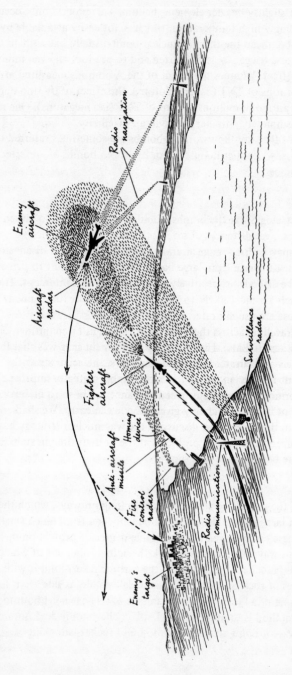

Note: The aircraft's navigation is aided by land-based radio, and it carries its own radar for detecting aircraft or other devices which may attack it. The defending side has radar for detection, and probably separate radar for directing its defending fighters or missiles, both of which may carry radar or homing devices.

Source: Based on drawing in Frank Barnaby (Director of SIPRI), 'Towards Tactical Infallibility', *New Scientist*, 10 May 1973, *58*, p. 348.

The Detectors

There are, of course, radar systems. They depend on sending out a short pulse of radio waves corresponding to a flash of light. This flash will be reflected from many things, including aircraft, rockets and what have you in the sky. Present-day receivers can pick up these reflected signals from enormous ranges and can very quickly decide how fast and in what direction the object is moving. This will allow one to decide whether the object is or is not part of an enemy attack. If a mistake were made in this decision, this might lead to a retaliatory attack, which had not really been called for. Extremely elaborate precautions have been taken to see that such mistakes do not occur, but there have already been some frightening incidents. A great deal of effort is being expended in America, and certainly in Russia, to improve the reliability of this component of the whole set-up, but it still remains one of the most dangerous areas.

The detection of submarines is much more difficult than that of airborne vehicles. Radar cannot be used under the sea, since electro-magnetic waves, at least those short enough to be useful in locating objects, are not transmitted through water. One is reduced to using pulses of sound waves instead of radio waves; but sound waves, of course, travel very much more slowly in the oceans. It is not much use detecting a submarine unless you can do so when it is a hundred or so miles away; by the time a sound wave reflected from a submarine at that distance has got back to the detector, the submarine will have been able to move quite a long distance. One solution seems to be to keep a large number of unmanned sound detectors scattered over vast areas of ocean, sending out radio signals to a central place when they hear anything – but if anybody tried this it would probably be pretty easy to fool the system by fake submarines, etc. Another, perhaps more promising, solution is to have sufficient anti-submarine vessels (either on the surface or themselves submarines) so that once an enemy submarine has been located even roughly, they can keep continuously on its track. So far as is publicly known, neither of these ploys can as yet be carried out successfully.

The Interceptors

The general principle of modern interceptors of aircraft or rockets is to have something – a small aircraft or a smallish rocket – which can be guided by a ground-based apparatus into the general neigh-bourhood of an attacking vehicle; when it gets close enough, it takes over its own guidance and 'homes' on to the vehicle and explodes either on contact with it or when it gets in near proximity to it. For the first part of the guidance the interceptor is controlled by a computerised calculation, based on what is known of the previous flight of the vehicle, of its position when the interceptor arrives, which, in the case of an aircraft might involve a time interval of as much as 10 minutes, but in the case of an intercepted rocket would have to be very much less. The interceptor's own homing method can either be detection of the sound, or more probably the heat, from the vehicle's engines, then guiding itself towards the source of heat; or the interceptor may send out a radar signal of its own and use that to locate its prey.

The interceptor used against long-range aircraft may be short-range fighter aircraft (possibly unmanned) or rockets. Those used against rockets must also be rockets, since aircraft would be too slow. They are known as ABMs (anti-ballistic missiles).

It is not particularly difficult to design homing interceptors against submarines, but as we have pointed out above, the difficulty is to find the submarines in the first place, so that the interceptors can be guided into close enough range for their homing apparatus to start operating.

The Deceivers

These are devices for deceiving the enemy's reactors or interceptors. The only deception one would wish to practise concerning the first part of the flight of a vehicle would be to conceal it. At the end of a vehicle's flight, just before the bombs are released, there would be little hope of concealing it, but it would be very useful to deceive the detectors as to exactly where it was and in what direction it was travelling, because this would upset the attempt to guide the interceptors into the right neighbourhood. Finally, of course, when the interceptors switch on their own homing devices, it would be most useful to make them home on to the wrong things.

There have been considerable and important developments in this respect in the last few years. The most important step has been to make it possible for one vehicle to carry several different and separate bombs. This has been done partly by a new system of launching which allows a vehicle to carry a heavier weight of explosive than when each bomb was set off from its own rocket-launcher. Usually a rocket has a first stage which burns a great deal of fuel to get the vehicle through the earth's atmosphere out into more or less empty space; then this part of the rocket is allowed to drop off and a much smaller rocket ignites to propel the bombs across the long distance through space; finally the section containing the explosive (the 're-entry vehicle') has to re-enter the atmosphere, where it is heated up by the friction of the air, and, like a meteor, would burn away completely unless made of the right material. Recently it has been found possible to use compressed air within the launching tube instead of the first-stage rocket, and thus save a lot of weight.

An even more important step has been not only to increase the number of bombs carried by one vehicle, but also to design a system which allows each bomb to be dropped on a different target. This has depended on being able to build highly elaborate navigational systems (which control the positions on which the bombs are to be dropped) in a micro-miniaturised form, so that each bomb can be given its own guidance. The first step in this was known as MIRV, which stood for Multiple Independently Targetable Re-entry Vehicles; in this system, the targets were selected and set into the guidance apparatus before the rocket was launched. Both the Americans and the Russians seem to be able to do this. A further step is called MARV; this stands for Manoeuvrable Re-entry Vehicle, the point being that the targets can be altered after the vehicle has already been launched. The point of both MIRV and MARV, of course, is that a given number of initial rockets can carry into the presence of the enemy a great many more separate bombs, which enormously complicates the task of detecting and intercepting systems.

The Targets

To the ordinary person the accuracy with which a rocket can be directed for three or four thousand miles on to a target on another continent. to fall within a radius of a mile or two of its mark, has been astonishing. But even so this is not really good enough to knock out a properly 'hardened' installation, such as a deeply buried rocket-launcher surrounded by thick concrete. This has meant that the theory of nuclear warfare has been based on rocket attacks on soft targets, that is to say, mainly on cities and centres of population, with the aim of killing off as many people as possible. It seems, however, that in the last year or two this already remarkable accuracy has been improved so that attacks on the hardened military targets have now to be seriously considered.

Nuclear Strategy[1]

The arms race between the United States and the Soviet Union is a textbook example of escalation by each side trying to go one better than the other — a 'symmetrical schismogenesis'. As we shall see later,

Figure 10.3: An Intercontinental Ballistic Missile Equipped with Multiple Re-entry Vehicles

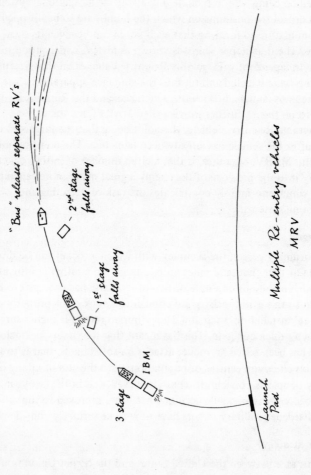

"Bus" releases separate RV's

2ⁿᵈ stage falls away

1ˢᵗ stage falls away

3 stage

I B M

Launch Pad

Multiple Re-entry vehicles
MRV

Source: G.W. Rathjens, 'The Dynamics of the Arms Race', *Scientific American*, April 1969; also published as Chapter 20 of Herbert F. York ed., *Arms Control* (W.H. Freeman & Co., San Francisco, 1974).

the two sides are just beginning, very tentatively, to bring the situation under control, by losing interest in that particular competition and turning attention to something else — a tactic which is passing under the name 'detente' in the international field today. But there are clear signs that the situation is simultaneously getting more complicated. The number of minor nuclear powers is growing, India being the most recent to join them, and it may start to increase quite rapidly. Many countries — Israel, South Africa, Japan, both Germanys, to name only a few — could make nuclear bombs tomorrow, and in a few years' time very many countries in Asia, Africa and South America could own at least a few A-bombs. And, of course, one major country, China, is set on making itself a great nuclear military power, comparable to the present big two. The theories of interacting systems are still far too under-developed to provide any clear concept of the kinds of run-away processes, or alternatively types of stable system, which one could look for in situations which involve many more than two actors, and those of very different strengths.

Games theorists at one time moved into the American military planning establishment (The Pentagon) in a big way, and tried to formalise the theory of war in strict mathematical terms.[2] But the results were rather disappointing. Games theory cannot in practice solve any problem except how to play safe, or as safe as may be — what it calls a 'minimax strategy'. It can help to solve that problem in complex circumstances, but that is hardly good enough, since that may not be what one wants to do in practice. The military equivalent to such a strategy is known as 'worst conceivable analysis'; e.g. Britain should plan how to defend itself if the USSR, or even France, launched an all-out nuclear attack. Obviously any effective strategy would be far too expensive to be practical, even if possible at all. In practice all nations have to gamble, to some extent, that the worst conceivable will not happen. The difficult questions to settle are how much to gamble, how much to invest in one's own capacities for attack, and suchlike. Here, games theory can give some hints about how to set about the problems, drawing up pay-off tables and the rest of it, but it cannot actually solve anything. The questions have to be discussed in their particularity rather than as examples of general principles. This we will now do.

The first idea about a nuclear war was that one side would try to get in first, to take the other side by surprise, and obliterate his nuclear armament so that he could not retaliate. This is the so-called counter-force first strike strategy. For a short time, America might

Figure 10.4: First and Second Strike Strategies

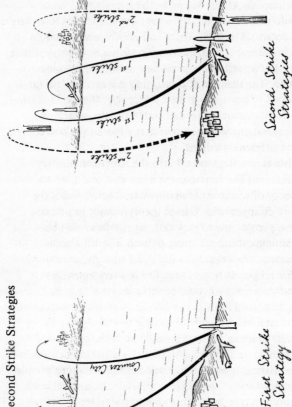

Note: In first strike strategy (left side) the attacking country tries to knock out the other side's forces as well as attacking his bases of production. In second strike strategy both sides try first to knock out the other's forces, and have enough of their own surviving then to attack the cities.

Source: Unknown; may be based on SIPRI Yearbook 1974, p. 55, or Elizabeth Young, *Farewell to Arms Control* (Penguin, 1972). pp. 179–80.

really have been able to achieve this against Russia and it is quite likely that at the present time it could be pulled off by America, and certainly by the Soviet Union, against China, and with not much more risk against Britain or France. It was not too long, however, before the size of the Soviet armaments became too large for this to become a practical proposition. The point then was for both sides to see that, however much they were taken by surprise, they would not lose everything and would be able to retaliate with a 'second strike strategy'. The second strike would, of course, have to be strong enough for its results to be unacceptable to the enemy who had got in first. If one side had destroyed half the other side's major cities by a surprise attack and most of its softer military establishment, there must have remained in being sufficient hard establishment to knock out half the attacker's cities in return.

This is perhaps appropriately named MAD (Mutually Assured Destruction) strategy.[3] It is the system that the two major powers, the United States and the Soviet Union (and thus the world as a whole), have been working on for the last few years. It has at least led to the first signs of effective international agreement in this field. The nuclear armaments of the two superpowers were so large that they both realised it was a mere waste of money to go on piling up more and more of the same types of weapons. Firstly, it was clear that they had both got into a situation of diminishing returns. The US Defence Secretary, McNamara, worked out, in 1972, how much damage would be done to the Soviet population or industry if a given quantity of bombs (measured in megatons) could be dropped on it (Figure 10.5). Clearly anything beyond 400 megatons would be largely wasted, since all major industry and heavily populated areas would already be destroyed; all that would be left to do would be the exercise un-appealingly referred to as 'overkill'. But, even by 1969, both sides had at least 1,000 land-based ICBMs each capable of carrying several megatons. Moreover, further expenditure on anti-missile defences (ABMs) did not look very attractive. They are exceedingly expensive, and although they will probably prevent some of the enemy's missiles getting to their targets, the enemy would only have to increase the number of ICBMs he sends over by a relatively small percentage to swamp any defensive ABM system that either side has contemplated so far.

The two sides therefore started Strategic Arms Limitation Talks (known as SALT) with one another, and did eventually agree to set limits to the numbers of intercontinental vehicles they would keep in

Figure 10.5: McNamara's Estimates (1972) of Effects of Attack by
USA on USSR with Various Tonnages of Bombs

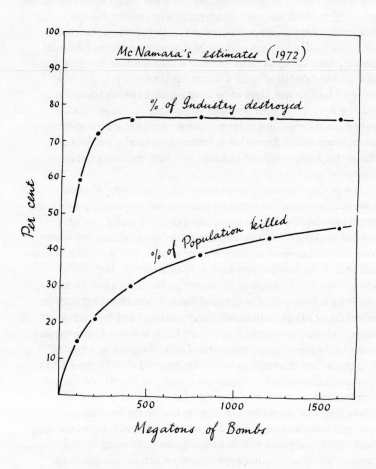

Source: Drawn from figures in Thomas Gordon Plate, *Understanding Doomsday*,
(Simon & Schuster, 1971), p. 17.

being and to the number of cities they would protect with interceptor
vehicles (ABMs). This was at least something, but it turned out to be
not very much. The SALT agreement limited numbers of vehicles,
but not the sophistication of the vehicles. The Americans first, and
then the Russians, MIRVed their vehicles, which meant that, although
the numbers of vehicles were frozen, their destructive power went on

increasing.

Now it seems possible that they can improve the accuracy so that attacks on hardened military sites are practical; this means that the whole second strike strategy comes in question again. The only effective counter to this situation must be either to harden the land-based launching sites still further, so that to knock them out would demand a degree of accuracy which would recede out of reach of the modern improved navigational methods, or to rely still more heavily on the difficulty of finding and destroying a submarine launcher. The first is probably the cheaper solution; pouring 10,000 tons of concrete, where one poured 100 tons before, is cheap compared to building nuclear submarine launchers. But it seems likely that it will be a further development of the submarine that the American-Soviet confrontation will tend to go in for.

Submarines are not, however, much use in the Soviet-China confrontation. This has not yet reached a scale where it plays a major role in the world's global power balances, but within the next two or three decades China will almost certainly become as massive a power factor in the nuclear field as the two super giants of today. Furthermore, the basic causes of conflict between China and Russia are likely to become much more polarised than those between the Soviet Union and the United States. On the ideological level the distinction between capitalism (increasingly controlled by government) and Lenin-Stalinist Communism (increasingly influenced by considerations of competitive efficiency) grows less; and at the material level the USA and the USSR have come into almost no immediate contact at all. On the other hand, Maoist decentralised do-it-yourself community action is ideologically poles apart from what the Soviet system has developed into. And materially these two systems meet face to face along the longest land frontier in the world — a frontier to the south of which in China, not too far away, is some of the most highly populated land surface to be found on the surface of the earth, while to the north of it, on the Russian side, are some of the largest remaining areas of very lightly populated country, difficult but with modern techniques not impossible to develop into localities capable of supporting civilised existence.

It does not look as though mankind can see much prospect in the immediate future of avoiding the essentially completely wasteful expenditure of resources required to carry on the nuclear race merely to preserve the *status quo*. America and Russia have got to find some way of keeping themselves safely stalemated, even in the face of MIRV,

MARV and improved accuracy. Even when they have done that — probably with the aid of submarines — the Soviet Union, if it wishes to retain its Siberian territory, has got to find some basis for an atomic stalemate between two powers which are not separated by a convenient ocean, but which both derive their strength from vast areas of solid land which come together at a line, across which in theory a man could stand with one foot in China and one in Russia.

A final, though probably important, point is that A-bombs (though not H-bombs) do not require elaborate technology in their manufacture, provided one can lay one's hands on refined plutonium. Plutonium is a by-product of most of the types of atomic energy plant which many countries are relying on to produce their electricity in the future, and there is a very real danger that criminals or terrorists may succeed in stealing sufficient plutonium to make one or even more A-bombs, which would be enormously powerful weapons of blackmail. People who have studied possible ways of guarding against theft or sabotage tend to conclude that the only real safeguard is for every use of atomic power — civilian as much as military — to be put under the tight control of some international body, and that this safeguard should be worked towards before it is forced on the world by some disaster which might have been averted.

Chemical and Biological Warfare[4]

Although global atomic war earns its place as a subject which no discussion on the man-made future could possibly omit, many people today make a surprisingly good job of pushing atomic war out of their consciousness with what has come to be called chemical and biological warfare (CBW). It is, in my opinion, a mistake to lump these two types of weaponry into the same category, so I will try to bring out some of the major points of controversy about them separately.

Biological Warfare

By this term is meant the attempt to use, as weapons of war, biological agents which cause disease, possibly even leading to death, either in the enemy people or in their livestock or crops. There is no doubt that all 'advanced' countries have devoted quite a lot of money and effort to developing more harmful strains of disease, germs or viruses, and to finding ways in which they could be disseminated and spread through an enemy population. Most of these efforts have been expounded to the public as research concerned with discovering what tactics and agents the enemy might utilise, so that we can find ways of counteracting them. Research devoted to finding out how to defend oneself, however, is almost completely indistinguishable from research devoted to finding out how to attack the other person.

The short point about biological warfare is that nobody has ever come up with any satisfactory idea as to how it could be used without being as much of a danger to the user as to the enemy. One may possess highly infectious and lethal strains of diseases such as anthrax or bubonic plague but so far there is no practical way to make sure that they kill only the enemy and not oneself. Throughout the last two or three brutally war-ridden decades, when there have been several nations quite ready to use anything they could find, there is no convincing evidence that anyone has ever really tried to use biological warfare; it seems to have been just too difficult to control. There have been claims that the Americans tried it against the Chinese and North Koreans at the time of the Korean War, but few people are convinced by the evidence, and if it did occur, it seems to have been highly inefficient.

Biological warfare can, I think, be written off as an important element in the relations between major bodies such as national states. If it has any importance in the modern world, it will be as one of the possible weapons of politically or religiously motivated fanatics, who feel that such wrongs and injustices as they suffer justify *any* aggression against the world at large. If anyone ever does use means of 'biological warfare', it is in my opinion most likely to be in the context of paranoid terrorism.

Chemical Warfare[5]

Although chemical warfare is conventionally classified along with biological warfare, under the general grouping CBW (chemical and biological warfare), it is really something very different. It would be hard to think of any aspect of military technology at the present day which does not depend on chemistry, from the simplest gunpowder to the most sophisticated modern explosives. All rifles, machine guns, mortars, cannons, bombs and surface-to-air missiles are devices essentially dependent on chemistry. The phrase 'chemical warfare' has, however, come to mean the use other than as explosives of chemical substances to reduce the enemy's capacity for opposition.

For example, one can make him feel so uncomfortable with tear gases, mustard gases and the like that the only thing he can think of is to get out and recover, and he has no energy left for opposition; or one can actually try to anaesthetise him, so that he loses consciousness; or one can attack him with a substance which affects him so that in a day or two most of his contribution to the active opposition will become minimal and he will have to be pulled back into hospital or some recovery area.

I think it is difficult to doubt that the majority of people in the world today feel that the use of chemical agents in this way — not as explosives where they are well accepted, but as non-lethal, or at least more gently lethal agents — is in some way unfair, indecent and immoral. There certainly is a strong feeling among many people, that when a civil demonstration of protest threatens to turn into a real riot, it is 'unfair' or 'indecent' for the police, or other official forces responsible for civil order, to use agents which are obviously chemical (tear gas or the like) instead of good old-fashioned truncheons, which immobilised the opposition by giving them concussion. Whether this is so is a question for each person to decide for himself.

The reaction of horror to the notion of chemical warfare is in fact not shared by many of the most progressive left-wing unorthodox scientists. J.B.S. Haldane, the most impeccably communist Guru of left-wing protest movements in the thirties, agreed completely with the London Metropolitan Police Chief whose job was to control demonstrations, that he would much rather be put out for a few hours by chemical warfare than be on the receiving end of Napoleon's recipe ('A whiff of grapeshot' propelled by a chemical explosive, but leaving a lump of metal somewhere in one's anatomy).

There are two special forms of chemical warfare which have been fairly widely used in recent times and which have come in for particular condemnation. First is the use of solidified petrol (napalm) as an incendiary agent, usually dropped from aircraft. This is undoubtedly a very unpleasant weapon, perhaps particularly because it lends itself so readily to being used against small, more or less defenceless, rural communities, as in South East Asia. However, I do not see that it is any worse than the high explosive bombs which have also been used so lavishly in that theatre of war. Possibly the greatest importance of napalm and similar weapons is the horror they arouse in many people, by their unusual nature. If this horror could spill over into a realisation of the equally great horror of many of the conventional weapons which we have grown to accept, the essentially irrational prejudice against napalm and other chemical agents, as opposed to other types of weapon, may in the end serve a good purpose.

Another special type of weapon is the use of herbicides to destroy the crops on which the enemy is relying for food, or the vegetation which he is using to cover his movements. This is a tactic which has been widely used by the Americans in South East Asia.[6] It does not seem to have been very successful in defeating the enemy. The most important criticism, however, is that there is a considerable likelihood that the effects on the ecology of the territory attacked may be long-lasting. It is true that in many areas of Vietnam the total destruction of vegetation and of the surface soil by heavy explosive bombing looks like having at least as long-lasting effects as the destruction by herbicides. In some regions in fact the effects of the herbicides seem to have been overcome in a few years by the natural regenerative properties of the ecosystem. In other regions, however, particularly in mangrove swamps along the coast, and in regions where the previously valuable forest timber becomes replaced by rather useless bamboo, technically qualified opinion seems to think that it will take at least a decade and possibly considerably more to bring the land back into a productive state. A form of weapon which seems to have brought comparatively little military advantage at the cost of long-lasting damage to the basic resources for human existence in the region con-cerned can only be considered extremely unsatisfactory from all points of view.

One general point of importance about all these unconventional agents of chemical and biological warfare is that, for the very reason that they are not yet conventionally accepted as parts of 'standard' weaponry, it may be easier to come to international agreements to ban their use than it is to ban the use of bombs, bullets and so on. Whether it would be easier to enforce this ban, should one of these weapons turn out after all to be useful, is another matter. However, the optimists can argue that they provide a way of getting a real process of disarmament at least begun; and this is certainly an essential, and possibly quite an important, step towards a thorough-going system of disarmament or arms control, which the world must eventually achieve if it is to attain anything like a stable order.

Other Developments in the Technique of War

The methods of waging war, like other technologies, are undergoing rapid change at the present time. Perhaps the most general character of the change is that the defence seems to be gaining the edge over the attack. In the last few decades, the tank and the dive-bomber — attacking weapons — have seemed almost irresistible. Recently, as in the Yom Kippur war in the Middle East, newly developed defensive weapons are at last coming near to controlling them. These weapons are essentially short-range rockets, which can either be controlled by the man who launched them so as to hit their target or which have built-in homing devices which lead them to the target. It looks as though they will lead to great alterations in the tactics of war, and perhaps in the ease with which frontiers can be defended in 'conventional' wars. But these are matters for the military specialist, and I do not think they earn a place amongst the major influences on the character of the man-made future.

Further Reading

A. Thomas Gordon Plate, *Understanding Doomsday* (Simon & Schuster, 1971). This discusses nuclear war only.

B. Laurence Martin, *Arms Strategy* (Weidenfeld & Nicolson, 1973) (more general).

C. Herbert F. York ed., *Arms Control*, readings from *Scientific American* (W.H. Freeman & Co., San Francisco, 1974).

D. One of the most thorough sources is SIPRI (Stockholm International Peace Research Institute), Sveavgen 166, S-113 46, Stockholm, Sweden. Their Yearbooks *World Armaments and Disarmament* are published annually by: Almquist & Wiksell, P.O. Box 62, S-107 20 Stockholm 1, Sweden; Humanities Press Inc., 303 Park Ave. S., New York 10010; Paul Elek Ltd, London.

The main Yearbooks are large and expensive. Short summaries of them are obtainable (free) from SIPRI.

Notes

1. See *The Nuclear Deterrence Debate*, SIPRI Yearbook 1974, Chapter 5, p. 55.
2. Anatol Rapoport, *Strategy and Conscience* (Harper & Row, 1964).
3. Ibid.
4. See *Problems of Chemical and Biological Warfare*, vol. 1 – 1972 onwards, SIPRI.
5. See Special Issue of Pugwash Newsletter, June 1974.
6. Matthew Meselson, 'Chemical and Biological Weapons', *Scientific American*, May 1970, and Herbert F. York ed., *Arms Control* (W.H. Freeman & Co., San Francisco, 1974), Chapter 3.

11 VALUES

Throughout the whole world, both in its developed and developing parts, there is a widespread feeling that the system of values by which man has guided his actions in the last few generations requires re-examination and almost certainly should be altered in many important respects. The basis for this feeling is partly a moral revulsion against some of the old value systems, but partly it is forced on us by the practical demands of world problems. The issues of population and food, urbanisation, transport, increased leisure, safeguarding the environment, and so on, may appear to be simple material questions, but deeper inspection shows that they involve questions of motivation and aspirations, and the value systems on which these are based.

The questions about values which trouble men's minds at the present time are both extraordinarily wide-ranging, leaving hardly any of our older ethical assumptions unquestioned, and also go extremely deep. In one short chapter of a book such as this, it is obviously impossible to discuss these questions as thoroughly as they deserve. My aim will be only to provide an introduction and to suggest in the notes, a few books and articles in which the reader can follow up those aspects in which he is especially interested. In my discussion I shall not go out of my way to try to assume a god-like impartiality and universal sympathy with all the different points of view which people are putting forward. This will be a personal and individual expression of opinion; I think justifiably so, since individuality is something on which I set a high value and which I should not wish to see diminished in the world.

From Primary 'Goods' to Ethical Values

The basic level from which we have to begin in considering values is those things which were 'good for' or 'advantageous' to the animals which were our evolutionary ancestors. These are such things as adequate food and health, and the ability to grow up successfully and leave offspring to contribute to the next generation in evolution. Evolution is brought about by the fact that some individuals of a species leave more offspring than others and therefore contribute more to future generations: a process known as natural selection. It is not such a simple process as it appears at first sight, and as many people think it to be. To be efficient in the face of natural selection requires not only that the animal be adapted to a particular mode of life in the ecological system in which it lives, but if a lineage of animals is to continue evolving for a long period it must be adapted in a way which is flexible enough to allow for modifications when the ecosystem changes, as it inevitably will. There is, rather surprisingly, no accepted short phrase for this combination of efficiency in meeting the immediate demands of today's ecology and flexibility sufficient to cope with the unforeseen demands that tomorrow may bring. In my book *The Ethical Animal*[1] I suggested calling it 'biological wisdom', but the term has not yet been generally adopted.

These 'goods' are relevant to subhuman animals. At that level of evolution, they can scarcely be considered ethical values, in the sense in which man uses these terms. One of the great problems for debate is whence arises the human sense of morality, which marks the difference between an animal good and an ethical value. Throughout most of the world and most of human history, it has been thought that moral values are a development, as it were, of qualities which are inherent in all aspects of nature, but which man has been able to realise and experience more explicitly than can other creatures. For people with such beliefs the human soul was only a fuller development of something in which all nature has a share.

There has been a tendency in western thought which is in sharp contrast with this. At the very beginning of the developments which led towards modern science, there was a powerful movement of opinion that mind is something of an entirely different character to matter. The prime exponent of this view was the French philosopher Descartes. What is known as 'Cartesian Dualism' asserts the separation of mind from matter as two quite different orders of existence. But the status of moral values (or 'the soul') was at first left much less clear – partly perhaps because questioning the orthodox doctrines of the Catholic Church was a dangerous pastime in those days. It was not very long, however, before philosophers of science (the key name in this connection is Hume) urged that values are also something quite different from matter, and that for the purposes of science matter must be considered quite without reference to any questions of value. This doctrine was the dominant view during the seventeenth, eighteenth and at least the first half of the nineteenth century. During this period most of science dealt with the inanimate things in the world; the only well-developed sciences were chemistry and above all physics. Physics, with its precise laws about the behaviour of clearly defined entities, was taken to be the paradigm example of what a science should be. It was confidently hoped by many that it would be found that everything could be explained by physics.

One of the important discussions about ethical values at the present time takes the form of an attack on science, which is based on the assumptions, firstly, that the whole of science is in fact founded on the views just expressed; and, secondly, that those views are the major cause for what is claimed to be modern western man's devaluation of nature and dehumanisation of his fellows. In my opinion, this anti-science counter-culture is right in many of the positive things it has to say — many of the values it praises are genuine and important ones — but there are several reasons why many of its negative arguments, against science, are only partially correct and even become dangerous by concealing the main point. Certainly nature should not be devalued, nor man dehumanised. But, in the first place, the Cartesian-Human-Newtonian view does not necessarily do this. In the second place, recent science, which has seen the rising importance of biology and the development of physics into much less simple mechanistic theories, is not nearly so much influenced by the Newtonian view as its critics suppose it always must be. Finally, and most importantly, the real villain in bringing about the sorry state of the world is nothing so far away as the metaphysical basis of science, but is rather a combination of much more down-to-earth value systems, those concerned with selfishness, individual power, material possessions and immediate comfort.

There is no space to refer to more than a minute fraction of the voluminous writings by these critics of modern science, but a good example to take is Theodore Roszak, because although he does eventually conclude that science takes the major blame for what he dislikes in today's world, he is at least aware of many of the points on the other side. In his recent book *Where the Wasteland Ends*[2] Roszak takes Newton rather than Hume or Descartes as the personification of science and Blake, who demanded an end to 'single vision and Newton's sleep', as the opposing hero. Roszak sees science as essentially the attempt to live up to Bacon's description of it.

We can give credit to Bacon and Descartes that there exists the tantalising assumption, basic to all scientific work, that a deper-sonalised method of knowing *can* be perfected — and that *only* such a method of knowing gains access to the reality of nature . . . We are agreeing that it is no loss to the scientist personally, or to the culture generally, to strip human thought of its most intimately personal qualities — its ethical vision, its metaphysical resonance, its

existential meaning ... With Bacon and Descartes, we are legitimising
an act of depersonalisation, a censorship of those very qualities of
mind and spirit which have always been regarded as indispensable to
the health of culture.[3]

He goes on to elaborate this point.[4]

Charles Gillespie [in *The Edge of Objectivity*[5]] goes to the heart of
the matter when he portrays the history of science as the aggressive
advance through culture of an 'edge of objectivity' ... The
scientific 'act of knowing', as Gillespie tells us, 'is an act of
alienation'. It is a forcing of experience out and away from the grip
of the personal.

The basic method of science was discussed at length in *Tools of
Thought*, where it was concluded that the 'classical scientific method',
which Roszak and Gillespie are writing about, is not so simple as they
allege, and is also by no means characteristic of the whole of the field
we commonly call 'science'. Here we are concerned with science not as
a method, but as something which gives rise to a philosophical outlook,
and thus to a system of ethics. It is easy enough to find distinguished
modern scientists who express views very similar to those Roszak
attributes to all scientists. For instance, the main point of Sir Peter
Medawar's recent book *The Hope of Progress*[6] is a defence of Bacon's
views about objectivity; and the main subject of Sir Karl Popper's
discussions of scientific method[7] is the investigation of how to attain it.
But Roszak himself knows that the matter is not so simple as all that.
For Newton the world was by no means totally depersonalised. Newton
wrote of himself:

I do not know what I may appear to the world, but to myself I seem
to have been only a boy playing on the sea shore, and diverting
myself, and now and then finding a smoother pebble or a prettier
shell than ordinary, whilst the great ocean of truth lay undiscovered
before me.

In so far as he followed the Cartesian principle of separating the world
into the human mind and non-human 'matter', the matter remained for him
quite as mysterious as the mind, being indeed pregnant with God. Writing
about the force of gravity, for which he had provided the quantitative
rules of operation, Newton wrote:

God, being present everywhere by His will, moves all the bodies in his infinite, uniform *sensorium*, and so shapes and reshapes according to His pleasure all parts of the universe, much more than our soul by its will is able to move the limbs of our body.[8]

Roszak in fact notes that

... we have observed how the initial effect of the scientific revolution was to vastly enhance the stature of man and the magnificence of nature. The dominant tone in the work of the early scientists is exuberant celebration. They exalt human understanding and glorify God's handiwork. That tone (though purged of its theological resonance) still lingers on today. But there has been mixed with it since the beginning a darker motif: the compulsive need to disenchant whatever was mysterious, immaterial, trans-cendent: in a word, to *reduce*... to reduce all things to the terms that objective consciousness might master.[9]

But does this tone merely 'linger'? Is this darker motif really a part of science? At another point Roszak writes,

There can be no question but that the worst vices to which the objective style of experience leads — callousness, authoritarian manipulation, simple indifference to the sensibilities of people and nature — are ancient and universal traits ... Mankind hardly required Bacon's *novum organum* to teach it such criminalities.[10]

I think Roszak has to squeeze his argument hard to persuade us that the blame falls on science and not on some of the other factors which affected civilisation before science arose and which go on affecting it now.

But first it is necessary to look again at whether science necessarily is based on the Newton-Cartesian single vision. The idea that this provides an acceptable account of the historical origins of science in the Europe of the fifteenth and sixteenth centuries is no longer in favour with professional historians of science.[11] They stress the con-tributions in the early days of other types of thought to the emergence of the new knowledge. There was, for instance, a movement which took biology and the phenomena of life as the central theme of the world. Aristotle was its great representative in classical times; and Harvey, the discoverer of the circulation of the blood, undoubtedly a

a significant contributor to the new science, was in the main a follower
of Aristotle. Also, there was a magical tradition which was remarkably
important, particularly in the development of chemistry. Its classical
representative was a (probably mythical) Egyptian magician, known as
'Thrice-Blessed Hermes' (Hermes Trismegistus). To early scientists,
the changes which can occur to a substance when it is heated or distilled
or mixed with something else, seemed so mysterious that it was
difficult to distinguish them from real magic; stone-like metal ores,
strongly heated, perhaps with charcoal, turned into bright shining
metal; a fluid metal, mercury, heated, might turn into a brilliant red
powder, one of its oxides; sulphur could be transformed into sulphuric
acid, or the bad-smelling gas we know as H_2S, or into a rubbery substance. No wonder that chemistry became mixed up with (in fact gets
its name from) alchemy, which the Arabs picked up in Alexandria and
carried (developing it as they went along) west along the shores of the
Mediterranean into Spain, from where Europe took it up again as an
ingredient in the new science. It merged into Neo-Platonism, which
was the opposition to Aristotelianism and was the main early strand of
thought which laid stress on the importance of mathematics, which
often seems almost as magical in its results as chemistry. In this form it
had a strong influence on such important early scientists as Copernicus,
Kepler and Newton. Mechanism, the 'single vision' of the world as made
up of machines, was only the third of the major traditions. Its classical
hero was, perhaps, Archimedes. It was not until the end of the sixteenth
century that it became important, first in France and a little later in
England. The mechanists, like Descartes, Hobbes and Boyle, who
claimed Francis Bacon as their great champion, actually misrepresented
his somewhat muddled views; Bacon's main importance was as an
exponent of a fourth component, the reaction of careful, exact, even
humdrum observation.[12]

We have to build up a comprehension of more complex things by
finding suitable ways of combining these simple basic entities. This last
line of thought was most fully developed by the naturalists, who defined
and classified animals and plants.[13] It asserts that our knowledge of
nature starts by observations; observations which, when they are
systematically prepared and arranged, are spoken of as experiments. An
observation requires an observer, and experiment an experimenter.
This type of thinking accepts that the basis of science includes a human
being, the scientist. The Cartesian splitting of things into two totally
different categories, the human mind over against non-human nature, is
fundamentally impossible; total objectivity is a myth and science cannot

be, and is not, based on it. Admittedly this point of view has been very unfashionable for most of the eighteenth and nineteenth centuries and is even now returning to favour only rather gradually. Nevertheless it has always been a possible view of science, and that alone is enough to show that science in itself does not necessarily give rise to what Blake and Roszak call the Newtonian single vision, with all the evil consequences which they claim to flow from it. The predominant and powerful influence of this particular view of science must have been brought about by causes outside science itself; and so, as I argued above, do many of the practical ill effects which Roszak blames on this mistaken view.

This view that science is based on experiments and observations rather than the totally objective reality of material particles like atoms and electrons allows us to believe that human values are just as real as anything else we can know about, since they are involved in the observations from which all our knowledge starts. We have still, however, to see how the biological 'goods' which are factors in the non-human animal world become human values with the evolution of mankind.

I do not wish here to discuss this philosophical problem at any length. It is clear that the difference between a human value and a biological good is connected with the fact that man is a social animal, who is able to formulate abstract mental concepts and to communicate them to his fellows, mainly by means of language. Thus, while animals are concerned mainly with goods that apply to them individually – their strength, health, food, sexual satisfaction and so on – man, in addition, becomes concerned with goods relating not only to him individually, but to him in relation to his fellows – values such as truthfulness, loyalty, friendship, love. I have expressed my own views about the evolutionary transition from biological goods to human values in a book called *The Ethical Animal*[14] in which I argue that the particular flavour which attaches to some possible human aims and which leads us to call them ethical values, arises from the way they are related to the processes going on in a child's mind at the time it learns to speak language.

Anti-science

There are, of course, several criticisms which may fairly be levelled against the science of today. One common but fairly trivial criticism, justifiable in its way, is that every new advance in scientific understanding raising more problems than it solves. Toynbee, in his overview of the whole of human history, *A Study of History*,[15] puts this point into perspective, perhaps best in a quotation he gives from Walt Whitman, 'It is provided in the essence of things, that from any fruition of success, no matter what, shall come forth something to make a greater struggle necessary.' This is surely the only reason why man has not been bored to death generations ago; because every insight he acquires by trying to solve one problem makes him realise there is some other question which he can accept as an interesting challenge.

Another criticism is that science has allowed itself to be carried away by the extraordinary successes of atomic theories in dealing with the physical world, so that it has tried to apply these much too rigidly to fields such as human and social behaviour, into which they can provide very little insight. This sort of failure is also a general danger for all man's activities. Arnold Toynbee again discusses it extensively and provides innumerable examples of it in the history of all civilisations, and in all manner of contexts. He speaks of three steps in the process, under their Greek names: *Choros*, 'the break-through'; *Hubris*, 'pride'; *Ate*, 'the fall'.

> What is palpably true of military action is also true of other human activities in less hazardous fields where the trail of gunpowder which leads from Choros through Hubris to Ate is not so explosive. Whatever the human faculty or the sphere of its exercise may be, the presumption that, because a faculty has proved equal to the accomplishment of a limited task within its proper field, it may therefore be counted on to produce some inordinate effect in a different set of circumstances, is never anything but an intellectual and moral aberration, and never leads to anything but certain disaster.[16]

There may well be some plausibility in arguing that Newtonian science was, in say the 1920s/1930s, at the brink where Hubris crumbles under one's feet and one finds oneself falling down the precipice into the Ate; but with the development of quantum mechanics, as basic aspects of physics, and of organicism, or Whiteheadianism, as a basis for biology, science has certainly done a great deal to rescue itself in time.

A similar point can be put in a much more powerful and potentially damaging way, which is the complement to the arguments for which we used Roszak as the mouthpiece. Roszak's criticism is 'idealist', in the sense that he supposes that the ideas of science (wrong, he thinks) have important effects on the ways (bad, of course) in which society runs itself. Neo-Marxists follow the example of Marx in turning idealism upside down. For them, science is a mere product of a culture whose nature is basically determined by political forces and in particular by economic forces. Society is not the fault of science; but science is the fault of society.

Now of course that science is produced in particular cultures – so far mainly in European-derived capitalist cultures – it does to some extent reflect the nature of the society which produced it. But there are strict limits to the extent to which the politico-economic forces can be effective in determining the nature of science. It is plausible to suggest that a competitive profit-motivated society or indeed any society, including a Soviet-type one, which allows itself to become obsessed by material possessions, will tend in its science to try to isolate factors in experience from one another, so that it can more easily concentrate on its chosen material values without having to bother about all the relations and interactions; it will tend to be atomistic in philosophy rather than holistic, to go in for 'things' rather than 'processes'; and perhaps to pursue more enthusiastically the material sciences, physics and chemistry, than the more biological or psychological ones (but remember that the former may genuinely be less difficult than the latter). But, however much politico-economic forces may direct the attention of scientists and influence the nature of the concepts they use, it seems to me indisputable that there is some basic structure of relationships in the make-up of the universe, which remains unaltered however we try to express it. To give an example. Chemists used to say that the stable compound of hydrogen and oxygen can be expressed in the formula H_2O, while compounds, which might be expressed as H_2O_2 or H_3O, were less stable. Now, a quantum chemist at present would not be wholly satisfied with that formulation; it does not include everything that we now know about these compounds. So it is not wholly 'objective' in the sense which some philosophers of science demand. But on the other hand, it does express some relationship which cannot be talked out of existence. And to that extent it is not alterable by any change in culture, politico-economic or other.

Too many scientists have forgotten for too long the degree to which their formulations of scientific theories are influenced by their own perceptual apparatus and by the interests and philosophical out-looks which they have picked up from the society in which they live. It is salutory for them to be reminded of this; but many also realise that their real concern is to try to increase our knowledge of the basic structure which men cannot change in the world around them, and many too are quite ready to try to look at science through the eyes of a differently motivated society — to develop, for instance, alternative technologies, or resource-conserving systems and the like.

Values and the 'Ecology Movement'

The recent and sudden great increase in concern, in the developed western nations at least, about the condition of natural ecosystems, and the realisation that the pollution and despoiling of them are rapidly approaching unacceptable levels, has led many people to ask which of our generally accepted value systems are to blame for producing this sorry state of affairs. Since much of the most obvious pollution comes from the industrial applications of science-based technology, many people immediately jumped to the conclusion that the root of the trouble was an overvaluation of science. The scientists, of course, replied that the cause of pollution and despoiling of nature was not science itself, but that science had been misused by industry.

The discussion that followed is not at all one-sided. One can take Theodore Roszak again as one of the more perceptive spokesmen of the anti-science group. He writes

> It might seem unfair to lay the blame for impending environmental disaster at the doorstep of the scientists. Granted, the rape of the environment has not been carried out by scientists, but by profiteering industrialists and myopic developers, with the eager support of a burgeoning population greedy to consume more than nature can provide, and to waste more than nature can clear away. But to absolve the scientific community from complicity in the matter is quite simply to ignore that science has been the only natural philosophy the western world has known since the age of Newton. It is to ignore the key question: Who provided us with the image of nature, that invited the rape, and with the sensibility that has licensed it? It is not, after all, the normal thing for people to ruin their environment. It is extraordinary and requires extra-ordinary incitement.[17]

Again, to take another quotation from that rather repetitious book,

> To accuse science of breaking faith between human beings and their environment may seem a harsh indictment. And yet, can any less dramatic — and demonic — conception of the scientific revolution do justice to the stupendous dynamism which has characterised

western civilisations for the last three centuries?[18]

But then in other places he just denies science that very demonic
dynamism he has just invoked for the rape of the environment.

> The basic effect of Newtonian mechanism was to produce a nature
> that was felt to be dead, alien, and purely functional. This estranged
> relationship with scientists and nature has remained unchanged; it is
> still what our science most irreducibly is.

But it is not just turning nature into a bit of a bore that Roszak has
set out to explain. It is 'attacking it with the sort of ferocity and
wantonness that one only vents upon a foe little trusted, much less to
be pitied'.[19] He cannot really have it both ways.

A more balanced view is expressed by John Black, a professional
ecologist:[20]

> ... ecological breakdown need not have occurred, had the scientific
> abilities of western civilisation been used in different directions, or
> used more wisely. . . . The reason is to be found not in science or
> technology alone, but in the whole complex of ideas on which
> western civilisation is based.

Black's book is largely concerned with the accusation that science
is only the latest phase in the development of Judaeo-Christian civilisation, and that the root values of western civilisation are the basic
causes of the evils to which the ecological movement has drawn
attention.[21] This accusation tends to go back to the account of the
Creation given in the book of Genesis. In Chapter 1, after creating man,

> God blessed them, and God said unto them, Be fruitful, and
> multiply, and replenish the earth, and subdue it: and have dominion
> over the fish of the sea, and over the fowl of the air, and over every
> living thing that moveth upon the earth.

This can be taken as a licence, if not an order, for what Roszak describes
as a ferocious and wanton attack. But, as Black points out, the Book of
Genesis contains two separate and different accounts of the Creation. In
the other version, given mainly in Chapter 2, in Black's words,

> God made the earth, but since there had been no rain, there was no

vegetation on it. Following the mist which watered the earth, preparing the soil surface for plant growth, God created man, and then
planted a garden for him to live in. Only then did God feel that man
should not live on the earth alone and created the animals and birds
as companions for him. Finding these inadequate for the purpose,
since although they could be a *help* to man, they could not be *meet*
for him, that is, suitable for him or equal to him, God made a
woman from Adam's rib, and brought her to him. Nowhere in (this)
narrative of the creation is man given dominion over the animals;
the only instruction he receives is that, with one important exception,
he might eat freely from every tree in the Garden.

So it is at least doubtful whether even early Christianity encouraged
man to attack his natural environment as an enemy to be subdued and
exploited. Certainly Christianity, up to at least the time of the
Renaissance, was quite as good as any of the rival civilisations in keeping
the world a fit place for human living. There were several great ecological
catastrophes of early civilisation — they did not occur in Christian lands.
The first civilisation of Mesopotamia ruined its environment and
destroyed itself by pushing its agricultural productivity more than the
circumstances could bear, leading to erosion of the fertile soil into the
rivers, and the silting up of the harbours. The ecology of most of the
eastern Mediterranean, particularly the northern shores of Africa, was
also ruined by exploitive agriculture, under civilisations dominated by
Greek, Roman and Islamic religions, not by Christianity. In contrast it
was medieval Christianity which turned the somewhat inhospitable
swampy tangled woodlands of northern Europe into stably productive,
agriculturally rich country.

It might be argued that all this changed about the time of the
Renaissance. Before that, Christianity had been indifferent to science
and technology, if not actually opposed to it. It judged proposed new
developments in the light of their moral acceptability, not their
technological promise, and on the whole it preferred to keep things
as they had been. During these centuries, the science which had
developed under the Greeks, and the technological skills of the near-
eastern civilisations, such as Egypt, survived by being taken over by
the invading Arabs, who carried them along the north coast of Africa,
and eventually into Spain, from where they spread at the time of the
Renaissance back into Europe.

This revival of the ancient learnings, accompanied by the Protestant
revolt against the Catholic Church, soon led to the appearance of

extreme Puritan sects, with their ethics of hard work and strict adherence to a number of literally-interpreted religious doctrines. The same period of history in Western Europe saw the consolidation of capitalism as the dominant mode of economic organisation. There has been an enormous amount of historical argument about the relations between these three great movements. For a long time the orthodox view was that capitalism could not have gained the importance it did, except in a Protestant society. In fact some of the most respected authors, such as Max Weber and R.H. Tawney, argued that one was in effect the cause of the other. Nowadays historians seem to be much more doubtful if the relation was so close. Many of the most extreme Protestants, such as the Scottish Highland Calvinists, or some of the English Protestants at the time of Cromwell, such as the Diggers, were anything but capitalists; while many of the Italian capitalist bankers remained good Catholics. In any case, the rape of the environment did not start until the rise of fairly massive industrial enterprises, some two centuries or so after Protestantism and capitalism had come on the scene. In the meantime, it was Protestant farmers in Britain who had created the English landscape we now so much admire as natural; and mainly Protestant immigrants into the United States who began to tame the wilderness into something slightly more like the Garden of Eden in which man finds it agreeable to live.

When industry did arise, from say the middle of the eighteenth century onwards, the connections between the basic technological inventions and anything which can be called science were much less close than many people nowadays seem to think. Nearly all the inventors were practical men coming out of workshops rather than laboratories. It was not until about the middle of the nineteenth century that professional science, of the kind which we call by that name today, began to be translated rather directly into the industrial technological processes which can plausibly be accused of raping the earth.

The uses to which technology is put are determined much more by things other than its origin, whether from craftsmen's know-how or from sophisticated scientific theories. For most of the last two centuries, man in the countries which we now regard as developed has been employing every technology he can put his hands to, primarily to further his own greed, for obtaining and keeping material goods. Just where this sense of greed has come from is more difficult to say. Partly, surely, from the breakdown of faith in Christianity, including its Protestant version, which usually involved some sense of stewardship, and partly from the rise of capitalism; but much the same has gone on in the only developed culture claiming to be non-capitalist, i.e. the Communist Soviet Union. Another strong influence was the extraordinary situation in which Europeans found themselves when they discovered the Americas, which were so rich in natural wealth and so poor in inhabitants. The early Spanish and Portuguese invaders of Central and South America set themselves almost immediately on a course of ruthless exploitation (undeterred by their Catholic faith). The early settlers of North America, primarily British, were at first more restrained (quite largely by their strongly held Puritan faith) but then again adopted the view that the continent was simply there to be exploited. It was, I think, primarily in North America that, in Roszak's words, 'the modern west has played the conquering hero in its dealing with nature'. Conceivably one could say this also of Australia, though the attack there was certainly less successful, perhaps because the environment was not such a push-over. I doubt if one could claim that this was western man's behaviour in New Zealand, or even in South Africa; and in Western Europe, most of such behaviour, which is quite recent, has been brought back from America as a returning wave of malpractices.

It is, I argue, the worship of Mammon, the Almighty Dollar, not Science, which has to bear the blame. It is Greed, Get Rich Quick, Turn a Quick Buck, Mine that Soil, Get Your Hands on That Gold, Squeeze Those Bastards Out, Control the Market, that provides the demonic drive to turn God's Own Country into God's Own Junk Yard; and it takes more than I can swallow of pseudo-psycho-analytical double-talk that all this is just an excusable over-reaction against the bland and dessicated view of the universe for which Newtonian science was told to take the blame.

Black finishes his book, *The Dominion of Man*, with the remark that:

> If western civilisation has failed, it has failed because it has been un-able to find a concept which would engender a feeling of respon-sibility for the use to which we put our control over nature, and at this late stage it is not easy to suggest one which would be com-patible with the rest of our world view. We have no means of knowing if, faced with far-reaching, even revolutionary changes in our environment, our fundamental approach to the world will change to allow a more stable relationship between man and nature within the framework of our existing society, or whether western society itself will have to be replaced. It is not easy to forecast where the building blocks for a new model of the Universe will be discovered.

This is a pessimistic view. There are some aspects of western civilisation which have been left fallow for a long time but which might
provide the basis for the kind of world review which Black calls for;
they will be discussed in the next chapter.

Does Ecology Provide a Standard?

It seems to be in the context of ecology that many of today's
generation first come into contact with the multi-level thinking which
demands giving attention simultaneously to many interacting components within a system. The value of this type of thought quite
rightly impresses them, but it sometimes tempts them to ask from
ecology more than that science can deliver. To quote Roszak again,

> Like all the healing arts, ecology is through and through judge-
> mental in character. It cannot be value-neutral. . . .What violates the
> natural harmony must be condemned; what enhances it be en-
> dorsed. . . Ecology is the closest our science has yet come to an
> integrative wisdom. It, and not physics, deserves to become the
> *basic* science of the future.[22]

I do not think that ecology, as the biologist studies it, does provide
an adequate basis for judgement. If a natural ecosystem is left to itself,
it relatively soon — in periods of say tens of years — gets into a more or
less stable state, in which it continues until disturbed, either by
evolutionary changes to some of its inhabitants or by forest fires, floods
or other natural disturbances. But these natural 'climax' ecologies are
by no means 'good' for man. Consider those that still exist on the planet's
surface: the Sahara, the Amazon basin, much of Siberia or the Canadian
Arctic. They are extremely unpleasant places, and static at that, with
little tendencies to change, let alone improve.

The best place to look for an aspect of science that gives one a notion
of dynamic improvement is the study of embryonic development. It is
difficult to deny that a full-grown rabbit is in some real sense 'better' —
more of a rabbit — than the fertilised egg out of which it grew. It is not
ethically better, but it seems to me undeniably better in some real, if
non-ethical sense. Ethical value, as I suggested above, arises only in
connection with man.

The relevance of ecology to human value is not so much that it
provides any basis for judgement, but that it shows the kind of thing
the judgement has to be about, namely a system of interacting
activity — different aspects of human personality, interacting with one

another and with natural and artificial surroundings — rather than single isolated traits.

The whole richness of the interacting system in which man is involved is also not fully expressed in his embryonic development, even if we include all his activities as a youth and adult. We really have to take into account more than just one lifetime, but rather the whole evolutionary succession. Human values inhere in what one might call 'human evolutionary ecology'. Unfortunately the science we have developed so far can hardly sketch even the crudest outline of this, which I consider the most basic science of the future.

If one is going to look to anything which could be called science to provide any worthwhile help in formulating human values, it will have to be scientific developments of this kind, which include man within their scope, rather than ecology of the normal kind which excludes him. When Thoreau said that 'In the wilderness is the salvation of mankind' (the motto of the Sierra Club in America), he was basically talking nonsense. Anything like a decent human life can put up with about 5 per cent of sheer wilderness, but not much more.

People who have thought profoundly about the values which should be served by the 'development' of the developing nations often turn towards the concept of development in the biological sense. In the 'Cocoyoc Declaration',[23] one group writes:

> Our first concern is to redefine the whole purpose of development. This should not be to develop things but to develop man. Human beings have basic needs: food, shelter, clothing, health, education. . . Development should not be limited to the satisfaction of basic needs. . . Development includes freedom of expression and impression, the right to give and to receive ideas and stimulus. . .

Values for a Post-industrial Society

Many of the people who are urging the importance of a new set of values, and are doing their best to define one, do not make an opposition to science the centre of their thinking, though it often remains part of it; nor do they all look to ecology to provide them with a pattern. They follow, indeed, such a large number of different paths that it is difficult to sketch an outline which does not leave out something of great importance. Perhaps one might say that most of the modern moralists start from one or other — and often from both — of two broad fields of concern. One of these is a moral objection to the so-called developed societies of the present day, mainly on the grounds

that they are dominated by greed. The other is the conviction that
social relations will have to change drastically for technological reasons;
either we shall find that we are running out of natural resources and
discover that we have to start being more thrifty in our use of them, or
that greater use of the computer and similar techniques will remove so
much of the routine tasks from men's shoulders that they will be faced
seriously with the difficult problem of how to use their leisure in a way
that makes it enjoyable.

As an example of a writer starting from the first field, one might
quote Philip Slater:[24]

> What is significant in the new culture is not a celebration of economic
> affluence, but a rejection of its foundation. It is not merely blindly
> reactive, but embodies the sociological consciousness that possessions
> actually generate scarcity. To accumulate possessions is to deliver
> pieces of oneself to dead things. Every time we buy something we
> deepen our emotional deprivation, and hence our need to buy some-
> thing. *This is good for business.*

From that rejection of the values he sees as underlying the present
economic functioning of societies, Slater goes on to conclude that

> There are an almost infinite number of polarities by means of which
> one can differentiate between the old culture and the new. The old
> culture tends to give preferences to property rights over personal
> rights, technological requirements over human needs, competition
> over co-operation, violence over sexuality, concentration over dis-
> tribution, the producer over the consumer, means over ends, secrecy
> over open-ness, social forms over personal expression, striving over
> gratification, Oedipal love over communal love. The new counter-
> culture tends to *reverse* all of these priorities.

Or again!

> The core of the old culture is scarcity. The flaw of the old culture
> is the fact that this scarcity is spurious — man-made in the case of
> bodily gratifications, and man-allowed or man-maintained in the case
> of material goods. The new culture is based on the assumption that
> important human needs are easily satisfied, that the resources for
> doing so are plentiful, but a certain amount of *work* is required to
> release the bounty that exists from the restraints under which it is

now placed.

There are also rather different approaches from the moral side. For instance, John Cage, well known as a composer of experimental music, is an eloquent exponent of the most extreme anarchism and repudiation of purpose or goal-seeking behaviour of any kind.

This approach resists presentation in a sequential logical form, but can perhaps be illustrated by the following quotations:[25]

> The truth is that everything causes everything else, we do not speak therefore of one thing causing another. There are no secrets.
> ... The purpose of one activity is no longer separate from the purpose of any other activity. All activities fuse in one purpose which is (cf. Huang-Po's Doctrine of Universal Mind) no purpose.
> ... The highest purpose is to have no purpose at all. This puts one in accord with nature in her manner of operation.... Where there is a history of organisation (art), introduce disorder, where there is a history of disorganisation (World Society), introduce order.
> ... There is nothing we really need to do that isn't dangerous.

Some of these ideas are not so far from the types of values advocated by people who approach the subject from the quite different starting point of considering what we should do with our lives when we have no longer to work so hard merely to stay alive. Again, pressures of space and time persuade me to give several quotations from one spokesman, rather than attempt an over-all inventory. So I will arbitrarily pick Gene Youngblood,[26] who uses the abstract and technically far-out cinema as a peg on which to hang some general remarks. 'When man is freed from the needs of marginal survival, he will remember what he was thinking before he had to prove his right to live.' Here I will interpolate a quotation from Alvin Toffler,[27]

> In that super-industrial civilisation of tomorrow, with its fast silent cybernetic intricacies, and its liberating quantities of time for the individual, art will not be a fringe benefit for the few, but an indispensable part of life for the many.

Going back to Gene Youngblood,

> Life becomes art when there is no difference between what we are and what we do ... The transition from culture that considers

leisure 'a problem' to a culture that demands leisure as a prerequisite of civilised behaviour, is a metamorphosis of the first magnitude, and it has begun. . . . Perhaps in the near future the whole process of living will be in this active seeking out of experiences.

Although one can glimpse some parallelisms or correspondences, or even convergences, in the novel values which these various thinkers are suggesting, there are still great divergences between them. There is an important line of thought which holds that in the near future civilised societies will be, and should be, more diversified in the systems of values which their citizens can follow with full social approval. Even if we shelve for later discussion the value system of the non-industrialised parts of the world (or even of the female members of the industrial society!), this point of view argues that we are seeing the emergence of an enormous variety of socially accepted life-styles.

As representative of this point of view, I shall again take a book by Philip Slater, but this time in collaboration with Warren Bennis,[28] and Alvin Toffler's book *Future Shock*,[29] a more worked-up, and perhaps more journalistically spiced-up, version of a similar point of view. Both start primarily with the technological-organisational situation, rather than the purely moral one. They lead on, however, not so much to the strong emphasis on each individual person doing his own thing, which is stressed in Slater, Cage and even Youngblood, but rather to smallish groups of people following together, for a time, a certain life-style, or working on a certain endeavour; though as they see it, an individual person would during his lifetime change quite often from one group to another — 'sub-culture hopping', as Toffler calls it. But with each change, he would feel himself not so much John Cage's individual, who 'keeps his head alert but empty' and 'takes it easy, but takes it' — but rather, all through life he is a member of a group, even if they are different groups at different times.

Warren Bennis argues that

The social structure of organisations of the future will have some unique characteristics. The key word will be 'temporary'. There will be adaptive, rapidly changing *temporary* systems. These will be task forces organised around problems to be solved by groups of relative strangers with diverse professional skills . . . This trend is already visible in the aero-space and construction industries, as well as many professional and consulting firms.[30]

As he sees it, man as we know him today needs to be 'revitalised'. And

> The elements of revitalisation are:
> An ability to learn from experience and to codify, store and retrieve the relevant knowledge.
> An ability to learn how to learn, that is to develop methods for improving the learning process.
> An ability to acquire and use feed-back mechanisms on performance, in short, to be self analytical.
> An ability to direct one's own destiny.[31]

He admits 'that the future I describe is not necessarily a "happy" one'. But he does go on to claim that

> fantasy, imagination, and creativity will be legitimate in ways that today seem strange. Social structures will no longer be instruments of psychic repression but will increasingly promote play and freedom on behalf of curiosity and thought.[32]

None of the suggestions about future value systems quoted so far has laid stress on a major concern of people in Europe and the developing countries, who seem to be placing more and more importance on decreasing inequalities between individuals within a nation and between nations. This is not a striving to achieve sameness or even an exact equality in income or material resources. It is, however, a very powerful world-wide movement arising from the conviction that inequality has been allowed to develop too far. The resources which support the life-style of an early-retired director of a large company (and his ideal wife) are too grossly superabundant by the standards of a night-watchman or office cleaner; and the standards of an industrial country as a whole are, even when averaged out over the whole population, some fifteen or twenty times those of the average person in the developing world. This, of course, causes political resentment, as soon as it becomes widely known through television or the cinema. But it has also provoked an ethical revulsion, not least among the richer people themselves. And a whole new system of values will have to be – and are being – evolved to meet the challenge.

One important factor, which the future will probably not be able to avoid, is the need to be less profligate of energy and natural resources. Only if the physicists do succeed in harnessing fusion power can the world even contemplate using energy as freely and wastefully as we have done, and even then the need to raise the standard of living of the developing parts of the world may set limits on the amount of energy in which we can allow ourselves to luxuriate. Again, it is almost impossible to see any new source for some of the rarer mineral resources which nowadays we are still treating as inexhaustible (see Chapter 4). For both these reasons the picture which Bennis presents, that we shall go beyond bureaucracy into 'the temporary society', is incomplete. Probably we shall go into a society in which the processes of manufacture will be required to produce objects and machines with much longer lifetimes, (possibly involving somewhat more servicing during these lifetimes) with the expenditure of a great deal less energy. It may well be that we shall have much more leisure and that we shall make more short-term temporary organisations of work, but the need to make things — of some types at least — which last a long time, and whose production does not absorb too much electricity or coal or oil, will probably call for the development of a kind of skilled craftsmanship which in the last few decades has tended to be pushed out of the world by mass production techniques. This type of skill, which allows a person the occasion to take a longer view than merely to the next weekly wage packet, has in the past always been one of the main factors around which individuals have built up their sense of self-respect and satisfaction. It may well become so again, though presumably in somewhat new ways which one can as yet hardly formulate in detail.

It certainly seems one of the values which the developing countries should try hard not to lose from their traditional value systems. They will certainly be going through unsettling periods of transition. There may well be strong attempts to transfer to them major manufacturing plants, operating by what have been the dominating systems of mass production. The injection of capital into their economies, which this involves, will at first sight seem very attractive and may indeed bring some advantages at least temporarily, but the transfers will have been made mainly because the citizens of the developed countries are finding the assembly line, and other methods involved in mass production, unattractive ways of spending their time, so that even at present a large amount of this work is actually carried out by immigrants into the developed countries from poorer ones. If we are really moving towards a future which places a greater value on quality and less on quantity, and which husbands its resources rather than squandering them, developing countries should think hard about the losses as well as about the gains involved in allowing the establishment of mass industries on their territories.

Another major influence on future value systems, which has not been mentioned so far, is the general desire, indeed the need, to bring about greater cohesion of mankind as a whole on a global scale. The practical requirement for this arises from the dangers of atomic warfare on a world scale, but it is also a general value which inspires many of the younger generation. We will have to consider the validity of many different value systems in connection with global unification.

The values can perhaps be classified into three classes.

(1)　Universal values which should be accepted by all members (individuals, nations, or other groups) who form the planetary society. Probably the most important of these universal values is the desire to identify with the whole human race. This does not exclude allowing some importance to more local loyalties, such as to nation, or even to groups within a nation; but there is unlikely to be much progress towards developing an effective global social organisation, unless adherence to mankind as a whole is given the primary position. It seems likely that such a value system almost necessarily implies granting greater importance to the quality of life than to the sheer quantity of any particular items, such as material wealth, numbers of persons and so on.

(2)　Conflicting values, a belief in which would disrupt the planetary society (e.g. some forms of exclusive nationalism, unrestrained aggressive competitiveness).

(3)　'Free' values, which do not conflict with the development of a global society, but are also not necessary foundations of it. Different groups could choose to express their individuality by developing one or other of these free values without doing any harm to the planetary society as a whole.

All value systems which stress the importance of trying to incorporate everybody into some coherent community with their fellows have a tendency to overlook the fact that different people have different tastes and want different things. Recent history has seen several examples of societies which set out, from a historical state of confusion and incoherence, with the aim to integrate themselves into something with an organic unity, only to end up a few years later in some form of totalitarianism. Hitler's Germany, Mussolini's Italy, Stalin's Russia were all examples.

The countries which have accepted the values of individualism and democracy have tended to go about solving this problem by the system of 'one man, one vote'. It is becoming clear that this does not always work very well either. On the one hand, the citizen may be offered only a restricted range of choices to vote for, and these choices may be selected for him by far-from-ideal political machines, such as party organisations. Again, if the democratic constitution gives absolute power to the majority, then some minorities may never be able to make their influence felt, e.g. the Blacks or Chicanos in the United States, the Catholics in Northern Ireland. Some new type of social apparatus, giving effect to the value of individuality, needs to be developed. Possibly we have been looking at things upside down, supposing that it is the duty of society to define the principles of unity and to make provision for individuals within it; instead perhaps we should give priority to the individual in all his differences from his fellows, and hope that it will require only a moderate amount of encouragement to allow the social unity to emerge as a result of the interactions between individuals. This is, I think, one of the principles that Mao was following in China, although that country seems to have oscillated between periods of imposition of unity from on top and periods when priority was given to decentralised freedom of individuals and small groups.

Probably there will be considerable 'free' values over the world as a whole. What were at one time preached as the virtues of the American 'melting pot', in which immigrants of all cultures and nationalities were to be moulded anew into a standard American citizen — although, of course, it was hoped he would be a very high quality citizen — do not seem likely to appeal to the world as a whole. It is doubtful indeed if they have actually worked out even in the United States itself. If, as one hopes, all the regions of the world, as different as North and South America, Europe, the Islamic world, the rest of Africa, the Soviet Union, China, India, South East Asia and so on, are going to work through to a post-industrial society, and achieve the feeling that the quality of their life is at least adequate, it is almost inconceivable that the different paths they will have to follow will lead to a uniform end result; much more likely there will be a wide range of types of society, each type containing within itself several, and perhaps many, life-styles.

One of the most important questions in all these problems concerning diversity in value systems and social organisation is the degree of autonomy granted to minorities. In the theory of standard western type of democracies, the majority has almost unlimited power to override any minority which it can outvote, although in practice a few well-organised minorities (e.g. powerful Trades Unions) can bully the majority. Some communist-type 'democracies' are based on the view that some far-seeing group (e.g. the revolutionary Working Class, or the Party) knows best what is good for everyone, and can override even a majority if it opposes them. The ideas about possible future value systems which have been discussed here all tend to emphasise the importance of making available a wide choice of value systems which are 'free' in the sense of not closing off other options for other people. Suitable social organisations for achieving this have not yet been worked out explicitly, though some societies, in some periods of history, have achieved a 'tolerance' which informally came near to filling this need. Discovery of a type of organisation which gives greater protection to freedom of choice in values is one of the most important problems which will have to be solved if the future is to be a happy one.

Amongst these 'local' loyalties there is one of a rather special kind — loyalty to sex. There is no doubt that practically the whole world, developed and developing, has for some centuries at least lived in male-dominated societies; possibly this was not always so definitely the case in some earlier agricultural pre-urban society. Certainly many women, particularly perhaps in developed countries, but not solely in them, see no reason why it should continue to be so.[33] The feminist movement involves one of the most active restructurings of value systems that is going on at the present time. It can be regarded as a 'free' value, in the sense that global society could exist even with considerable differences in the values which were given, in different parts of it, to ensuring similarity of treatment and opportunity for men and women.

Further Reading

A. Dennis Gabor, *The Mature Society* (Secker and Warburg, 1972).
B. Theodore Roszak, *Where the Wasteland Ends* (Doubleday, 1972).
C. C.H. Waddington ed., *Biology and the History of the Future* (Edinburgh University Press, 1969).
D. Erich Jantsch, *Design for Evolution* (Braziller, 1975).
E. E.F. Schumacher, *Small is Beautiful* (Blond & Briggs, 1973).
F. Nigel Calder, *Technopolis* (Simon & Schuster, 1970).
G. Gordon Rattray Taylor, *Rethink* (Secker & Warburg, 1972).
H. Andrei Sakharov, *Progress, Co-existence and Intellectual Freedom* (Andre Deutsch, 1968).
I. A. Tiselius and S. Nilsson eds., *The Place of Value in a World of Facts*, Nobel Symposium 1970 (Interscience, 1971).

J. A. Peccei, *The Chasm Ahead* (Macmillan, 1969).
K. Harvey Brooks, 'Technology and Values: New Ethical Issues Raised by Technological Progress', *Zygon*, 8, 17–35, 1973.
L. Peter Harper, ' "Soft Technology" and Criticisms of the Western Model of Development', *Prospects 3*: 183–192, 1973.
M. Eric Ashby, 'Science and Anti-Science', Bernal Lecture, 1971, *Proc.Roy.Soc.*(Lond.), *B, 178*: 29–42.

Notes

1. C.H. Waddington, *The Ethical Animal* (Allen & Unwin, 1960; University of Chicago Press, 1967).
2. Theodore Roszak, *Where the Wasteland Ends* (Doubleday, 1972).
3. Ibid., p. 146.
4. Ibid., p. 159.
5. Charles Gillespie, *The Edge of Objectivity* (Princeton University Press, 1960).
6. Peter Medawar, *The Hope of Progress* (Methuen, 1972).
7. Karl Popper, *Objective Knowledge* (Clarendon Press, 1972).
8. Quotation from Newton taken from D.P. Walker, *The Ancient Theology* (Cornell University Press, 1972), p. 255.
9. Roszak, *Wasteland*, p. 227.
10. Ibid., p. 158.
11. A good account of recent views is Hugh Kearney, *Science and Change 1500–1700* (Weidenfeld & Nicolson, 1971). For a more detailed recent account of the influences of Bacon, Newton and the founding of the Royal Society, see Frances A. Yates, *The Rosicrucian Enlightenment* (Routledge & Kegan Paul, 1972), particularly pp. 118–39 and 171–205.
12. C.H. Waddington, 'The New Atlantis Revisited', Bernal Lecture, 1975, *Proc.Roy.Soc.* (Lond.), *B* 1975, *190*: 301.
13. There seems to have been little recent discussion of the influence of the early naturalists. See C.E. Raven, *Synthetic Philosophy in the 17th Century*, Herbert Spencer Lecture (Blackwell, Oxford, 1945).
14. See note 1.
15. Arnold Toynbee, *A Study of History* (Abridged version, Oxford University Press, 1946) vol. 1, pp. 189 and 349.
16. Ibid., p. 349.
17. Roszak, *Wasteland*, p. 212.
18. Ibid., p. 156.
19. Ibid., p. 157.
20. John Black, *The Dominion of Man: The Search for Ecological Responsibility* (Edinburgh University Press, 1970).
21. Another good discussion is Thomas Sieger Derr, *Ecology and Human Liberation* (World Council of Churches, Geneva, 1973).
22. Roszak, *Wasteland*, p. 368.
23. 'The Cocoyoc Declaration', reprinted in *Development Dialogue*, September 1974, p. 88.
24. Philip Slater, *The Pursuit of Loneliness* (Allen Lane, 1971).
25. John Cage, *A Year from Monday* (Wesleyan University Press, 1969), and see C.H. Waddington ed., *Biology and the History of the Future* (Edinburgh University Press, 1969).

26. Gene Youngblood, *Expanded Cinema* (Dutton, NY, 1970).
27. Alvin Toffler, *Future Shock* (Random House, 1970).
28. Warren Bennis and Philip E. Slater, *The Temporary Society* (Harper & Row, 1969).
29. See note 27.
30. Bennis, *The Temporary Society*, p. 73.
31. Ibid., p. 71.
32. Ibid., p. 75.
33. There is no need to give references to the enormous polemical literature, but for a relatively cool look, see 'Changing Women in a Changing Society', *American J. Sociology*, vol. 78, no. 4, January 1973 (published separately by Chicago University Press, ed. J. Huber, 1973).

12 PUTTING THE PIECES TOGETHER

The first eleven chapters have given sketches of the main dynamic factors operating in the most important problem areas in the world of today. As has been repeatedly emphasised, in every area the situation is changing very fast, so no account of it can be quite up to date in detail. The best one can hope is to understand in principle the fundamental processes involved, and have an idea of the existing situation, which is not too outrageously out of date. The main difficulty in making some sort of sense of the whole situation is, however, not that of keeping up to the minute; it arises because all the processes involved are interlocked with one another in complex ways, so that the birth-rate affects not only the future demands for food but also the patterns of leisure, of city development and transport, and to some degree or other every one of the other items which has come into the book. How can one in any way synthesise the whole of this complex of interactions, so as to arrive at some sort of unified picture, rather than be reduced simply to a state of total confusion?

The computer is, of course, extremely good at handling large numbers of items in relation to one another. It is much better than the human brain in accepting masses of detail without being swamped. The first attempt to arrive at a synthesis of what all this mass of interacting processes might produce over the next few decades took the form of a 'simulation' on a computer. A group under Meadows at MIT collected a number of key variables as being amongst the most important for mankind as a whole (the population and total number of persons; the industrial output per head; the food available per head; pollution levels, remaining stocks of non-renewable resources such as metals, fossil fuels, etc.). They worked out the main causal processes affecting these items, and also did their best to ascertain the value of the variables from 1900 up to the present. They wrote a programme for a computer which enabled it to calculate reasonably accurately these past values, and it was then allowed to run on so as to give forecasts of the values from the present time up to the year 2100. These results predicted a disastrous decline in the availability of natural resources, which would force reductions in industrial output and food output, and eventually of population. This seemed so depressing that a number of assumptions were changed to see if any alterations from the present policy would

331

produce better results. For instance, suppose they had been unduly pessimistic about the amount of resources available, what would happen then? The computer predicted that there would be a staggering rise in industrial pollution, which would eventually in itself be sufficient to reduce first food output, then industrial output and then population. Quite a number of different assumptions were tried and in nearly every case some disaster eventually occurred. In fact, according to this model, the only way of avoiding eventual disaster for the world was by strict control of industrial working and of food output and by the stabilisation of population numbers.

This work was done as the Club of Rome's project on 'The Predicament of Mankind', and published and very widely disseminated in 1972, in a book called *The Limits to Growth*.[1] It raised considerable public interest and discussion. Many people realised for the first time that mankind really is facing an unprecedented set of difficulties. However, there were a great many points on which this computer simulation was open to question.[2] There was, for instance, a very obvious limitation that it lumped the whole world together, without taking average figures for the globe as a whole. Whereas, of course, situations are exceedingly different in, say, industrialised Western Europe or North Africa and the regions of Asia, Africa and South America, and so on. Again, one could always quarrel with the estimates of fuel sources, rate of population growth and so on. A more fundamental point was made by people who argued that the world does not actually operate in the way that the computer model implied. The computer programme was based on a series of fully determined interactions, comparable to those between chemical substances in solution. It supposed that a given level of industrial production used up natural resources at a given rate, and simply went on doing so. It failed to take into account many checks and balances that are part of the real world. Many orthodox social scientists pointed in particular to the operation of the market mechanism for fixing prices. If a raw material becomes scarce, its price will rise and industrialists will either use less of it or find some substitute. According to orthodox economic theory this is an automatic regulatory mechanism, which is built in to the world system and prevents it running away into the sort of disasters predicted by the computer.

Not everybody has been impressed by the effectiveness of the orthodox social science mechanisms in the world of today. The first major upset of the smooth running of the world system in recent years — an upset which persuaded many people that the Club of Rome was right

in saying that the system at present was highly dangerous and unstable
— was the sudden fivefold increase in the price of one of the most basic
of raw materials, oil. This increase was not due to the operation of the
market in the orthodox sense, but was brought about by a conscious
political decision. In fact one has to conclude that although it is
justifiable to criticise the first Club of Rome computer simulation for
leaving out of account various regulatory or controlling systems, which
actually exist, this defect cannot be remedied merely by bringing the
market into consideration. We have to look much more deeply into the
nature of organised systems which involve man and his society.

The expression 'general systems theory' is quite a fashionable one
nowadays, but in my opinion it is always necessary to ask oneself what
exactly is meant in the particular instance when one comes across it; it
usually does not refer to any coherent body of theorems about the
nature of systems and the way in which they interact. At the worst, and
by no means infrequently, one is presented with a 'systems analysis' of
something, when what is offered is a diagram consisting of a series
of nouns naming various items in the system, each noun probably
written in a rectangular box, and each box being connected with most
or all of the others by arrows going in both directions. This is simply a
pseudo-analysis and is an excuse for failing to think clearly enough to
specify precise verbs for what one noun does to the other, to replace
the completely imprecise arrows. It is because of its frequent debasement
to this level that I avoid the use of the phrase 'systems analysis' when
possible. What we need to do now is to consider the nature of certain
types of systems, but we will not call it 'systems analysis'.

In the previous book *Tools of Thought*, we considered several types
of systems which are relevant in the present context, for instance the
distinction between closed and open systems. A 'closed system' consists
of a series of interacting processes which operate inside an impenetrable
envelope. Nothing relevant to the operations of the processes can
come into the system from outside, or go out from the system to the
outside through that envelope. Such systems are rare in practice. In
some ways the world as a whole is close to a closed system, although
it, of course, still receives energy from sunlight and radiates a little
heat back. But apart from this exchange of energy it can be said to
operate in isolation from the rest of the universe. In an 'open system'
there is no impenetrable envelope; things important to the actions of
the system can come in and go out again. Any particular region of the
earth's surface, such as the United States or Europe, is, of course, an
open system, in that it can import things from other parts of the world

and export other things to them.

The next most important distinction between types of systems is whether they are mechanistic, adaptive or purposive. A 'mechanistic system' is one in which the rules of operation are laid down from the start and are not altered whatever the external circumstances may be. An 'adaptive system' is one which has some way of altering its internal behaviour in relation to the external circumstances in which it is placed. Finally, a 'purposive system' is one which involves entities which can formulate purposes and act so as to achieve them. There are several important subdivisions to be recognised within each of these categories. A mechanistic system may be uncontrolled in the sense that its fixed set of rules allows it simply to go on until it blows up or disappears or in some other way 'runs away'. The accusation against the Meadows world simulation was that it was an uncontrolled mechanistic system. The mechanistic system operates on a set of rules which involves controlling actions, so that, for instance, if one item gets too large the rules specify that the processes producing it will be slowed up and its growth inhibited. The classical free market of the economists is supposed to act as one such controlling system, but there can be many other kinds of internal control written into the basic rules of the mechanistic system. An adaptive system is one which involves a subtler form of control than this. Since the controlling forces are influenced by factors external to the system itself, probably all living systems, certainly all highly evolved ones, are adaptive in this way. They have means of registering the nature of the external environment and allowing this to bring about modifications of their behaviour. One type of adaptive system — and the most common type — is one in which the external environment modifies the behaviour of the system in such a way as to keep something constant, since something may be the state of the system, such as for instance the level of oxygen in the blood of the human body. A man goes up to the high altitude mountains where there is less oxygen in the atmosphere, his heart beats faster so as to keep constant the oxygen level of his blood: this is known as 'homeostasis'. On the other hand, what is kept constant may be a direction of change. For instance one can do all sorts of things to a developing embryo and it will react, not so as to keep itself constant, but to keep itself developing in the normal way to produce a normal adult: this is called homeorhesis. Another way to describe this type of system is to say that it is 'goal-seeking', i.e. it reacts in such a way as to reach some preset goal. Systems of this kind do not have to be living; they can, for instance, be easily designed by human engineers. The first and most famous example was the governor invented by James Watt to keep constant the steam pressure in the cylinder of his steam engines. If the pressure rose too high and the engine ran too fast the governor acted to open a valve and so reduce the steam pressure and bring the speed back to normal. There are now, of course, many more sophisticated devices of this kind, for instance thermostats on refrigerators, and all sorts of electrical stabilising devices, from those on ordinary television sets, to the extreme complexity of those on military or space rockets. Most of the biological adaptive or goal-seeking mechanisms have been built up by the processes of natural selection during evolution.

The next category of systems are those which are purposive. The simplest form of purposive action is to be able to choose between two alternative goals and set in action the appropriate goal-seeking machinery. New mechanistic philosophers may question the possibility of this, but in practice all human affairs are run as though man does possess some free will or freedom to choose which goals to follow. In fact, many animals behave as though they also could do this. For instance, they seem to be able to choose whether to run away from an enemy or to stand and fight. This would not be an appropriate place to engage in a long philosophical discussion about the exact sense in which one can or cannot be justified in talking of free will. The point here is that in considering the problems facing mankind and what we can do about them, we are in a situation which always has been, and undoubtedly will continue to be, treated as though it involved free agents. In fact, we treat ourselves and our fellow beings as though we have something which goes beyond the mere ability to choose between a number of known purposes or goals and which is an actual ability to create new goals which nobody else has thought of before.

The point of this divergence into the nature of systems is its implications for what we ought to be meaning when we speak of synthesising the diverse facets of the world's problems. We obviously cannot be satisfied with any uncontrolled mechanistic model such as the first simulation made by the Meadows team; but even if this model were improved (for instance by considering the world in terms of many different regions rather than as a global whole, and by introducing various types of controlling mechanisms, either automatic controls such as the classical market, or even consciously applied controls such as the action of the OPEC countries or other legislative actions that might be taken) the system would not give us everything we need. However, a greatly improved model for computer simulation has been developed as the second stage action by the Club of Rome, under the control of Mesarovic and Pestel.[3] As they themselves point out, their model should be regarded only as a tool which can help us in understanding the nature of the material we are dealing with. What we really have to do is to *make* the Man-Made Future. That means formulating purposes and trying to find ways of attaining them; probably they will, to a considerable extent, have to be new purposes. What these models can do is to tell us something about the nature of the material out of which the future world has got to be made; a craftsman needs to know whether he is to work with wood or steel, and he would like to have much more precise details about the character of his material than these broad categories. The justification of the computer simulations is that they are one of the ways of helping us to describe more precisely the general character of the broad basic material with which we are working. The snag is that they are very difficult for anyone but a specialist to understand, and of necessity they go into much more detail than anyone but a professional administrator is likely to be able to use — and personally I wish I were convinced that there were many professional administrators who could make good use of them.

For the ordinary person the main contribution he can make is to help in the creation of appropriate new goals and purposes. Here it is necessary to consider the goals and purposes of the individual and of society separately, and immediately a certain paradox or discrepancy emerges. It is for the individual that we are fully convinced of the reality of free will and of creative purposiveness; if one can call these 'spiritual' powers, to use an unfashionable term, then can or do societies have similar powers? There are many organised societies (such as various forms of tyrannies or police states) in which one might legitimately consider that the society as a whole has less creative freedom to form its own purpose than the individual is capable of, even though the potential freedom of the individual may be curtailed. On the other hand, in fully democratic societies — or some might argue even in societies ruled by benevolent dictators, if such exist — creative spiritual freedom may be as great as that of the individual, and possibly even greater, since it avoids the inevitable limitations of any single personality. Paradox, if it is such, arises because although the creative freedom of societies may be in many cases in doubt, the actual power of a society to influence future events is, of course, very much greater than that of any single individual. This is a dilemma which can be solved at one extreme by the 'drop-out' philosophy of developing a personal spiritual value, and letting the world go hang, or at the other extreme by conceding all power to the state and serving its purposes without any regard to any individual values of one's own.

Few people are likely to be satisfied with either. In practice both the social and the individual ends are very closely involved with one another. The action which seems most called for at a social level will demand considerable changes in personal purposes or systems of value, and again attempts to realise fully people's personal systems of value seem to demand changed social arrangements and types of behaviour.

Action at the social level is, of course, political action. It is certainly not part of my purpose in this book to advocate particular political solutions. However, I think it is in order to suggest the general character of the problems for which political solutions will have to be found. The problem amounts to nothing less than discovering a new way in which the whole world can arrange its affairs — economic, industrial, agricultural and social. To express this in a way as independently as possible of my own personal prejudices I shall quote from an interim report, dated June 1975,[4] of another group, set up by the Club of Rome. This one was co-ordinated by the Nobel Prize-winning economist, Jan Tinbergen of Holland. His task was to review how the present international order was working, and the interim report (and presumably the final one, which is expected in another year or so) is mainly concerned with the need for a New International Order. Here are some of the main points from it:

> In recent years we have come to realise that despite considerable achievements in many fields the path along which we have chosen to travel seems destined to disaster and despair . . . and as we struggle to make sense of our present predicament, the future, like some gigantic tidal wave, threatens to consume us . . . On the whole, the developed countries of the world have demonstrated considerable reluctance to initiate and support change . . . having derived much of their wealth from cheap resources and raw materials of the developing countries, they still refuse to give the Third World free access to their markets. . .
> . . . It is increasingly recognised that the key to development resides in the satisfaction of individual and collective basic needs within the framework of policies geared to specific sets of circumstances and relevant institutions. These needs concern food and water, health care, education, shelter and clothing, as well as security and freedom, equity and participation; in short, all that pertains to a life of dignity and modest prosperity. As such,

emphasis must be placed on identifying and satisfying minimum requirements, especially in view of the limitations imposed by natural resources . . .

1.7 The enormity and complexity of the world's problems have clearly demonstrated the inadequacy of existing international structures to serve mankind as a whole. If we are indeed to make sense of our future, more than marginal changes to the status quo will need to be made. In the light of the intransigence of the developed world, it is the Third World which has taken the initiative in pursuing radical alternatives. Having largely achieved political liberation, they are now involved in a struggle for economic liberation. This can only be achieved through the creation of a New International Order that serves the fulfilment of basic aspirations of developed as well as developing countries. The changes of direction implied here are in fact complementary and should definitely not be regarded merely as altruistic sacrifices from the former to the interests of the latter.

1.8 It is important that the current demand of the developing countries for a New International Order be perceived in its correct perspective. Firstly, the basic objective of the emerging trade union of poor nations is to negotiate a new deal with the rich nations through the instrument of collective bargaining. The essence of this new deal lies in their obtaining greater equality of opportunity and in securing the right to sit as equals around the bargaining tables of the world. No massive redistribution of past income and wealth is being demanded: in fact, even if all the demands were added up, they do not exceed about 1 per cent of the GNP of the rich nations. What is really required, however, is a redistribution of future growth opportunities. Secondly, the demand for a New International Order should be regarded as a movement, as part of an historical process, to be achieved over time, rather than in any single negotiation. Like the political liberation movement of the 1940s and the 1950s, the movement for a new economic deal is likely to dominate the next few decades and cannot be dismissed casually by the rich nations.

Tentative Results, Proposals and Recommendations

2.1 Our fundamental strategy must be one of a continuing process of change. Through the convergence of several forces presently at work we seem, however, to have arrived at a moment of historic discontinuity which, if the opportunity it offers is properly used, could result in fundamental and constructive changes to the present world order. This would be in line with the request for a New International Order, based on peace, justice and environmental integrity. The new order must guarantee a life of dignity for all; this would require a very considerable improvement in the living conditions of the poorest and most disprivileged groups.

2.2 To achieve the new order, the manner in which the existing power structure (technological, economic/military and political) functions will have to be changed. Since existing privileges and power domination seem to be at the root of many present evils and injustices within as well as between nations, and since privileges and power are seldom given up voluntarily, an effort to examine, formulate and make widely known the long-term common interest of all peoples and nations in human survival, in peace, justice and decency would seem to be of particular importance. What must be aimed at, as the crucial point for exercise of power, is the political decision-making process in the privileged and strong developed nations. It should be stressed that changes to the existing power structure, at both national and international levels, could be accomplished without resort to physical violence: we can have recourse to other means which can prove just as formidable, provided that enlightened political statesmanship is exerted.

2.3 The enormous differential between the world's rich and poor is widening rather than narrowing. In 1970, an individual living in the richest part of the world (defined so as to include one-tenth of the world's population) had 13 times more real income than an individual living in the poorest part (defined in a similar way). This ratio and the political dangers which it implies must be deemed absolutely unacceptable and every effort must therefore be made, firstly, to prevent a further enlargement of the differential and, secondly, to reduce it in the shortest possible time to an acceptable limit.

2.4 To establish the magnitude of the tasks involved, three alternative quantitative world futures – embracing population growth, food production and per capita incomes – have been investigated. These futures assume the absence of cataclysms, disintegration in the advanced countries and violent social and economic change. . .

2.5 The investigations suggest that if:
– no limit to world food production is assumed;
– the developing world is able to achieve a proposed per capita income growth-rate of 5 per cent per annum;
– the growth of per capita incomes in developed countries

maintains its present rate (approximately 3.3 per cent
per annum);
 − the 'low' population forecasts of the UN are assumed;
then the ratio between rich and poor countries could be reduced
from 13:1 to 6:1 over a 40 year period (taking 10 per cent at both
ends). This ratio could be reduced to 3:1 on the basis of the following:
 − 5 per cent growth-rate in developing countries;
 − a growth-rate of only 1.7 per cent in developed countries
   (approximately half the existing growth-rate so as to
   attain zero growth in about 40 years);
 − a maximum growth in world food production of 3.1
   per cent per annum (compared with 2 per cent at
   present);
 − a population growth of 0.1 per cent less than the 'low'
   UN forecasts . . .

2.6 The alternatives investigated are based upon several important
assumptions and considerations. They assume that the developed
world will, within the next few years, overcome the problems of
the present depression. The figures mentioned are 40 year averages
and meant to suggest gradual changes in the direction indicated. They
further assume that the link between the developed and developing
countries will gradually be reduced, for example through the
emergence of rational groupings in the developing world.

2.7 The ratio of 3:1 is equivalent to the present ratio, considered
barely acceptable, between rich and poor regions within the EEC.
This ratio could only be achieved between the regions and countries
of the world, at least on the basis of the assumptions made, over a
period of 40 years.

2.8 Acceptance and attainment of this ratio must be viewed as a
precondition for a peaceful world. The implications of this ratio are
many. They imply structural changes in international relationships
and modifications to the existing market system. They further imply
a concerted attack on world poverty as well as the stimulation of
growth in the poor regions of the world. It should also be noted that
policies geared to attain this ratio at the international level must be
combined with measures designed to reduce income inequalities
within countries, especially those of the developing world.

The magnitude of the changes in the international order which
Tinbergen's group say are essential may seem impossibly large and quite
impracticable to bring about in the time available. However, I think

many people underestimate the rapidity with which social changes can occur. It has taken a very few years for the Moslem Arab group of oil-producing states to become the equals of the industrialised western world in financial terms. John Platt and others[5] have made a study of the speed with which 48 important social changes have occurred in the last few decades, and the over-all conclusion is that surprisingly large changes can become effective surprisingly rapidly when the time is right for them.

How right is the time for the kind of changes Tinbergen's group are considering? On the level of international economics and politics great pressures are building up for radical and important changes in the relations between the world's different regions. However, as they make clear, these changes will only be accepted by democratic states if individual citizens accept them as just and valuable. The pill which the citizens of advanced countries may find difficult to swallow is that they are required to reduce their average rate of over-all growth to half or even less. This leaves them considerable liberty to redistribute the growth that does occur. It does not imply that the poorer sections of their communities must have the same modest increase in standard of living as the richer citizens. However, if the over-all average is to be lower and the poor are to overcome their present disabilities in housing and other amenities at a reasonably fast rate, this will inevitably imply that the standard of living of richer people will have to fall. Can one suppose that they could be persuaded to accept this as just and right?

It should be remembered that here the phrase 'growth-rate' is being applied to a standard of living which is defined in strictly material or indeed monetary terms. As we have pointed out before, monetary income is not the same thing as genuine human satisfaction. Until very recently most people have acted as though it were, and this is indeed one of the major causes of our difficulties. However, there is now beginning to be a reaction against this. At least a minority, but probably a growing one, is beginning to feel that it should measure what it gets from life in terms which go deeper than pounds and pence and dollars and cents. Schumacher, with his slogan 'small is beautiful' and writings such as his essay on Buddhist economics, is obtaining a response from many people to his plea to pay more attention to what gives true satisfaction than to what merely enables one to purchase hardware or commercialised entertainment. Ivan Illich[6] is another powerful advocate of a similar line of thought, though in my personal estimation he somewhat spoils his case by exaggeration. The various hippie back-to-nature alternative technology movements mostly contain a strong element of this type of value system, which often is carried so far as to cut their adherents completely adrift from any type of social or political action. What the Tinbergen group seems to be advocating is a political reorganisation of the international order in accordance with value systems which place their emphasis on these types of individual human satisfactions.

It seems that both the components necessary for dealing with the world's crisis are at least in existence and probably growing: on the one hand, social pressures with some political and economic power behind them, and, on the other, individuals who are willing to strive after goals of fulfilment of a kind different to those which have motivated the historical changes of the last century or so. The real question for the young generation of today is, I think, whether these two forces can be brought together to co-operate quickly enough to save the world before some mischance pushes it irretrievably into a disastrous breakdown.

Notes

1. Donella H. Meadows, Dennis L. Meadows, Jørgen Randers and William W. Behrens, *The Limits to Growth* (Universe Books, New York; Earth Island, London, 1972) was the first attempt to explore the complexities of the World Problem, sponsored by the Club of Rome.
2. There are many criticisms of its manifest imperfections. *Thinking about the Future*, Science Policy Research Unit of Sussex University (Chatto and Windus, 1973) is particularly concerned with technical defects; *Report on Limits to Growth*, Task Force of the World Bank, chaired by Mahbub ul-Haq, 1972, emphasises the need to consider the special needs of the developing countries; *Policy Sciences* special number, June 1974, includes a wide range of comments including a defence by Jay Forrester, who had laid the foundations of the model which the Meadows report expanded, as well as considerable emphasis on human decision-making; the last point is particularly discussed in Ervin Lazlo ed., *The World System; Models, Norms, Variations* (Braziller, New York, 1973).
3. M. Mesarovic and E. Pestel, *Mankind at the turning point*, the second report of the Club of Rome (Hutchinson, 1975).
4. *Reviewing the International Order*, Interim Report, June 1975, Project RIO, Rotterdam.
5. Karl Deutsch, John Platt and Dieter Senghaas, 'Conditions favouring Major Advances in Social Sciences', *Science*, 5 February 1971, *171*, 450.
6. See for example Ivan Illich, *Tools of Conviviality* (Calder & Boyars, 1973) and *Energy and Equity* (Calder & Boyars, 1974).

APPENDIX: ADDITIONAL READING AND NOTES ON THE LITERATURE

There has always been a trickle of books focusing on exploring possible or even probable human futures: from H.G. Wells, and before him Jules Verne, and many more authors even earlier. W.H.G. Armytage, *Yesterday's Tomorrows* (Routledge & Kegan Paul, 1968) is a good general survey, and Norman Cohn, *The Pursuit of the Millennium* (Paladin, 1970) is a detailed study of the Utopian cults of the Middle Ages. However, in recent years the pace has changed. The volume of books published about the future has increased so much that it threatens to become unmanageable. Anyone who starts as a casual reader, with plenty of other interests to fill his time, is quite likely to be overwhelmed, reduced to reading snippets here and there without any plan or coherence, or seduced into one particular line as the only true answer to everything.

The reading lists which follow, and those at the end of the chapters, attempt to provide some clues through that maze of literature, like Ariadne's thread. I have made a choice, and put it down in black and white. Of course it is, it must be, a personal, subjective, choice; but I have tried to ensure that most sensible views are represented, and that most of the important factors affecting the future are discussed independently in my own text.

List A is a small selection of books which are very general and broad in treatment, and which could be used as the basis of a university course, the set books which every student will have read. *List B* is a further set of rather similar books, some more restricted in their field, together with a list of useful periodicals and bibliographies. At the end of each chapter is key reading material in connection with the topics of that chapter, more specialised than that in Lists A and B, but still at an 'intelligent reader' level, together with *References*, which are the sources for facts, or alleged facts, quoted in the text or illustrations, and providing recent references into the depths of the specialised literature.

Reading List A: General

Best, Fred ed. *The Future of Work* (Prentice Hall, 1973)
Calder, Nigel ed. *Nature in the Round. A Guide to Environmental Science* (Weidenfeld & Nicolson, 1973)

Gabor, Dennis *The Mature Society* (Secker & Warburg, 1972)

Jantsch, Erich *Design for Evolution* (Braziller, 1975)

McHale, John and Magda Cordell McHale *Human Requirements. Supply Levels and Outer Bounds: a Framework for Thinking about the Planetary Bargain* (Aspen Institute for Humanistic Studies, Aspen, Colorado, 1975)

Mesarovic, Mihajlo and Eduard Pestel *Mankind at the Turning Point, The second report to the Club of Rome* (Dutton, 1974; Hutchinson, 1975)

Parsons, Jack *Population versus Liberty* (Pemberton, 1971; Prometheus Books, 1973)

Roszak, Theodore *Where the Wasteland Ends* (Doubleday, 1972)

Schumacher, E.F. *Small is Beautiful: a study of Economics as if People mattered* (Blond & Briggs; Harper & Row, 1973; Abacus, 1974)

Waddington, C.H. *Tools of Thought about Complex Systems* (Jonathan Cape; Paladin; Basic Books, 1976)

Waddington, C.H. ed. *Key Points, a collection of important articles about man's future**

Reading List B: Other Recommended Books, Periodicals and Bibliographies

Albertson, P. and M. Barnett eds. 'Environment and Society in Transition', *Annals of the New York Academy of Science. 184*, June 1971, is a lengthy report of a conference with much good, but also much feeble, material in it.

Calder, Nigel *Technopolis* (Simon & Schuster, 1970). First-rate journalistic coverage of most of the field.

Commoner, Barry *The Closing Circle* (Jonathan Cape, 1972)

Ehrlich, Paul R., Anne H. Ehrlich and John Holdren *Human Ecology: Problems and Solutions* (W.H. Freeman, 1973)

These last two books are by two of the leading 'doomsters', the Ehrlichs emphasising population and Commoner pollution. Read in conjunction with the battle between them in *Environment, 14*, 23–26 April 1972 and *Bulletin of the Atomic Scientists, 28*, May and June 1972, together with *Comment in Science, 177*, 21 July 1972, and review of Commoner by Waddington in *Nature, 237*, 9 June 1972.

Martin, James and A.R.D. Norman *The Computerised Society* (Prentice Hall, 1970; Penguin, 1973).

*Professor Waddington died before making the final selection for this Anthology. However, his preliminary selection is listed as reading list C. Janet Higgs, 1976.

Peccei, Aurelio *The Chasm Ahead* (Macmillan, 1969) gives the views, a few years ago, of the founder of the Club of Rome.

Sakharov, Andrei *Progress, Co-existence and Intellectual Freedom* (Andre Deutsch, 1968)

Scientific American Readers (W.H. Freeman): There are a number of volumes of selected articles from the *Scientific American*, which are mentioned in the notes to the appropriate chapters, but which taken together can be considered as a rather voluminous but comprehensive treatise at a popular level.

Taylor, Gordon Rattray *Rethink: a Paraprimitive Solution* (Secker & Warburg, 1972)

Thring, M.W. *Men, Machines and Tomorrow* (Routledge & Kegan Paul, 1973)

Tiselius, A. and S. Nilsson eds. *The Place of Value in a World of Facts* (Nobel Symposium, 1970; Interscience, 1971) is a report of an important early conference.

Waddington, C.H. ed. *Biology and the History of the Future* (Edinburgh University Press, 1972). A pithy exchange of views between eight leading people including a social scientist, Margaret Mead, and a practising artist, John Cage.

Ward, Barbara and René Dubos *Only One Earth* (Andre Deutsch, Penguin, 1972)

Ward, Barbara 'The Cocoyoc Declaration', reprinted in *Development Dialogue*, September 1974, p. 80 and *Bulletin of the Atomic Scientists*, March 1975, p. 6.

Periodicals

The Bulletin of the Atomic Scientists, which tried to persuade people to rename it *Science and Public Affairs* for a time (Educational Foundation for Nuclear Sciences, Chicago), is one of the oldest and still one of the best journals. It began from the problems of nuclear war, but now deals with a much wider field.

Ceres (Food and Agriculture Organisation of the UN, Rome) and *Population Bulletin* (Population Reference Bureau, Washington) are good value on food and population respectively. *The DOE Library Bulletin* (DOE, Marsham Street, London) lists current publications in many of the fields discussed here. *The Ecologist* (Wadebridge, Cornwall) and *Environment* (Scientists' Institute for Public Information, St. Louis, USA) start out from the problems of pollution, but spread their interests quite widely, although sometimes rather idiosyncratically. *Ekistics* (Athens Centre of Ekistics of the

Athens Technological Organisation, Greece), starting out from
urbanisation, covers a broad field by means of condensed articles
from many journals, and has some good bibliographies. The Athens
Centre of Ekistics also produces an extensive, and rather expensive,
service, *The Ekistics Index*, a computerised index of current literature.
Futures and *The Futurist* (Institute for the Future, Washington and
IPC Science and Technology, London; The World Future Society,
Washington, respectively) are the two main journals dealing with
all aspects of the future. *The Scientific American* (more popular)
and *Nature* and *Science* (rather more technical) have many articles
about a broad range of topics, although tending towards the 'hard
science' side.

Bibliographies

Peter Harper 'Directory of Alternative Technology', in *Architectural
Design*, November 1974, April, May 1975
A. Blanbried (compiler) *The Ethical and Human Value Implications of
Science and Technology: A Preliminary Directory Reviewing
Contemporary Activity* (Dept. of Physics, Program on Public
Conceptions of Science, Harvard University, June 1974)
John A. Moore ed. *Science for Society*, bibliography for the Commission
on Science Education (American Association for the Advancement
of Science, 1970)
Lynton K. Caldwell ed. *Science, Technology and Public Policy*, volumes
1 & 2, a selected bibliography (Indiana University, 1967)
Wilcox, Leslie *et al. Social Indicators: Societal Monitoring*, an annotated
bibliography (Elsevier, 1972)
Also the *DOE Annual List of Publications* cites many bibliographies
produced by DOE library on specific topics, e.g. *148N* Recycling and
the Recovery and Use of Waste Materials; *149* Environmental
Pollution; *164* Energy Resources.

Tape Recordings

Extensive collections of tape recordings of lectures, discussions, etc., are
available both from the World Futurist Society and the American
Association for the Advancement of Science, 1515 Massachusetts Ave.
NW, Washington, DC, 20005.

List C

Professor Waddington's notes are depicted in capitals, and papers found
amongst those he had collected together for the Anthology are marked *.

Other papers included in the list are best guesses from amongst his books, journals and reprints.

Futures Read-in: Anthology

BARILOCHE, *Latin American World Model*; A. Herrera *et al.*, Club of Rome Technical Symposium, *Towards a global vision of Human Problems* (Tokyo, 1973)

BIOLOGY AND THE HISTORY OF THE FUTURE (PARTS OF?)

CENTRAL SECTION OF NON-SERIAL QUOTES. *The personal environment, a non serial treatment of non linear phenomena. Mock up.* Prepared as an alternative third Man-Made Future book

CHANDRASEKHAR, S. *DEMOGRAPHY, DEVELOPMENT & ECOLOGY: India, a case study.* Commonwealth Human Ecology Council meeting, Malta, 1970

COCOYOC DECLARATION, *Bulletin of the Atomic Scientists*, March 1975

DOXIADIS (SOME, WHAT?) 'The Future of Human Settlements' in A. Tiselius and S. Nilsson eds., *The Place of Value in a World of Fact*, Nobel Symposium 14 (Wiley – Interscience, 1970), p. 307

GABCR, Dennis (PROPER PRIORITIES), 'The Proper Priorities of Science and Technology', Fawley Lecture 1972, University of Southampton

HARPER, PETER (THREATS AND PROMISES OF SCIENCE AND OF ALTERNATIVE TECHNOLOGY) *'Ludd Rides Again', *New Humanist*, June 1972, p. 59; 'In search of allies for the soft technologies', *Impact of Science on Society, 23*, 1973, 287–305

KING, ALEXANDER (NEW THRESHOLD) 'Another kind of growth: Industrial society and the quality of life', Donald Davies Memorial lecture, Institute International Studies, 1973 (or Club of Rome document)

Kishida, J. *et al. Toward a global vision of Human problems. Policy studies to world problematique.* Club of Rome Technical Symposium, Tokyo, 1973. (WHOLE OF THE JAPANESE STUDIES, TOKYO)

LOVINS, AMORY 'WORLD ENERGY STRATEGIES', *BULLETIN OF THE ATOMIC SCIENTISTS*, May and June 1974

MARUYAMA, Magorah, *'HUMAN FUTURISTICS AND URBAN PLANNING', *AIP Journal*, September 1973. *'Hierarchists, Individualists and Mutualists', *Futures*, April 1974. **'Symbiotization of cultural heterogeneity: Scientific epistemological and ethetic bases', *General Systems 18*, 1973, 127–35

MEAD, MARGARET (SELECTIONS FOR NEW LIVES) *Interview with

Edward Shiller in *Newsweek*, 25 August 1975

NEEDHAM, Joseph. *'History and Human Values: A Chinese perspective for world science and technology', lecture given to Canadian Association of Asian Studies, Montreal, 1975

PAPANEK (SOME), selection from *Design for the Real World* (Thames & Hudson, 1972)

Peccei, Aurelio and Manfred Siebker 'LIMITS TO GROWTH IN PERSPECTIVE', paper submitted to Economic Committee of the Parliamentary Assembly of the Council of Europe, December 1972

PLATT, John *'WHAT WE MUST DO', *Science 166*, 1115–21; *'DIVERSITY', *Science 154*, 1132–9; (BIOMEDICAL PAY OFFS) 'The Urgency and the Pay-offs for Biotechnical R & D', IUBS symposium, *Biology relevant to Human Welfare*, Seattle, 1971

Von Hippel, Frank 'NUCLEAR REACTOR SAFETY', *BULLETIN OF THE ATOMIC SCIENTISTS*, October 1974

WILSON, CARROLL (SUSTAINABLE SYSTEMS) 'Notes on sustainable systems', Club of Rome Technical symposium, *Towards a global vision of Human Problems*, Tokyo, 1973

**Professor Waddington had been looking unsuccessfully for a paper by Maruyama for inclusion in the Anthology on the comparison of Navajho and Japanese cultures; this paper was discovered after his death.

INDEX